THE
MILLENNIUM
PROPHECIES

AND THE
NEW JERUSALEM

Bill Salus

Author of the
NOW, NEXT, LAST, & FINAL Prophecies

The MILLENNIUM Prophecies and the NEW JERUSALEM

First printing October 2021

Publisher: Prophecy Depot Publishing
Customer Service: 714-376-5487
P.O. Box 5612
La Quinta, CA 92248

www.prophecydepotministries.net

ISBN: 978-1-7377901-0-5

Interior and cover by Mark Conn
Artist Matthew Salhus
Editor Karol Bankston
Researchers Ned Bankston and Brad Myers

Printed in the United States of America

Acknowledgements

Heartfelt thanks to my wife, children, grandchildren and friends who inspired me to write this book. A further debt of gratitude is extended to Ned and Karol Bankston, Bill and Beverly Williams, Ladd Holton, Brad Myers, Bob and Lynette Holmes, Mark Conn, Scott and Deborah Bueling, our Prophecy Depot Ministry Partners and all those who in one way or another, through prayer, encouragement, support, research, or otherwise, genuinely blessed this book.

Contents

Chapter 12

Introduction

The MILLENNIUM Prophecies
and the NEW JERUSALEM Book

Imagine it's sometime in the not-so-distant future, let's ARBITRARILY take the year 2030 AD. Envision at this randomly selected time that seven years of divine judgments have passed between, (2023-2030 AD), that have virtually rendered the planet uninhabitable. Major seas, rivers and streams were turned to blood, greatly diminishing the drinking water supply. Additionally, massive fires and scorching heat have burned up a majority of the vegetation, eliminating most food sources.

As if the above was not bad enough, throw into the equation that one-third of mankind has been killed by two-hundred million demons, the global economy has collapsed and a great earthquake has destroyed major cities, toppled tall mountains and detached every island from its foundation. Add into the mix as a final measure, a barrage of 100-pound hailstones have pummeled what was left of the depleted planet and killed many more within mankind.

These treacherous seven years of severe tribulation have caused the assembling of the most formidable array of world armies at Armageddon for *"the battle of that great day of God Almighty,"* which is prophesied in Revelation 16:14. Unbelievably, after all the devastation identified in the two paragraphs above, Satan, the Antichrist, the False Prophet and the three look like frog demons of Rev. 16:13-14 have somehow convinced most of humanity that it can win a war against God and bring about an end to His judgments!

ROLL, CAMERA ACTION!!! WHAT HAPPENS NEXT?

Some of you might be thinking this story makes for a good Hollywood movie script, but if you have been following this end time book and DVD series, you realize that these are prophetic foretellings, rather than fictional accounts, and this book is not a futuristic novel. To the contrary, the above scenario is the foretold climactic conclusion predicted in the Bible that leads to the SECOND COMING of JESUS CHRIST!

Let's hit rewind before answering what happens next.

BOOK 1: The NOW Prophecies – The first printing of this book was in February of 2016. It was the first book of this series and it addressed the unfulfilled biblical predictions that lacked any further preconditions. These represented the Bible prophecies that could happen anytime between then and NOW, meaning at this present time.

(You can read the summary list of the prophecies covered within this entire book series on their individual promotional pages at the back of this book.)

BOOK 2: The NEXT Prophecies – This book was released in October of 2018. It explained the biblical predictions that still had some minor preconditions, which prevented the prophecies from finding final fulfillment. Most of the prerequisite requirements will be removed upon the completion of the NOW Prophecies.

BOOK 3: The LAST Prophecies, the Prophecies in the First 3 ½ Years of the Tribulation – Published in October of 2019, this book introduced the Seven-Year Tribulation Period and explored the prophecies that would happen during the first half of this period.

BOOK 4: The FINAL Prophecies, the Prophecies in the Last 3 ½ Years of the Tribulation – This book hit the shelves one year later in October of 2020. It addressed the prophecies foretold to happen at the midpoint and last 3 ½ Years of the Seven-Year Tribulation Period.

In essence, the first four books of this series were written to escort the reader from NOW until the SECOND COMING of JESUS CHRIST, which is the answer to the question above of; "what happens next," at the end of the gloomy scenario?

How the last days scenario introduced at the beginning of this chapter ends, is that Jesus Christ returns to the earth and defeats the Antichrist and his armies. Then Jesus Christ, the Messiah, establishes His throne in Jerusalem and reigns with a rod of iron for a Millennia.

BOOK 5: The MILLENNIUM Prophecies and the NEW JERUSALEM explains how Jesus mops up the planetary mess and creates a new earth that is suitable for Him and (1) His Bride the Church, (2) the Old Testament Saints, (3) the Tribulation Saints and (4) the faithful Jewish remnant and (5) the surviving Gentile believers to inhabit and function in their respective roles.

If you are reading this book, you fall into one of seven categories, five of which DO HAVE a place in the Millennium and two that DON'T. The five that DO are enumerated in the preceding paragraph and the two that DON'T are revealed at various points within this book. Unfortunately, there will be many people who DON'T make it into the MILLENNIUM. The intention of this book is to ensure that you are not among them.

The Premillennial, Amillennial and Postmillennial Perspectives

This book presents the Millennium from the Dispensational Premillennial perspective. Dispensations are defined periods or ages through which God administers His plans for humanity. The dispensations are briefly summarized as follows;

1. *Innocence:* Between the Creation and the Fall of Man, (Adam and Eve), in the Garden,

2. *Conscience:* Between the Fall and the Flood, (of Noah),

3. *Human Government:* From the Flood to Abraham, (a period of repopulating the earth),

4. *Promise:* From Abraham to Moses, (a Promised Land for a Chosen People),

5. *Law:* From Moses to Jesus, (righteousness acquired through works),

6. *Grace:* From Pentecost to the Rapture—the Church Age, (righteousness administered via grace for those who received Jesus Christ through faith),

7. *Judgment:* From the Rapture to the Millennium, (the seven-seals, seven-trumpets and seven-bowl judgments),

8. *The Kingdom:* The 1000 Year Reign of Christ that begins with the 2nd Coming.

9. *The Eternal Order:* The everlasting era without an end, whereby God and Jesus Christ dwell forever with the good angels and all the saved souls.

Dispensational Premillennialism teaches that the Rapture of the Church will occur prior to the Seven-Year Tribulation Period, and both, (the Pre-Tribulation Rapture of the Church, followed by the Seven-Year Tribulation Period), will occur before the final return of Christ to Earth. As such, Jesus Christ returns to reign upon the earth prior to the inception of the 1000-year Millennium, i.e. Pre-Millennium.

There are opposing views, namely Amillennialism and Postmillennialism. Amillennialists do not expect a future literal thousand-year reign, but tend to believe the thousand years mentioned in the Bible is not a literal number but a symbolic number and represents the tail end of the time we are in now, the Church Age.

The Greek prefix *"A"* means *not (having)* or *without.* Breaking down the word *"A"* as a negation prefix means, *"A"* (not having) *Millennium* (1000-years).

The Roman Catholic Church is among the denominations that adheres to the Amillennial perspective. Below is a quote from the respected Catholic apologist, Tim Drake, about the Catholic Church's view on this topic.

> *"The Catholic Church is "amillennial," meaning that it believes that Christ's second coming and the last judgment will happen at the same time.*

> *According to Colin Donovan, theologian at EWTN,*
> *the Church "teaches that Christ already reigns in*
> *eternity (1 Cor 15:24-27) and that in this world*
> *his reign … is found already in the Church.".…*
> *Therefore, we believe "He will come again in glory*
> *to judge the living and the dead." Our belief is that*
> *the rapture will take place at the end of the world,*
> *and not until then."[1]*

In other words the Catholic Church, which teaches that it's the one and only true Church on earth, believes that it is co-reigning on the earth while Christ is reigning through it from heaven. Amillennialism is also common among some Protestant denominations such as, Lutherans, Anglicans, Methodists and more.

Postmillennialism, as the prefix "post" suggests, is the belief that Jesus Christ returns after the passing of the thousand years that is identified six times in Revelation 20. This view was championed by many of the English Puritans who believed that a huge awakening was soon to occur amongst Jews and Gentiles before the Lord's return. This view has continually lost momentum following the horrific tragedies that characterized the two World Wars in the first-half of the twentieth-century.

Since Scripture speaks of the Millennium as a time of peace and great prosperity, these World Wars, which further led to more Mideast conflicts and other major regional wars worldwide, have blatantly contradicted the Postmillennial view. The same could be said of the Amillennial perspective. Things are worsening around the globe, which suggests that the Amillennial denominations are failing miserably at their jobs as Christ's earthy co-regents.

A worsening world infers that Satan is not bound for a thousand years, but is hiding in plain sight. The next chapter points out that Satan will be imprisoned in the bottomless pit during the millennium, but at the time of the authoring of this book, the devil has the whole earth under his sway.

> "We know that we are of God, and the whole world lies under the sway of the wicked one." (1 John 5:29).

This chapter is not provided to exhaustively explain the teachings of Amillennialism or Postmillennialism, nor is it intended to debate these opposing views. However, as you read through the entirety of this book, it should become obvious that Jesus Christ is scheduled for a Pre-Tribulation return for His Church and a Premillennial return for HIS SECOND COMING!

2

The Seventy-Five Day Interval Prophecies

The Seventy Five Day Interval Period

	Midpoint	Endpoint	
			• Antichrist & False Prophet Cast Into Lake Of Fire
			• Satan Bound For 1000 Years into Bottomless Pit
			• Faithful Jewish Remnant Returns to Israel
First Half	*Second Half*		• Removal of Abomination of Desolation
of the	*of the*		• Restoration of the New Earth
Trib-Period	*Trib-Period*		• The Resurrections
			• The Judgement Seat of Christ
			• The Resurrection of the Old Testament Saints
			• The Resurrection of the Tribulation Saints
			• The Judgement of the Gentile Nations

3.5 Years	3.5 Years	
1260 Days	1260 Days	◄——— 75 Day Interval ———►
42 Months	42 Months	

One of the lesser taught prophetic time periods is the Seventy-Five Day Interval. This interval period appears to occupy the opening seventy-five days on the Millennial calendar. The Abomination of Desolation happens at the midpoint of the Tribulation Period, which will sometimes be abbreviated as Trib-period in this book. This momentous event sets in motion the last 3 ½ years of the Trib-period which totals 1260 days, but Daniel 12:11-12 quoted in the image below introduces an additional 75 days of importance that extend beyond these allotted 1260 days.

Timeline of the End Times

Midpoint of Trib-Period		Daniel 12:12 75-Day	M
"And from the time *that* the daily sacrifice is taken away, and the abomination of desolation is set up, there *shall* be one thousand two hundred and ninety days. Blessed is he who waits, and comes to the one thousand three hundred and thirty-five days." Daniel 12:11-12		I n t e r v a l	I L L E N N I U M
Last 3.5 Years of Trib-Period ◄——— 1260 Days ———►		(1335-1260) 75 Days	

Daniel informs that whoever survives these additional seventy-five days will be blessed. This is because those who somehow manage to live through the Seven-Year Trib-period and Seventy-Five Day Interval will enter into the Millennium and populate the nations. The inference is that some will be transported into the Messianic Kingdom, but others won't. The chapter entitled, *"Introduction to the Judgment of the Nations,"* will distinguish between those who do and don't receive a passport into the Messianic Age. That chapter also reveals the brutal end of those who don't make the cut!

As the timeline image at the beginning of this chapter illustrates, this interval period is packed with powerful prophetic events. The next few chapters will address the following prophecies that seemingly find fulfillment during the 75-day interval;

- The Antichrist and False Prophet are Cast into Lake of Fire – (Rev. 19:20),

- Satan is Bound for 1000 Years in the Bottomless Pit – (Rev. 20:1-3),

- Removal of the Abomination of Desolation – (Daniel 12:11-12),

- Restoration of the New Earth – (Isaiah 65:17, 66:22, 2 Peter 3:10-13),

- The First Resurrections – (Rev. 20:4-6),

- The Judgment Seat of Christ – (Romans 14:10-12, 2 Corinthians 5:10, 1 Cor. 3:10-15),

- The Resurrection of the Old Testament Saints – (Isaiah 26:19 and Daniel 12:2),

- The Resurrection of the Tribulation Saints – (Rev. 7:9-14, 20:4),

- The Marriage Supper of the Lamb – (Rev. 19:9),

- Judgment of the Gentile Nations – (Matthew 25:31-46).

3

The Antichrist and False Prophet are Cast Alive into the Lake of Fire

"And I saw the beast, (*the Antichrist*), the kings of the earth, and their armies, gathered together to make war against Him, (*Jesus Christ*), who sat on the horse and against His army. Then the beast was captured, and with him the false prophet who worked signs in his presence, by which he deceived those who received the mark of the beast and those who worshiped his image. These two were cast alive into the lake of fire burning with brimstone. And the rest were killed with the sword which proceeded from the mouth of Him who sat on the horse. And all the birds were filled with their flesh." (Revelation 19:19-21, NKJV; emphasis added)

There will be no place for the Antichrist and False Prophet on the restored earth in all its splendor during the Millennium. This diabolical duo is given a one-way ticket to the Lake of Fire. As they watch in shock the vultures feast upon the flesh of their defeated armageddonite[2] armies, while they are still breathing, Jesus Christ casts them alive into their final hellish abode.

As the timeline below illustrates, the careers of this terrible tag-team are short-lived. The Antichrist's claim to fame roughly spans the seven years of tribulation and the False Prophet thrives in the limelight for approximately three and one-half years.

The Careers of the Antichrist & False Prophet in the 7-Year Tribulation

Rev. 6:1-2 Antichrist rides in as the white horseman of the 1st Seal Judgement **Daniel 9:27, Isaiah 28:15** Antichrist confirms a treaty with Israel that starts the 7-years of Tribulation **Rev. 17:3, 7** Antichrist forms an alliance with the Harlot world religion **Rev. 17:2** Antichrist aligns with the Ten Kings	Rev. 6:1-2 Antichrist has the Ten Kings desolate the Harlot **Rev. 13:3, 12, 14** Antichrist resurrects from the dead **Daniel 9:27** Antichrist desolates the Temple & exalts himself as god **Rev. 13:15** False Prophet orders the making of, & gives life to, the image of the beast **Rev. 13:16** False Prophet requires everyone to take the mark of the beast **Rev. 13:17** Antichrist rules over a chashless global society	Daniel 11:40-44 Antichrist wages and wins wars **Zechariah 13:8** Antichrist attempts Jewish genocide **Rev. 13:15, 20:4** Antichrist has Christians beheaded **Rev. 16:10** Antichrist kingdom goes dark and economy shuts down **Rev. 16:16** Antichrist and armies go to Armageddon **Rev. 19:19-21** Antichrist, False Prophet & armies are defeated at Armageddon	Rev. 19:20 Jesus Christ kills the armies at Armageddon, captures the Antichrist & False Prophet and casts them alive into the Lake of Fire
First 3 ½ Years	Midpoint	Second 3 ½ Years	75-Days

The First 3 ½ Years of the 7-Year Tribulation Period

Rev. 17:16 - Antichrist has the Ten Kings desolate the Harlot global religion.

Daniel 9:27, Isaiah 28:15-18 – At some point after his arrival on the white horse, the Antichrist confirms a treaty between Israel and Death and Sheol (Hades) that starts the 7-Year Tribulation.

(These top two events could find fulfillment in the Post-Rapture / Pre-Tribulation Gap Period, which is introduced in The NEXT Prophecies book. This gap likely exists because it's not the Rapture that starts the 7-Year Trib-period, rather it's started when the Daniel 9:27 treaty gets executed).

Rev. 17:3, 7 - Antichrist forms an alliance with the Harlot world religion.

Rev. 17:12 - Antichrist aligns with the Ten Kings.

The Midpoint of the 7-Year Tribulation Period

Rev. 17:16 - Antichrist has the Ten Kings desolate the Harlot global religion.

Rev. 13:3, 12, 14 - Antichrist resurrects from the dead.

Rev. 11:7-12 - Antichrist kills the Two Witnesses, but three-and-a-half days later they resurrect and ascend up into heaven.

Daniel 9:27 - Antichrist desolates the Temple and exalts himself as god.

Rev. 13:15 - False Prophet orders the making of, and gives life to, the Image of the Beast.

Rev. 13:16 - False Prophet requires everyone to take the Mark of the Beast. ***But readers beware! No one who takes the mark of the beast will enter the millennium!***

Rev. 13:17 - Antichrist rules over a cashless global society.

The Last 3 ½ Years of the 7-Year Tribulation Period

Daniel 11:40-44 - Antichrist wages and wins wars.

Zechariah 13:8 - Antichrist attempts Jewish genocide.

Rev. 13:15, 20:4 - Antichrist has Christians beheaded.

Rev. 16:10 - Antichrist kingdom goes dark and economy shuts down.

Rev. 16:16 - Antichrist and armies go to Armageddon.

Rev. 19:19-21 - Antichrist, False Prophet & armies are defeated at Armageddon.

The 75-Day Interval

Rev. 19:20 - Jesus Christ kills the armies at Armageddon, captures the Antichrist & False Prophet and casts them alive into the Lake of Fire.

It's hard to know the precise chronological order of 75-day interval events but logically, it would seem that before Jesus Christ makes His victory ascent up to the Mount of Olives he will need to get rid of the Antichrist and False Prophet.

> "Then the Lord will go forth And fight against those nations, As He fights in the day of battle. And in that day His feet will stand on the Mount of Olives, Which faces Jerusalem on the east." (Zechariah 14:3-4a)

Thus, it would appear that one of the first prophecies to find fulfillment in the 75-day interval is the casting alive of the Antichrist and False Prophet into the Lake of Fire. Jesus Christ wins the war at Armageddon at the end of the Tribulation period and then promptly boots these two villains off the planet.

The Lake of Fire is the fourth and final abode of the Antichrist and the second and final of the False Prophet. The False Prophet lives on the earth, his first address, until he gets cast into the Lake of fire, which becomes his final habitat, but the Antichrist's abodes are:

1. The Earth: he emerges out of the revived Roman Empire to dwell upon the earth – (Daniel 9:26),

2. The Bottomless Pit, *aka.* the Abyss: he gets killed by a mortal head would and gets confined into the Abyss – (Rev. 13:3,12,14, 11:7, 17:8),

3. The Earth: he relives upon the earth after his resurrection for approximately another 3 ½ years during the second-half of the Trib-period – (refer to the verses in #2 above),

4. The Lake of Fire: he gets cast alive into the Lake of Fire –
    (Rev. 19:20).

The Antichrist and his cohort the False Prophet seem to have the Lake of Fire to themselves throughout the Millennium. This will give them lots of time to reflect upon their extremely regrettable earthly activities. At the end of the thousand years they will welcome in the multitude of undesirables identified in the verse below that get judged at the Great White Throne of Rev. 20:11-15.

> "But the cowardly, unbelieving, abominable, murderers, sexually immoral, sorcerers, idolaters, and all liars shall have their part in the lake which burns with fire and brimstone, which is the second death." (Rev. 21:8)

In *The Final Prophecies* book, I give a graphic description of the details that take place at Armageddon. This battle concludes the 7-Year Tribulation Period. By way of brief review:

1. While the defiant armies march toward Armageddon, they are shaken by the greatest earthquake in history. As a result, the cities of the nations fell, every island fled away, and the mountains were not found. (Rev. 16:18-20),

2. After the devastating earthquake, the armageddonites near their battlefield and are pummeled by 100-pound hailstones. (Rev. 16:21),

3. Then, as they ready their weapons for warfare they look up to see vultures licking their beaks while flying overhead preparing to feast upon their flesh. (Rev. 19:17-18),

4. Lastly, Jesus Christ returns in His Second Coming and single-handedly kills the armies and captures the Antichrist and False Prophet, who then get cast alive into the Lake of Fire. (Isaiah 63:1-6, Rev. 19:20).

In the end analysis, the Trib-period ends with nothing short of a wholesale slaughter of the disobedient world armies, but what about the rebellious peoples that sent their sons off to wage this no-win-war? How do these insubordinate civilians meet their demise?

It turns out that they are the subjects of a subsequent blood bath, which will be explored in the chapter entitled, "*The Slaughter of the Goat Gentiles.*" These two massacres seemingly happen within about a 75-day window period. One ends the Trib-period, while the other sets the stage for life in the Millennium.

4

The Final Destinations of Satan, the Fallen Angels and Demons

By now, you might be wondering when you will be reading about the great news and exciting facts concerning life in the Messianic Age. Rest assured, those chapters are forthcoming and you will discover that in the Millennium:

- The world will be restored to Garden of Eden-like conditions – (Ezekiel 36:33-36),

- The pending God-given promises to Abraham will be fulfilled – (Genesis 12:2, 15:18),

- The Messiah will live upon the earth and govern it justly – (Isaiah 9:6-7),

- The peoples will all speak the same language and praise the Lord with one accord (Zephaniah 3:9),

- World peace will prevail – (Isaiah 9:7),

- The planet will be filled with the knowledge of the Lord – (Isaiah 11:9),

- The creation will again co-exist in perfect harmony with mankind – Isaiah 11:6-8),

- The Church Age and Tribulation Saints will co-reign with Christ – (Revelation 20:4-6).

Yes indeed, life in the Millennium will be extremely blessed, just like Daniel 12:12 below says. *"Blessed is he who waits, and comes to the one thousand three hundred and thirty-five days."* The *blessed is he*, is the one who is granted access into the Messianic Kingdom.

One of the primary reasons that Millennial life is blessed is because during the Seventy-Five-Day Interval, the last seventy-five days of *"the one thousand three hundred and thirty-five days,"* the evildoers are purged out. They are forbidden to further promote lawlessness upon the earth upon its restoration.

The prior chapter revealed the ends of the Antichrist and False Prophet, and this chapter will track the final destinations of Satan, his fallen angelic cohorts and their demon troublemakers. Charting Satan's end is easy, and so we'll start with him, but knowing precisely where the fallen angels and demons are relocated is a bit more challenging. Their likely final abodes will conclude the chapter.

The Abyss: the Fifth Abode of Satan

(The seven abodes of Satan are identified later within this chapter).

> "Then I saw an angel coming down from heaven, having the key to the bottomless pit and a great chain in his hand. He laid hold of the dragon, that serpent of old, who is *the* Devil and Satan, and bound him for a thousand years; and he cast him into the bottomless pit, and shut him up, and set a seal on him, so that he should

> deceive the nations no more till the thousand years were finished. But after these things he must be released for a little while." (Rev. 20:1-3)

Having read through about a dozen commentaries on these three verses, some of them relatively complex, I discovered that this simple quote below from Meyers NT Commentary seems to say it best.

> *"An angel, descending from heaven, binds Satan with a great chain, and casts him into the abyss for one thousand years."*[3]

In other words, there is no need to complicate this prophecy by allegorizing or spiritualizing it because it can be interpreted literally. The undeniable prophetic fact is, *"that serpent of old, who is the Devil and Satan,"* is going to be confined in the bottomless pit, *aka* the abyss, during the entire Millennium. As such, *"he should deceive the nations no more till the thousand years"* are over.

The Devil is going to be restrained in his fifth abode and unable to further deceive mankind. According to John 8:44, Satan is a liar, deceiver and a murderer. 1 John 5:19 informs that the whole world is under the sway of this wicked being. This sort of behavior, coming from this powerful of a being, is not conducive to Millennial living and as such, it won't be tolerated in the Messianic age.

The next few sections will discuss the restraint, the manner and location of the restraint, what's being restrained and why it's being restrained.

The Restraint

At the time of the authoring of this chapter, Satan is being partially restrained, but according to 2 Thessalonians 2:5-12, a time is coming when this hindrance will be completely removed. Upon removal of the restraint, the Devil and his demonic forces will use power, signs and lying wonders to promote all unrighteous deception among those who perish, because they did not receive Jesus Christ as their Savior, that they might be saved. This satanic scenario is specifically strategized to promote lawlessness upon the earth so that it will embrace the Antichrist and his global agenda.

Even though Satan is partially restrained now, he along with the help of his minions are still able to:

1.   Influence the whole world, (1 John 5:19, Matthew 4:8-9),

2.   Manipulate populations to do evil things, (Job 1:15, 17),

3.   Invoke natural disasters, (Job 1:19),

4.   Inject diseases upon people, (Job 2:7),

5.   Manipulate circumstances to harass people (Ephesians 6:11-12, 2 Corinthians 12:7).

I have also put forward in my book entitled, *The FINAL Prophecies*, that the UFO phenomena and the apparitions of the Virgin Mary, (Queen of Heaven), may also be designed by the Devil to deceive people in these last days.

The list above identifies some of Satan's capabilities while he is operating under partial restraint. Christ won't allow any of these scenarios, let alone the forthcoming unrestrained events whatever they are, to be performed under His watch during the Messianic Kingdom. Therefore, the Devil must be restrained.

Man's Sin Nature Still Exists in the Millennium

Satan's restraint during the Millennium is especially necessary because people living on the earth at that time will still have a sin nature.

> "No more shall an infant from there *live but a
> few* days, Nor an old man who has not fulfilled
> his days; For the child shall die one hundred
> years old, But the sinner *being* one hundred years
> old shall be accursed." (Isaiah 65:20)

Isaiah appears to be informing that a person will have up to
one-hundred years to receive Christ as their Messiah. It seems hard
to fathom that even though Jesus Christ is living upon, and ruling
over, the earth in the Millennium, that some people will reach
one-hundred years and still not receive Him as their Savior.

The Earth Revisited: the Sixth Abode of Satan

Revelation 20:3 says that after Satan's 1000 years of confinement
in the abyss, "*he must be released for a little while.*" (Rev. 20:3c). The
reason for the release of Satan is identified in the passage below.

> "Now when the thousand years have expired,
> Satan will be released from his prison and will go
> out to deceive the nations which are in the four
> corners of the earth, Gog and Magog, to gather
> them together to battle, whose number *is* as the
> sand of the sea. They went up on the breadth of
> the earth and surrounded the camp of the saints
> and the beloved city. And fire came down from
> God out of heaven and devoured them. The devil,
> who deceived them, was cast into the lake of fire
> and brimstone where the beast and the false
> prophet *are*. And they will be tormented day and
> night forever and ever." (Rev. 20:7-10)

The Devil gets released to lead a multitude, "*whose number is as
the sand of the sea,*" of unbelievers into a final battle at the end of
the Millennium. The fact that these peoples get devoured implies
that they are unbelieving sinners that are subject to deception.
No wonder, according to Rev. 2:27 and elsewhere, Jesus Christ

must rule with a rod of iron and not a feather. More on this battle, which is different than the Gog of Magog war in Ezekiel 38, will be discussed in the chapter entitled, *"The Magog Invasion in the Aftermath of the Millennium."*

The Manner and Location of Satan's Restraint During the Millennium

The manner of restraint is a forceful eviction from the planet. Satan does not vacate willingly but, the *"angel coming down from heaven, having the key to the bottomless pit and a great chain in his hand,"* must *"cast him into the bottomless pit, and shut him up, and set a seal on him."*

According to Rev. 12:9, which happens around the midpoint of the Trib-period, Satan gets cast out of heaven with one-third of his fallen angel friends. When they are confined to the earth, they are furious. Rev. 12:12 warns, *"Woe to the inhabitants of the earth and the sea! For the devil has come down to you, having great wrath, because he knows that he has a short time."*

Exactly, *"a short time!"* More precisely, about 3 ½ years! What's worth noting, is that a single no-name angel is able to *"cast him into the bottomless pit, and shut him up, and set a seal on him."* What happened to his fallen angel cohorts? Why are they unable to fight off this one angel? The plights of these bad angels will be discussed at the end of this chapter.

The Seven Abodes of Satan

The location of the restraint is Satan's fifth abode. The Bible tells us that Satan, at various points of his career, occupies seven separate addresses.

1.   The First Abode: The Throne of God.

2.   The Second Abode: The Mineral Garden of Eden.

(The first two abodes are to be found in Ezekiel 28:11-15).

3. The Third Abode: The Atmospheric Heavens – (Ephesians 2:2 and 6:12). Presently, the Devil shares dual citizenship between earth and heaven.

4. The Fourth Abode: The Earth – (Rev. 12:7-12). This happens at the midpoint of the Trib-period.

5. The Fifth Abode: The Abyss – (Rev. 20:1-3). This happens at the beginning of the Millennium.

6. The Sixth Abode: The Earth Revisited – (Rev. 20:3). This happens at the end of the Millennium and only lasts until the final Gog of Magog battle ends in Rev. 20:7-9.

7. The Seventh Abode: The Lake of Fire – (Rev. 20:10). Satan gets cast here after losing the battle in #6 above. This seems to be his final abode.

The Lake of Fire: Satan's Seventh Abode

"The devil, who deceived them, was cast into the lake of fire and brimstone where the beast and the false prophet *are.* And they will be tormented day and night forever and ever." (Rev. 20:10)

In my book entitled, *The FINAL Prophecies*, I neglected to mention Satan's sixth abode, which is the earth revisited, and thus only listed six abodes, but technically there are seven as per the list above.

Exploring What's Being Restrained and Why

It is commonly taught that the restraint upon Satan is removed at the time of the Rapture. Thus, only the generation of people who miss out on the Rapture will truly be able to know the extent of what's being restrained.

Whatever the unhindered power, signs and lying wonders end up being, they cannot be allowed a repeat performance during the Millennium. Since Satan can't be trusted because he is a liar, deceiver and a murderer, he must be fully, not partially, restrained! Therefore he will be restrained and he will go kicking and screaming into the abyss.

The Final Destination of the Fallen Angels and Demons

As previously mentioned, *"knowing precisely where the fallen angels and demons are relocated is a bit more challenging."* As such, I reached out to the following Bible prophecy experts to get their thoughts about where these bad satanic minions wind up. The panel included Dr. David Reagan, Dr. Ron Rhodes, Dr. Mark Hitchcock, Dr. Andy Woods and TV Hosts Gary Stearman, LA Marzulli and Nathan Jones. I have incorporated some of their comments in the appendix entitled, *"The Fate of the Fallen Angels and Demons."*

What we can comfortably conclude thus far is that first the Antichrist and False Prophet are cast into the Lake of Fire and then at the end of the Millennium, Satan ends up there too. What about Satan's forces, the fallen angels and demons? Will they wind up there also?

First of all, let's put this into a population perspective by addressing how many of these bad beings we are talking about? An uncertain estimate in no particular order is broken down as follows:

- 3 = the unholy trinity of Satan, Antichrist and the False Prophet,

- 3 = the three frog-like evil spirits of the Sixth Bowl Judgment, (Rev. 16:13-14),

- 200,000,000 = demonic army of the Sixth Trumpet Judgment, (Rev. 9:16),

- (?) = the innumerable swarm of the locust of the Fifth Trumpet Judgment, which is separate from the 200 million above and appear to also be demonic forces, (Rev. 9:3)

(It's important to note that we are not told what happens to these two groups of demons above after they fulfill their evil purposes upon the earth. Apparently, they are still residing on the earth co-existing with Satan throughout the Trib-period).

- (?) = the other massive crowd of garden variety demons that are not included above, or in (Mark chapter 5 and elsewhere),

- (?) = the one-third multitude of the angels that are cast out of heaven alongside Satan at the midpoint of the Trib-period, (Rev. 12:4, 9),

- (?) = the untold host of fallen angels that were imprisoned in Tartarus from the flood at the time of Noah, (2 Peter 2:4). They are reserved for judgment and appear to be distinct from the one-third of the fallen angels of Rev. 12:4, 9.

Due to the unknown amounts in question (?), we don't have a precise number of these non-human wicked ones, but it's safe to say there are millions if not billions of them. The point of this mathematical equation is to be reminded… that they all got to go! This amounts to a massive relocation that must happen prior to *"the one thousand three hundred and thirty-five days, prescribed in Daniel 12:12."*

This multitude doesn't even include the unsaved humans, most of them with the mark of the beast on their right hand or forehead, that survive the Trib-period. They got to go too! Their plight is the subject of upcoming chapters that deal with the judgment of the Gentiles.

The Destination of the Fallen Angels

With their head coach Satan ultimately imprisoned in the Abyss, it's hard to imagine that these subordinates will function independently and be privileged to relocate elsewhere. It was previously mentioned that Satan's cohorts seem nowhere to be found when a single no-named angel chains him up in the Abyss. Is this because they are also handcuffed in some manner at the time?

The panel of experts adequately point out in the appendix, that we are not specifically told what happens to the fallen angels, but the predominant thinking is that they are also confined to the Abyss with Satan. Dr. Andy Woods put it this way in the appendix.

> "*My working assumption has always been that the demons will be with Satan in the abyss (Rev. 20:2-3) since, according to passages like Matthew 25:41 and Revelation 12:7, the demons, or the fallen angels, seem to be under Satan's authority. So, wherever Satan is they will be also. However, this is just assumption on my part.*"

Nathan Jones added an interesting timing twist in his quote. Jones said,

> "*Well, there's one possible clue in 1 Corinthians 6:3, "Do you not know that we shall judge angels? How much more, things that pertain to this life?" At what point would Christians be judging angels? It could either be at the Sheep-Goat Judgment or at the Great White Throne. I believe the former fits the timeline better. But it's just a hypothesis.*"

The Sheep and Goat Judgment is the subject of an upcoming chapter, but the good point that Nathan Jones makes is Christians won't be judging the good angels, but the fallen ones. It's my view that the timing of this judgment is likely during the 75-day interval and likely corresponds closely with when Satan gets cast into the Abyss. So my vote is that this is also when the bad angels are judged, found guilty as charged and are likewise confined to the Abyss.

Yes, it's speculation, but it is the most sensible view that I have found thus far. However, the Demons appear to have a different displacement.

The Displacement of the Demons

> "*It is commonly believed that fallen angels and demons are one and the same. In fact, they are frequently used as synonyms in the Judeo-Christian literature of the last several hundred years. However, it turns out that ancient rabbis Early Church fathers believed that they were separate and distinct entities... When we examine the Biblical record, we see the attributes and activities of angels and demons are different.*"[4] (Chuck Missler and Mark Eastman)

The quote above points out that fallen angels and demons are apparently different types of intelligent beings. Although they are on the same satanic team, they have differing attributes and activities. A few basic comparisons between these two evil groups are:

1. *Angels can be good / Demons are always evil* – Angels are inherently good, that is, unless they are fallen angelic followers of Satan. According to Hebrews 1:14, good angels function as "ministering spirits sent forth to minister for those who will inherit salvation." On the flip

side, a fallen angel intentionally creates havoc for believers according to Ephesians 6:12. All biblical accounts of demons are always bad. Calling a demon good would be an oxymoron.

2. *Angels can travel between heaven and earth / Demons are restricted to the earth.* The biblical book of Job informs that Satan, as a fallen angel, participated in a meeting that took place in heaven. In Job 1:7 and 2:2, Satan boasted that he had returned *"From going to and fro on the earth, and from walking back and forth on it."* This historical account illustrates that angels have the ability to travel between heaven and earth. In fact, there are numerous examples in the Bible, like in Daniel 10:10-13 and Matthew 28:2, whereby angels have traveled to the earth on a mission. In contrast, there are no biblical accounts of demons traveling between earth and heaven.

3. *Angels can appear human / Demons must inhabit humans* – The angel Gabriel appeared to Mary in Luke 1:26-28. Hebrews 13:2 suggests that a good angel in his effort to minister to a believer, could actually appear as a stranger in human form. Conversely, demons are purely evil spirits looking for a human body to inhabit. Christ called them unclean spirits and pointed out in Matthew 24:43-45, that a person can be inhabited by more than one of them at a time. This is also demonstrated in Mark 5:1-17 and Luke 8:26-39.

4. *Angels don't appear as animals / Demons can inhabit animals* – Apart from the fact that the angel of the Lord, spoke through the mouth of a donkey in Numbers 22:28-30, and the Holy Spirit appeared as a dove in Matthew 3:16, there appear to be no reasons to assume that angels appear as animals. In fact, these two above miraculous events don't count because in the case of the donkey, the angel of the Lord represents a Christophany, which is a

visible manifestation or appearance of Christ before His human incarnation, and the Holy Spirit is a member of the Godhead and not an angel. Thus, it was the Godhead functioning within the donkey and the dove. However, demons can inhabit animals according to the swine story in Mark 5:1-17 and Luke 8:26-39, insects like locusts as per Rev. 9:1-10 and amphibian frog-like beings in Rev. 16:13-14.

5.   *Angels come from God / Demons could come from fallen angels* – This is a DEBATABLE POINT, but worth considering. According to Psalm 148:2-5, it appears that angels were created by God. The verse below suggests the same, and could imply that God also created demons.

> "For by Him all things were created that are in heaven and that are on earth, visible and invisible, whether thrones or dominions or principalities or powers. All things were created through Him and for Him." (Colossians 1:16)

However, there are three reasons that I don't believe that God created demons:

First, there is no clear verse in the Bible that specifically identifies the origin of demons.

Second, God does not create unclean evil things. Some might argue this point by saying some laws provided in Leviticus 11 prohibit the eating of some animals, fish and birds because they are considered unclean, but those laws were put in place over two millennia after the fall of Adam and Eve in the garden. It's doubtful that these species were created unclean, rather these Levitical laws may be intended for good practical dietary purposes.

Third, in ancient texts like the Dead Sea Scrolls and the Book of Enoch, demons are presented as the disembodied spirits of the dead Nephilim giants who perished at the time of the great flood. I have explored this controversial subject matter in an article entitled, *Are Demons the Disembodied Spirits of the Nephilim?*

The Demon Inhabited Animals in Desolated Places Theory

Some believe that the evil spirits of demons, or at least some of them, will exist on the earth during the Millennium, but that they will be confined to the desolated places of historic Babylon and ancient Edom.

In a future chapter some of the geography of the earth will be presented. Places like Israel (Ezekiel 36:33-36), Iran (Jeremiah 49:39), Egypt, (Isaiah 19:23-25, Ezekiel 29:13-14) Assyria, (Isaiah 19:23-25) Jordan (Jeremiah 49:6) and elsewhere will be restored from the devastation that happens in the prophetic end times wars of Psalm 83 and Ezekiel 38. However, Babylon and Edom will not be restored, but will remain desolate wastelands during the Millennium. These two locations will be uninhabitable for humans, but possibly suitable for demon-possessed birds and animals.

Edom (Southern Jordan) in the Millennium

Ancient Edom is located in modern-day Southern Jordan. As part of Edom's punishment for persecuting the Jewish people, Joel 3:19 says that "*Edom* [in the Millennium will be] *a desolate wilderness, Because of violence against the people of Judah, For they have shed innocent blood in their land.*"

In the passage below, Isaiah gives a more graphic description of Edom in the Millennium.

> "Its streams shall be turned into pitch, And its dust into brimstone; Its land shall become burning pitch. It shall not be quenched night or day; Its smoke shall ascend forever. From generation to

generation it shall lie waste; No one shall pass through it forever and ever." (Isaiah 34:9-10)

Isaiah says that *"No one shall pass through it forever and ever."* This means that due to the dreadful atmospheric and topographic conditions described above that this territory will be uninhabitable for humans. However, Isaiah 34:11-15 explains that:

- The pelican and the porcupine shall possess it and also the owl and the raven shall dwell in it. (Isaiah 34:11),

- It shall be a habitation of jackals and a courtyard for ostriches. (Isaiah 34:13),

- The wild beasts of the desert shall also meet with the jackals, and the wild goat shall bleat to its companion; also the night-monster shall rest there. (Isaiah 34:14)

- There the arrow snake shall make her nest and lay eggs and hatch, and gather them under her shadow; there also shall the hawks be gathered, everyone with her mate. (Isaiah 34:15).

Before explaining how these birds and animals may be demon possessed, let's also describe the similar conditions that Babylon finds itself in during the Millennium.

Babylon in the Millennium

(Babylon) "It will never be inhabited, Nor will it be settled from generation to generation; Nor will the Arabian pitch tents there, Nor will the shepherds make their sheepfolds there." (Isaiah 13:20)

In the verse above, Isaiah points out that Babylon will never be inhabited by humans again. Jeremiah 50:39-40 echoes this statement, *"It shall be inhabited no more forever, Nor shall it be dwelt in from generation to generation. As God overthrew Sodom and Gomorrah And their neighbors," says the Lord, "So no one shall reside there, Nor son of man dwell in it."*

Jeremiah 51:41-43 explains that the future condition of *"Babylon has become desolate among the nations! ... Her cities are a desolation, A dry land and a wilderness, A land where no one dwells, Through which no son of man passes."*

Although, no humans will inhabit Babylon during the Millennium, Jeremiah 50:39 informs that Babylon will be a home for the wild desert beasts, jackals and ostriches. The passages in Isaiah 13 below also allude to these wild life-forms.

> "But wild beasts of the desert shall lie there; and their houses shall be full of doleful creatures; and owls shall dwell there, and satyrs shall dance there. And the wild beasts of the islands shall cry in their desolate houses, and dragons in their pleasant palaces: and her time is near to come, and her days shall not be prolonged." (Isaiah 13:21-22, KJV)

Isaiah states that Babylon will be inhabited by *"doleful creatures, owls, satyrs, wild beasts and dragons."* The Brenton Septuagint Translation below helps to further clarify the potentially demonic nature of these creatures.

> "But wild beasts shall rest there; and the houses shall be filled with howling; and monsters shall rest there, and devils shall dance there, and satyrs shall dwell there; and hedgehogs shall make their nests in their houses. It will come soon, and will not tarry."[5]

Both of these translations allude to "satyrs." The Strong's Lexicon translates the word "satyrs" as: *a masculine noun referring possibly to a he-goat, or it may refer to a demon possessed goat like the swine of Gadara (Mt 8:30-32).*[6] In 2 Chronicles 11:15, the word "satyr" is translated as devils in the KJV and goat idols in the ESV.

According to Fausett's Bible Dictionary, satyrs in Leviticus 17:7 is translated in context as, "they shall no more offer ... sacrifices unto devils" (seirim) i.e. to the evil spirits of the desert, literally, "shaggy goats," hence applied to an object of pagan worship or a demon dwelling in the desert (2 Chronicles 11:15; Isaiah 13:21; Isaiah 34:14).[7]

One last quote to help potentially find the intended interpretation for satyr comes from Eugene M. McCarthy PHD Genetics.

> "*The Greeks used the word satyr to refer to a different sort of animal. Instead of goat-human hybrids, as the Romans imagined them, a Greek would have described a satyr as a cross between a human and a horse, more like a centaur.*"[8]

After digesting the above translations of Isaiah 13:21-22 and the definitions of "satyr," it's likely that the life-forms that Isaiah describes are not the basic birds and animals that you are familiar with. These could be demons, demon possessed animals or maybe even demon possessed hybrids that are partially human and animal, like a chimera.

Hybrids are animals which occur from the mating of two different species. A chimera is an animal composed of cells with two different DNA sets; they form when two embryos merge and grow as one.

Are the life-forms in Edom and Babylon Demons, Demon Possessed, or hybrids?

As stated earlier, there are some notable prophecy teachers who suggest that the birds and animals described in the verses above could either be demon-possessed, or actual demons and not literal birds and animals. If this is the case, then it appears that the displaced demons, at least some of them, are confined during the Millennium within the uninhabitable geographies of Edom and Babylon.

Addressing Isaiah 34:8-15, Dr. Arnold Fruchtenbaum writes:

> *"These animals as we know them cannot live in a place of burning pitch and burning brimstone. Two clues in this text show that these are not literal birds and animals... The word wild goats actually means "demons in goat form." The word translated night-monster means "night demons." Like Babylon, Edom will also be an abode of demons."*[9]

Dr. Tony Garland says something similar to Fruchtenbaum in the quote below.

> *"It appears that both Babylon and Edom (Isa. 34:8-17) will be dwelling places for demons during the Millennial Kingdom. It is obvious that the animal inhabitants, as we know them, mentioned in Isa. 13:20-22 and Jer. 50:39-40, cannot live in a place of continual burning pitch and brimstone and so there cannot be literal animals. . . . This place of continual burning and smoke will be a place of confinement for many demons during the Kingdom period. . . . In fact, the Hebrew word translated wild goats refers to demons in goat form."*[10]

There is another possible support for this demon-possessed theory found in the Revelation 18 passage below.

> "After these things I saw another angel coming down from heaven, having great authority, and the earth was illuminated with his glory. And he cried mightily with a loud voice, saying, "Babylon the great is fallen, is fallen, and has become a

> dwelling place of demons, a prison for every foul spirit, and a cage for every unclean and hated bird!" (Rev. 18:1-2)

Some believe that these two verses allude to the literal location of Babylon inside of Iraq. In my book entitled, *The FINAL Prophecies*, I put forward the possibility that this specific reference to Babylon could represent the city of Rome. I connect the fall of this Babylon to the desolation of the Harlot world religion in Revelation 17:16. If that's the case, then perhaps Rome could also be a location of demons during the Millennium.

My personal view is that Edom in Jordan and Babylon in Iraq will likely be where the demons are displaced to during the Millennium. I believe there is scriptural support for this theory. Whether or not Rome is another location of demons in the Millennium is speculation on my part.

Conclusion

In the end analysis, the final destination of Satan, the fallen angels and the demons appears to be as follows:

- *Satan* gets cast into the abyss for the duration of the Millennium, (Rev. 20:1-3). Then he returns to the earth for a short interval of time to mount one final battle against God, (Rev. 20:7-9). Upon failing again to win that last war, the Devil ends up in the Lake of Fire forever, (Rev. 20:10), with the Antichrist and False Prophet and all the unbelievers that get judged at the White Throne Judgment. (Rev. 20:11-15).

- *The Fallen Angels* likely follow the same downward path that's set for Satan. They probably spend the Millennium imprisoned in the abyss and then ultimately wind up in the Lake of Fire.

- *The Demons* probably spend the Millennium strictly confined in the uninhabitable areas of Edom, Jordan, Babylon, Iraq and maybe even the city of Rome. Although I favor this possibility, the other option is that the demons could also be cast into the abyss with Satan. Ultimately, it would seem sensible that no matter where they are incarcerated during the Millennium, that they would also end up with Satan in the Lake of Fire after the thousand years have passed. This is speculation, but not beyond the realm of possibility.

The important point is that neither Satan, the Antichrist, the False Prophet, the Fallen Angels nor the Demons will be able to interact with the humans living upon the planet during the Millennium. All of these evil beings will be detained and prevented from influencing people and world affairs during the thousand-year Messianic Kingdom. However, after the Millennium, Satan will be loosed for a final confrontation with God.

5

The Faithful Jewish Remnant Returns to Israel

Thus far, this book has attempted to chronologically order the events of the 75-day interval as they segue into the Millennium. Although the order of prophetic events may not precisely follow the sequence laid out so far within this book, they have been ordered in a way to enable the reader to travel step-by-step in the shoes of the peoples that will experience these future events.

Having confined Satan, the fallen angels and demons, the Antichrist and False Prophet, and destroyed the bad kings of the earth and their armageddonite armies, it's time for the Lord to restore and repopulate the planet for the Millennium. Once the inhabitants are approved and provided their millennial passports, we can develop where they reside and how their lands are restored.

> *"Israel within the period of the Messianic Kingdom is a major theme of the Old Testament Prophets. Indeed, it was the high point of Old Testament prophecy and every writing prophet with the exception of Jonah, Nahum, Habakkuk, and Malachi had something to say about it."* (Dr. Arnold Fruchtenbaum)[11]

The process of repopulating appears to begin with the return of the Jews back into their historic homeland of Israel. During the Great Tribulation Period, a remnant of surviving Jews were exiled in ancient Edom, (Southern Jordan). At the inception of the Millennium, they need to depart from Edom, which according to Isaiah 34:9-10 will be an uninhabitable wasteland throughout the 1000-year period, and return to a restored Jewish state.

Contrary to the teachings of replacement theologians, God is not done with the Jew! The Church has not replaced Israel because standing at the threshold of the Millennium, awaiting accomplishment, are the unfulfilled unconditional covenantal promises that God gave to Abraham and his descendants. These prophecies require the existence of the Jewish race in the Millennium. These important God-given assurances specify that Abraham is to have:

- *A great name, father a great nation and be a blessing to all of the families of the earth*, (Genesis 12:2-3). The Hebrew word for *great*, which is the same word used in "*great name*" and "*great nation,*" is "*gadol.*" It can be interpreted as exceedingly greater, the greatest, a larger more prominent, marvelous and mighty name and nation.[12]

- *Descendants forever*, (Genesis 13:15, 15:5-6, 22:17). A great nation needs a "Chosen People" to occupy it. The Jewish race had to survive through the Trib-period for this to come true.

- *A homeland* that extends from the river of Egypt to the great river, the River Euphrates, which courses through modern-day Syria and Iraq, (Genesis 15:18). A great nation requires a "Promised Land" for its citizens. Israel has yet to fully encompass all of this territory.

Presently, the size of Israel is approximately 8,550 sq. miles, which is just under the size of the state of New Jersey, (8,729). Some estimates suggest that the Promised Land spans approximately 300,000 sq. miles.[13] This much Promised Land can facilitate a lot of Chosen People in the Millennium.

> *"Blessing I will bless you*, (Abraham), and multiplying *I will multiply your descendants as the stars of the heaven and as the sand which is on the seashore; and your descendants shall possess the gate of their enemies."* (Genesis 22:17, NKJV; emphasis added)

This verse assures that Abraham will, at some time in his future, have an abundance of descendants and that they will possess the gate(s) of their enemies. This hasn't happened historically on this large of a scale and currently the population of Israel rates 100th in a headcount among the nations.[14]

In no way does this ranking qualify as the number of stars in heaven or grains of sand on the seashore. Moreover, there are sizeable Arab states with gates that have been historic enemies of Israel, such as Syria, Jordan and Iraq, who possess major portions of the Promised Land.

In order for God to fulfill this oath, this all must change. Israel will need to grow both in population and landmass. This implies that during the Millennium they significantly expand their citizenry and boundaries. Along the way, Israel must take possession of *"the gate of their enemies."* Since the Millennium is not characterized by wars, this presupposes that the capturing of some Arab territories by Israel happens prior to the Millennium.

> "He, (*the Lord*), shall judge between the nations, And rebuke many people; They shall beat their swords into plowshares, And their spears into pruning hooks; Nation shall not lift up sword against nation, Neither shall they learn war anymore, (*during the Millennium*)." (Isaiah 2:4, NKJV; emphasis added)

In my book entitled, *The NOW Prophecies*, I explain how the expansion of Israel likely takes place incrementally. Before the Trib-period, Israel seems to capture Jordan (Jer. 49:2), Gaza, the West Bank and Southern Lebanon (Obadiah 1:19-20) and a portion of Egypt (Isaiah 19:16-18). The balance of territory would then be given to Israel in the Millennium.

- *An Eternal King* to reign over his descendants. A great kingdom needs a qualified King to rule over it. This King will be Jesus Christ, Who according to Revelation 17:14 and 19:16, is the "King of Kings." This aspect is an amplification of the Abrahamic Covenant that was issued through a promise made to King David. It is commonly referred to as the "Davidic Covenant."

  "When your days are fulfilled and you rest with your fathers, I will set up your seed, (*the Messiah*), after you, who will come from your body, and I will establish his kingdom. He shall build a house for My name, and I will establish the throne of his kingdom forever." (2 Samuel 7:12-13, NKJV; emphasis added)

The following is the prophetic chain of messianic events that ultimately finds final fulfillment in the Eternal King, Jesus Christ, sitting upon the Davidic Throne in the Millennium.

1. *The Seed of the Woman*: at the time of the fall of Adam and Eve in the Garden of Eden, the Messiah was identified as the "Seed."

    "And I will put enmity Between you and the woman, And between your seed and her Seed; He shall bruise your head, And you shall bruise His heel." (Genesis 3:15)

2. *The Seed of Abraham*: The lineage through which the Messianic Seed would follow, was through Abraham, Isaac and Jacob, who are the patriarchal fathers of the Jews.

"In your, (*Abraham*), seed all the nations of the earth shall be blessed, because you have obeyed My voice." (Gen. 22:18, NKJV; emphasis added)

"And I will make your, (*Abraham's son Isaac's*) descendants multiply as the stars of heaven; I will give to your descendants all these lands; and in your seed all the nations of the earth shall be blessed; because Abraham obeyed My voice and kept My charge, My commandments, My statutes, and My laws." (Gen. 26:4-5, NKJV; emphasis added)

"And behold, the Lord stood above it and said: "I *am* the Lord God of Abraham your father and the God of Isaac; the land on which you, (*Jacob*), lie I will give to you and your descendants. Also your descendants shall be as the dust of the earth; you shall spread abroad to the west and the east, to the north and the south; and in you and in your seed all the families of the earth shall be blessed." (Gen. 28:13-14, NKJV; emphasis added)

3.   *The Seed of David:* Read 2 Samuel 7:12-13 above. David was from the lineage of Judah, who was Jacob's fourth son. Jacob had twelve sons, who are commonly called, the "Twelve Tribes of Israel." This is fitting because the Lord renamed Jacob as Israel.

"And He said, "Your name shall no longer be called Jacob, but Israel; for you have struggled with God and with men, and have prevailed."" (Gen. 32:18)

A title of the Messiah in the Bible is, "The Lion of the Tribe of Judah."

"But one of the elders said to me, "Do not weep. Behold, the Lion of the tribe of Judah, the Root of David, has prevailed to open the scroll and to loose its seven seals."" (Revelation 5:5)

4. *The Virgin Birth:* In order for the Messianic Seed to be born as God in the form of a man, He had to be born of a virgin.

    "Therefore the Lord Himself will give you a sign: Behold, the virgin shall conceive and bear a Son, and shall call His name Immanuel." (Isaiah 7:14)

5. *The Immaculate Conception:* In fulfillment of all the above prophecies, the Seed as Jesus Christ, was born of the Virgin Mary.

    "Then the angel said to her, "Do not be afraid, Mary, for you have found favor with God. And behold, you will conceive in your womb and bring forth a Son, and shall call His name Jesus. He will be great, and will be called the Son of the Highest; and the Lord God will give Him the throne of His father David. And He will reign over the house of Jacob forever, and of His kingdom there will be no end." (Luke 1:30-33)

•   *An Eternal Law* to govern his descendants. This promise is also an amplification of the Abrahamic Covenant and it's referred to as the "New Covenant." The antiquated old Mosaic law will be replaced by a new one, (Jeremiah 31:31-33). "*But this is the covenant that I will make with the house of Israel after those days, says the LORD: I will put My law in their minds, and write it on their hearts; and I will be their God, and they shall be My people,*" (Jer. 31:33). The eternal law is founded upon the two primary principles of love as expressed by Jesus below.

> "Jesus said to him, "'You shall love the Lord your God with all your heart, with all your soul, and with all your mind.' This is the first and great commandment. And the second is like it: 'You shall love your neighbor as yourself.' On these two commandments hang all the Law and the Prophets." (Matthew 22:36-40).

After Jesus Christ returns in His Second Coming and wins the major war at Armageddon, the likely sequence of events regarding the return of the Jews into Israel are:

1. *Jesus Christ makes His victory ascent up to the Mount of Olives.*

    > "Then the Lord will go forth And fight against those nations, (*in the battle of Armageddon*), As He fights in the day of battle. And in that day, (*after victory is achieved*), His feet will stand on the Mount of Olives, Which faces Jerusalem on the east." (Zechariah 14:3-4a, NKJV; emphasis added)

2. *Jesus Christ establishes His throne in Jerusalem.*

    > "At that time Jerusalem shall be called The Throne of the Lord, and all the nations shall be gathered to it, to the name of the Lord, to Jerusalem. No more shall they follow the dictates of their evil hearts." (Jeremiah 3:17)

3. *Jesus Christ will pour out the Spirit of grace upon the Jews,* (Ezekiel 36:27, Zech. 12:10), which will:

    a.   Cause the Jews to look upon Jesus Christ as "whom they pierced," alluding to His crucifixion. (Zech. 12:10),

b. Prompt a great period of mourning that starts in Jerusalem and then sweeps across all of Israel. (Zech. 12:11-14).

The following passage is important to read and understand because it explains the process of how the events identified in number #3 above happen.

> "And I, *(Jesus Christ),* will pour on the house of David and on the inhabitants of Jerusalem the Spirit of grace and supplication; then they will look on Me, *(Jesus Christ),* whom they pierced. Yes, they will mourn for Him as one mourns for his only son, and grieve for Him as one grieves for a firstborn. In that day there shall be a great mourning in Jerusalem, like the mourning at Hadad Rimmon in the plain of Megiddo. And the land shall mourn, every family by itself: the family of the house of David by itself, and their wives by themselves; the family of the house of Nathan by itself, and their wives by themselves; the family of the house of Levi by itself, and their wives by themselves; the family of Shimei by itself, and their wives by themselves; all the families that remain, every family by itself, and their wives by themselves." (Zechariah 12:10-14, NKJV; emphasis added)

These verses imply that prior to this period of national mourning, the Old Testament Saints will have resurrected. This would include the family households of David, Nathan, Levi and Shimei and their respective wives.

This national mourning will likely occur for the duration of the first thirty days of the Seventy-Five Day Interval Period. Thirty days of grieving finds historical precedent in the cases of Moses and his brother Aaron.

> "So Moses the servant of the Lord died there
> in the land of Moab, according to the word
> of the Lord. And He buried him in a valley in
> the land of Moab, opposite Beth Peor; but no
> one knows his grave to this day. Moses *was* one
> hundred and twenty years old when he
> died. His eyes were not dim nor his natural
> vigor diminished. And the children of Israel
> wept for Moses in the plains of Moab thirty
> days. So the days of weeping and mourning for
> Moses ended." (Deuteronomy 34:5-8)

It's interesting to note that the above passage clearly states *no
one knows* the location of *Moses' grave to this day*. This even includes
Satan according to the verse below.

> "Yet Michael the archangel, in contending with
> the devil, when he disputed about the (*location of
> the*) body of Moses, dared not bring against him
> a reviling accusation, but said, "The Lord rebuke
> you!" (Jude 1:9, NKJV; emphasis added)

According to Matthew 17:3-4, Moses has already resurrected,
so the location of his grave is no longer a matter of importance,
but his brother Aaron will likely be resurrected with the Old
Testament Saints and be among the mourners. Aaron was also
grieved for thirty days when he died.

> "Now when all the congregation saw that Aaron
> was dead, all the house of Israel mourned for
> Aaron thirty days." (Numbers 20:29)

The resurrection of the Old Testament Saints is prophesied in
the verses below.

> *"Your dead shall live; Together with my dead body
> they shall arise. Awake and sing, you who dwell in*

dust; For your dew is like the dew of herbs, And the earth shall cast out the dead." (Isaiah 26:19)

"And many of those who sleep in the dust of the earth shall awake, Some, to everlasting life, Some to shame and everlasting contempt." (Daniel 12:2)

Those who resurrect *"to everlasting life,"* apparently do so at the inception of the Millennium and that includes the Old Testament Saints, but those who awake *"to shame and everlasting contempt,"* seemingly show up at the end of the Millennium. They have a part in the White Throne Judgment described in Rev. 20:11-15.

4. *The branches of Jewish government are established.* These branches are explained in the chapter entitled, *"The Millennial Government: The Jewish Branch."*

5. *The Eternal Law is established.*

    "David My servant shall be king over them, and they shall all have one shepherd; they shall also walk in My judgments and observe My statutes, and do them." (Ezek. 37:24)

6. *A covenant of everlasting peace is given to the Jews.* Up to this future point, the Jews only experienced periods of temporary peace on earth, but this Millennial covenant promises them a permanent peace.

    "Moreover I will make a covenant of peace with them, and it shall be an everlasting covenant with them; I will establish them and multiply them, and I will set My sanctuary in their midst forevermore." (Ezek. 37:26)

7. *The Abomination of Desolation is taken down.* In preparation for the fulfillment of #8-#10 below, the Abomination of

Desolation that the Antichrist set up in the Third Jewish Temple at the midpoint of the Trib-period, needs to be removed. This happens on day 30 within the 75-Day Interval. Some believe this is the "Image of the Beast" in Revelation 13:14-15 and that it gets set up in the most sacred part of the Temple called, the "Holy of Holies." The Abomination of Desolation is alluded to in Daniel 9:27 and Matthew 24:15.

"And from the time *that* the daily *sacrifice* is taken away, and the abomination of desolation is set up, *there shall be* one thousand two hundred and ninety days." (Daniel 12:11)

8.   *The Millennial Temple gets established.*

"My tabernacle also shall be with them; indeed I will be their God, and they shall be My people. The nations also will know that I, the Lord, sanctify Israel, when My sanctuary is in their midst forevermore." (Ezek. 37:27-28).

9.   The Millennial Jewish Priesthood is appointed and the Temple Sacrifices begin.

"And the Levites who went far from Me, when Israel went astray, who strayed away from Me after their idols, they shall bear their iniquity. Yet they shall be ministers in My sanctuary, as gatekeepers of the house and ministers of the house; they shall slay the burnt offering and the sacrifice for the people, and they shall stand before them to minister to them." (Ezek. 44:10-11)

10.   *The Feast of Tabernacles* and likely the other Jewish Feasts are initiated for continued celebration and commemoration.

"And it shall come to pass that everyone who is left of all the nations which came against Jerusalem shall go up from year to year to worship the King, the Lord of hosts, and to keep the Feast of Tabernacles." (Zech. 14:16)

Summary

The Israel of today that ranks 149 in territorial size among 190 plus nations, will be a GREAT NATION in the MILLENNIUM.[15] Then, the Jewish state will be heavily populated and large in landmass. This can't be necessarily said of other nations at that time. For instance, Egypt will also exist as a nation in the Millennium. It will be restored after forty-years of desolation.

"I will make the land of Egypt desolate in the midst of the countries that are desolate; and among the cities that are laid waste, her cities shall be desolate forty years; and I will scatter the Egyptians among the nations and disperse them throughout the countries." (Ezekiel 29:12)

Unlike the expanded nation of Israel, Egypt, which is presently the most populated Arab state in the world, will become the lowliest nation existing with the Messianic Kingdom.

"I will bring back the captives of Egypt and cause them to return to the land of Petros, to the land of their origin, and there they shall be a lowly kingdom. It shall be the lowliest of kingdoms; it shall never again exalt itself above the nations, for I will diminish them so that they will not rule over the nations anymore. No longer shall it be the confidence of the house of Israel, but will remind them of their iniquity when they turned to follow them. Then they shall know that I am the Lord God." (Ezekiel 29:14-16)

In the Millennium, Jerusalem will be the headquarters of the global government. Israel will be filled with new and old (resurrected) descendants of Abraham. It will be a blessed country and a delight to the Gentile nations.

> ""And all nations will call you blessed, For you will be a delightful land," Says the LORD of hosts." (Malachi 3:12)

In addition to the Faithful Jewish Remnant that departs from exile in Edom to return into Israel, the other surviving Jewish believers that are scattered throughout the world will be returning in the "*arms*" and upon the "*shoulders*" of the Gentiles.

> "Thus says the Lord God: "Behold, I will lift My hand in an oath to the nations, And set up My standard for the peoples; They shall bring your sons in *their* arms, And your daughters shall be carried on *their* shoulders; Kings shall be your foster fathers, And their queens your nursing mothers; They shall bow down to you with *their* faces to the earth, And lick up the dust of your feet. Then you will know that I *am* the Lord, For they shall not be ashamed who wait for Me."" (Isaiah 49:22-23)

These above verses imply that Anti-Semitism will cease to exist in the Millennium. Isaiah further states that among the Jews that return to Israel out of all the nations, some will become priests.

> "Then, (*the Millennium*), they shall bring all your, (*Jewish*), brethren for an offering to the Lord out of all nations, on horses and in chariots and in litters, on mules and on camels, to My holy mountain Jerusalem," says the Lord, "as the children of Israel bring an offering in a clean vessel into the house of the Lord. And

I will also take some of them for priests and Levites," says the Lord." (Isaiah 66:20-21, NKJV; emphasis added)

In closing, if you think that God's done with the Jew, then the Bible implores you to think otherwise. The worst thing that a believer wants to happen is for God to forego the unfulfilled unconditional pledges that were made to Abraham by abandoning his descendants. That would make the God of the Bible a promise-breaker and it would shatter the assurances a believer has in their eternal salvation.

Fortunately, God is not going to disappoint the Jewish descendants of Abraham, Isaac and Jacob, but is going to fulfill every last unfulfilled promise that He gave to their patriarchal fathers. He will complete this process in the Millennium.

6

The Resurrections in the Millennium

he prior chapter noted a couple of the verses that referenced the resurrection of the Old Testament Saints. During the Millennium, there will be two spectacular resurrections. These will likely take place during the 75-Day Interval Period and could occur simultaneously. In addition to the Old Testament Saints, the Tribulation Saints will also raise from the dead.

There are at least sixteen resurrections identified within the Bible. Ten are historical and six are forthcoming. None of these appear to be "*near death*" experiences, rather they all seem to be classified as clinically deceased individuals. The resurrections listed below with the triple (***) asterisks represent those who received eternal bodies when they are raised from the dead.

The past resurrections include:[16]

1. Resurrection of the widow's son in Zarephath (1 Kings 17:17–22),

2. Resurrection of the Shunammite's son (2 Kings 4:18–37),

3. Resurrection of the man thrown into Elisha's grave (2 Kings 13:20-21),

4. Resurrection of Jairus' daughter (Mark 5:36-43),

5.   Resurrection of the young man at Nain (Luke 7:11-15),

6.   Resurrection of Lazarus (John 11:38–44),

7.   Resurrection of unknown saints during the crucifixion (Matt 27:52–53),

8.   (These two verses do not tell us if these resurrected ones received eternal bodies).

9.   (***) Resurrection of Christ (Matt 28:1-6),

10. Resurrection of Tabitha/Dorcas (Acts 9:36–42),

11. Resurrection of Eutychus (Acts 20:7–12),

The prophesied resurrections of the future include:

1.   (***) Resurrection of the Church (i.e., Rapture, 1 Thess 4:13-18; 1 Cor 15:51-53),

     A support verse for the Rapture also being the resurrection of the Church Age saints is: "*In a moment*, in the twinkling of an eye, at the last trumpet. For the trumpet will sound, and *the dead will be raised* incorruptible, and *we shall be changed*." (1 Cor. 15:52, NKJV; emphasis added)

2.   (***) Counterfeit Resurrection of the Antichrist (Rev. 11:7, 13:3, 12, 14, 17:8),

     (This appears to be a real resurrection performed by Satan, but approximately 3 ½ years afterward the Antichrist is cast alive into the Lake of Fire as per Rev. 19:20).

3.   (***) Resurrection of the Two Witnesses (Revelation 11:11),

(We are not told who these Two Witnesses are, or if they resurrect into eternal bodies, but the assumption is that they do receive permanent bodies). The timing, ministries and identities of these Two Witnesses are explored in great detail within my book entitled, *"The LAST Prophecies, The Prophecies in the First 3 ½ Years of the Tribulation."*

4.   (***) Resurrection of Old Testament Saints (Isaiah 26:19; Daniel 12:2),

5.   (***) Resurrection of the Tribulation Saints (Rev. 7:14-15, 20:4),

6.   (***) Resurrection of the Wicked (Rev. 20:5, 11-15).

(This resurrection happens after the 1000-year Millennium).

Like the resurrections in the past, the ones in the future will happen independently from each other, with the possible exception of the resurrection of the Old Testament and Tribulation Saints. The resurrection of the Church in the Rapture will conclude the Church Age and it will include all the people who became believers in Christ within this period.

Subsequently, the Antichrist resurrects around the midpoint of the Trib-period. Shortly thereafter, he kills the Two Witnesses in Jerusalem and according to Rev. 11:11, they resurrect three and one-half days later.

The resurrection of the Old Testament Saints should include every believer of God from the time of Adam and Eve until the beginning of the Church Age. The only exceptions would be Elijah and Enoch, who were previously raptured, and those identified in #7 above, who were resurrected as per (Matt 27:52–53). The resurrection of the Tribulation Saints would include all those who receive Christ between the Rapture and His Second Coming at the end of the Trib-period.

The Marvelous Resurrections

All past resurrections have caused people to marvel. The examples below point to the potential power that a resurrection has over the minds of the masses.

The Resurrection of Jesus Christ

Matthew 20:2 explains that Mary Magdalene *raced* to inform the apostles that Jesus Christ had risen. Thomas was astonished. He *doubted* it and said:

> "Unless I see in His hands the print of the nails, and put my finger into the print of the nails, and put my hand into His side, I will not believe." (John 20:25b)

The Rapture Resurrection of the Church Age Believers

When, without warning, millions vanish from the earth in the resurrection of the Church in the Rapture, those left behind will most certainly be shocked and bewildered. Heavily saturated Christians countries, like America and the UK will likely fall into panic as they grieve the loss of their loved ones and experience their societal functions begin to rapidly falter.

The Resurrection of the Antichrist

In the future when the Antichrist is resurrected we are informed that the masses marvel and it becomes a major turning point in his career that causes many people to follow him.

> "And I saw one of his, (*Satan's*) heads, (*the Antichrist*), as if it had been mortally wounded, and his deadly wound was healed. And all the world marveled and followed the beast. So they worshiped the dragon who gave authority to the beast; and they worshiped the beast, saying, "Who is like the beast? Who is able to make war with him?" (Rev. 13:3-4)

The Resurrection of the Two Witnesses

Undoubtedly, at the midpoint of the Trib-period, after three and one-half days of celebrating the death of the Two Witnesses, the celebrators will be startled to see them resurrect and ascend to heaven in Rev. 11:7-12. To top it off, Revelation 11:13 says when they resurrect and ascend that; "*In the same hour there was a great earthquake, and a tenth of the city fell. In the earthquake seven thousand people were killed, and the rest were afraid and gave glory to the God of heaven.*"

The Resurrection of the Old Testament Saints

Like all of these cases above, when the Old Testament (OT) Saints reappear on the earth to live in the Millennium, the world will marvel. Imagine the scene at the time.

Survivors of the Antichrist's Holocaust

1.   The surviving Faithful Jewish Remnant will have survived the slaughter of two-thirds of their countrymen killed in the land of Israel by the Antichrist (Zechariah 13:8). This episode occurs in the second three and one-half years of the Trib-period.

This assessment needs some qualifying in order to hammer home the joyful intensity of what likely happens when the Faithful Remnant finally meets their resurrected ancestors, the OT Saints.

Try to wrap your head around the mindsets of the survivors from the horrors of the Hitler Holocaust. You've seen the historic agonizing photos of starving Jews in concentration camps during World War II. Houses looted, woman raped, dear friends lost and close families ripped apart and in most cases never reunited. This period ranks as one of the worst times in Jewish history. The prophet Ezekiel said it best when he prophesied from his dry bones vision over 2500 years before the Holocaust happened.

> "Then He said to me, (*Ezekiel*), "Son of man, these, (*extremely dry and brittle*), bones are the whole house of Israel. (*They represent the Jewish race*). They indeed say, '*Our bones are dry, our hope is lost, and we ourselves are cut off.*' Therefore prophesy and say to them, 'Thus says the Lord God: "Behold, O My people, I will open your graves and cause you to come up from your graves, and bring you into the land of Israel, (*which means that the Jews were living outside of Israel during the Diaspora*)." (Ezekiel 37:11-12, NKJV; emphasis added)

Ezekiel's prophecy came true and after the Holocaust, the Jews returned to their ancient homeland of Israel in 1948. This terrible saga in Jewish history serves as a foreshadowing of the coming horrific genocidal campaign of the Antichrist during the second 3 ½ years of the Trib-period.

> "Behold, the day of the Lord is coming, And your spoil will be divided in your midst. For I will gather all the nations, (*led by the Antichrist*), to battle against Jerusalem; The city shall be taken, The houses rifled, And the, (*Jewish*), women ravished. Half of the city shall go into captivity, But the, (*faithful*), remnant of the people shall not be cut off from the city." (Zechariah 14:1-2, NKJV; emphasis added)

This sounds like a repeat performance of what happened when the Nazis raided Jewish homes and raped Jewish women. However, this assault isn't limited to a single nation of German perpetrators, but it involves *"all the nations."* The NLT version says, *"The city will be taken, the houses looted, and the women raped."* In the process it can be estimated that millions of Jews will be slaughtered as per the passage below.

> ""And it shall come to pass in all the land, (*of Israel*)," Says the Lord, *"That* two-thirds, (*of the Jews*), in it shall be cut off *and* die, But *one*-third, (*the Faithful Jewish Remnant*), shall be left in it: I will bring the *one*-third through the fire, (*of the Trib-period*), Will refine them as silver is refined, And test them as gold is tested. They will call on My name, And I will answer them. I will say, 'This *is* My people'; And each one will say, 'The Lord *is* my God.' ""(Zechariah 13:8-9, NKJV; emphasis added)

In the verses below, Isaiah provides more details of the events that will transpire inside of Israel during this dreadful scenario. He alludes to what happens promptly after the false covenant of Isaiah 28:15 and Daniel 9:27 gets annulled by the Antichrist at the midpoint of the Trib-period.

> "Your covenant with death will be annulled, And your agreement with Sheol will not stand; When the overflowing scourge, (*of Zechariah 14:1-2 above*), passes through, Then you, (*Jews in Israel*), will be trampled down by it, (*as per Zechariah 13:8 above*). As often as it goes out it will take you; For morning by morning it will pass over, And by day and by night; It will be a terror just to understand the report." For the bed is too short to stretch out *on,* And the covering so narrow that one cannot wrap himself *in it."* (Isaiah 28:18-20, NKJV; emphasis added)

Do you get the picture painted by these above prophetic passages? It's the Holocaust in turbo mode. The Nazi Holocaust operations were generally initiated on October 12, 1940, when the Warsaw Ghetto was established. Then, Hitler's crusade to eliminate the Jews lasted about four and one-half years until April 29, 1945, when the last concentration camps of Dachau were liberated by the Americans and Ravensbruck by the Soviets.

By comparison, this killing spree, although it happens throughout the second-half of the Trib-period, could cause the most casualties in the first few weeks or months. In this future case, a majority of the Jews will be sitting ducks living in Israel, rather than scattered throughout Europe. They are ripe for the slaughter of all the world armies commanded by the Antichrist.

Forced into Exile to Avoid Genocide

2. The Faithful Jewish Remnant will have just spent three and one-half years of exile in Edom and they will be making their way back into Israel led by the Messiah. Fresh on their minds will be the horrors of the Antichrist led holocaust that just happened. It was this dreadful scenario that forced them into exile and they were on the chopping block next. If the Messiah didn't return, there would be no surviving Jews at all.

Returning to Israel with the Messiah

3. As the Faithful Jewish Remnant enters their homeland, probably without warning, they might see their ethnicity restored by the appearances of their patriarchal descendants, Abraham, Isaac, Jacob and his twelve sons, King David and prophets such as Isaiah and Jeremiah. There will likely be millions of resurrected Old Testament Jewish Saints. Millions killed by the Antichrist, but maybe millions resurrected by the Lord.

What a marvelous moment for this faithful remnant of Jews to experience. It's likely that some of those killed by the Antichrist were dear friends and close family members of the survivors. It's bound to be a bittersweet time. Yes, the Messiah is leading them home, but some of these returning Jews might still be mourning the loss of their loved ones and thinking that they won't be seeing them again. These devastating memories don't just disappear. Grieving is a process and the deeper the loss, the longer the mourning.

When lo and behold, a Levite runs into Levi, or a Benjamite meets Benjamin. Unless these Old Testament heroes are resurrected elsewhere, which makes no sense, they will be residing in the Promised Land. What a family homecoming this scenario will be. They will probably be quickly forming into a long line to meet their father Abraham.

The Resurrection of the Tribulation (Jewish) Saints

For those returning Jews, alluded to above, that might still be mourning the loss of their loved ones that got killed by the Antichrist, they may discover that their loved ones, if they were believers, are also resurrected at the time as the Old Testament Saints. Imagine in the example above that when the Levite runs into the resurrected Levi, that standing next to his ancient ancestral kin is the Levite's recently resurrected son, who had been killed by the Antichrist.

The Family Reunion of the Faithful Remnant with the Jewish OT and the Jewish Tribulation Saints

What follows, is a speculative explanation of why such a marvelous family reunion makes sense and might happen. This next section is intended to stimulate the readers interest in the Millennium and raise their hopes to the high heavens.

First, when a Jew becomes a believer during the Tribulation period, that Jew becomes a Tribulation Saint. This is similar to when a Jew becomes a believer during the Church Age, even though they become a Messianic Jew, that Jew becomes a Church Age Saint. Church Age Saints and Tribulation Saints are comprised of both Jews and Gentiles. Anyone who becomes a believer during the Tribulation becomes a Tribulation Saint.

Second, when the Tribulation Saints are resurrected, they all appear to be raised from the dead at the same time. It doesn't matter if they are Jew or Gentile, or whether they died in the Post-Rapture / Pre-Tribulation gap, or the first or second half of the seven-year Trib-period.

(The Post-Rapture / Pre-Tribulation Gap Interval, which spans the period of an unspecified time, is explored in my book entitled, The NEXT Prophecies*).*

Third, it seems highly likely that the Old Testament Saints and Tribulation Saints are resurrected at the same time.

Fourth, it also seems probable that when the Jewish OT and Tribulation Saints are resurrected, they will likely be resurrected in the land of Israel.

A historical example is found in the case of Jesus Christ, Who was a JEW! He rose from the same tomb that He had been buried in (Matt. 28:1-6). Also, according to the passage below, Jesus will at some point be touching down at the same place, and in the same manner, from which He had ascended.

> "Now when He, (*Jesus Christ*), had spoken these things, while they watched, He was taken up, and a cloud received Him out of their sight. And while they looked steadfastly toward heaven as He went up, behold, two men, (*likely angels*), stood by them in white apparel, who also said, "Men of Galilee, why do you stand gazing up into heaven? This *same* Jesus, who was taken up from

you into heaven, will so come in like manner
as you saw Him go into heaven."" (Acts 1:9-11,
NKJV; emphasis added)

Jesus Christ soared up to heaven miraculously without the
assistance of an aircraft and He will return to earth in the same
way. Moreover, according to Luke 24:50-52, Jesus ascended from
Bethany, which was on the eastern slope of the Mount of Olives.
Zechariah 14:4 predicts that the feet of Jesus will stand again on
the Mount of Olives.

Fifth, in addition to the probability that the Jewish OT Saints
and Jewish Tribulation Saints *resurrect at the same time* and *return
to the same place* of Israel, they could possibly be paired together
by genealogies upon arrival. Remember that each of Jacob's twelve
sons is destined to inherit a designated tribal territory within
the Promised Land. It is likely that during the Millennium these
twelve tribes of Israel will reside within their respective regions.

Perhaps, the resurrected Jewish Tribulation Saints will be
matched up with their ancestral tribes upon being raised from the
dead. This has the makings for a grand generational family reunion.

In summary, although the third, fourth and fifth points above
involve some speculation, the possibilities that a Jewish OT Saint
and a Jewish Tribulation Saint might resurrect at the same time,
return to the same place and be aligned by ancestry are not far-
fetched. If this is the case, then what a marvelous family reunion
may occur when the Faithful Jewish Remnant returns to Israel.

The Old Testament and Tribulation Saints are Guests of the Marriage Supper of the Lamb

In addition to the five recent points just identified, there is
another point to mention. This sixth clue fits better in this section
but it adds believability to the Faithful Jewish Remnant family
reunion scenario. One of the stellar celebrations that kicks off

the Millennium and seems to happen near the end of the 75-Day Interval, is the "Marriage Supper of the Lamb."

> "And I heard, as it were, the voice of a great multitude, as the sound of many waters and as the sound of mighty thunderings, saying, "Alleluia! For the Lord God Omnipotent reigns! Let us be glad and rejoice and give Him glory, for the marriage of the Lamb, (*Jesus Christ*), has come, and His wife, (*the raptured / resurrected Church Saints*), has made herself ready." And to her it was granted to be arrayed in fine linen, clean and bright, for the fine linen is the righteous acts of the saints. Then he said to me, "Write: 'Blessed *are* those, (*resurrected OT and Tribulation Saints), who are called to the marriage supper of the Lamb!*' " And he said to me, "These are the true sayings of God.""" (Rev. 19:6-9, NKJV; emphasis added)

The Marriage Supper, or sometimes alluded to as the marriage feast or wedding banquet, is an important part of the traditional Jewish wedding. Jesus Christ represented by the "Lamb of God," (John 1:29), was born a Jew, so the context of this passage is the Jewish Wedding model.

The Church in typology, is the Bride of Christ as depicted in 2 Corinthians 11:2, Ephesians 5:22-27 and Rev. 19:7-9 above. If you want to learn more about this wedding model, you can read my online article entitled, "*The Bride of Christ and the Jewish Wedding Model.*"[17]

The important points made in Rev. 19:6-9, are that the customary Marriage Supper can't happen until the groom is ready, the bride is adorned and the guests have arrived. The guests appear to be the resurrected OT and Tribulation Saints.

"The fourth stage of the Jewish wedding system is the marriage feast which lasted seven days...The Old Testament and Tribulation saints make up the friends of the bridegroom. Now that they have been resurrected, the wedding feast can take place." (Dr. Arnold Fruchtenbaum)[18]

The following parable of the wedding banquet that was taught by Christ helps to gain a better understanding of who the blessed guests are that *"are called to the marriage supper of the Lamb!*

"Jesus spoke to them again in parables, saying: "The kingdom of heaven is like a king who prepared a wedding banquet for his son. He sent his servants to those who had been invited to the banquet to tell them to come, but they refused to come." "Then he sent some more servants and said, 'Tell those who have been invited that I have prepared my dinner: My oxen and fattened cattle have been butchered, and everything is ready. Come to the wedding banquet.' "But they paid no attention and went off—one to his field, another to his business. The rest seized his servants, mistreated them and killed them. The king was enraged. He sent his army and destroyed those murderers and burned their city. "Then he said to his servants, 'The wedding banquet is ready, but those I invited did not deserve to come. So go to the street corners and invite to the banquet anyone you find.' So the servants went out into the streets and gathered all the people they could find, the bad as well as the good, and the wedding hall was filled with guests. "But when the king came in to see the guests, he noticed a man there who was not wearing wedding clothes. He asked, 'How did you get in here without wedding clothes, friend?' The man was speechless. "Then the king told the attendants, 'Tie him hand and foot, and throw him outside, into the darkness, where there will be weeping and gnashing of teeth.' "For many are invited, but few are chosen." (Matthew 22:1-14)

Before submitting my thoughts about this parable, I will provide you with a good quote about this parabolic passage from Dr. Arnold Fruchtenbaum.

> "*The point of the parable is that those who were originally bidden to the wedding feast, the Pharisees and the Jewish generation of Jesus' day will not partake of the feast (the Kingdom) due to their commitment of the unpardonable sin. However the Jews of the Tribulation generation will. But this will include only believers; the unbelievers will be cast into the outer darkness and excluded from the Messianic Kingdom.*"[19]

(Fruchtenbaum teaches that the unpardonable sin in this case was the rejection of Jesus Christ as the Messiah by the Pharisees on their accusations of Him being demon possessed as per Matthew 12:24. This amounted to the national rejection by Israel of Jesus Christ).

I believe the parable of the wedding feast could be interpreted as follows:

- "*He sent his servants to those who had been invited to the banquet to tell them to come, but they refused to come.*" (Matt. 22:3)

This likely represents the rejection by the religious leaders of Israel of Jesus Christ as the Messiah at His First Coming. Jesus is the Groom and *his servants* could represent His apostles and disciples. (STRIKE ONE)!

- *"Then he sent some more servants... But they paid no attention and went off... seized his servants, mistreated them and killed them."* (Matt. 22:4-6 abbreviated)

This might allude to the Jewish generational rejection of Jesus Christ as the Messiah and their continued disdain toward His disciples. In general, Jews still reject Christ (the Groom) as their Messiah and are not typically fond of Christians (the Bride of Christ). (STRIKE TWO)!!

- *"Then he said to his servants...go to the street corners and invite to the banquet anyone you find...So the servants went...and gathered all the people they could find...and the wedding hall was filled with guests."* (Matt. 22:8-10 abbreviated)

This section deals with the invited guests who accepted the invitation, so it can't allude to either the Groom, Bride, or those apostate religious leaders of Israel who rejected the invitation in the upper two bullet points. Therefore, through a process of elimination, it appears to be representing the OT and Tribulation Saints. The fact that the *"wedding hall was filled with guests,"* infers that these two groups are resurrected, alive and available to attend the feast.

- *"But when the king came in to see the guests, he noticed a man there who was not wearing wedding clothes...The man was speechless...Then the king told the attendants, 'Tie him hand and foot, and throw him outside, into the darkness, where there will be weeping and gnashing of teeth."* (Matt. 22:11-13 abbreviated)

The King seemingly represents God, the Heavenly Father of the Groom Jesus Christ, and the Father-in-Law of the Bride the Church, but who is this uninvited guest? He is a fish out of water who belongs in Hades, where there exists *darkness, weeping and gnashing of teeth*, rather than this banquet hall.

Since the King has arrived to see the guests, this means that the timing of His visit is when the marriage supper is taking place, which is likely during the 75-Day Interval. The unwelcome guest who is not properly dressed, would likely be dealing with unbelievers on earth at the time the wedding feast is occurring. Apparently this guest, as a representation of unbelievers, is still alive on earth at the time.

Matthew 22:10 seems to also suggest this when it points out that the wedding hall was filled with "*both bad and good*" guests. "*So those servants went out into the highways and gathered together all whom they found, both bad and good. And the wedding hall was filled with guests.*"

As odd as this possibility sounds, an upcoming chapter will point out that a judgment awaits unbelievers during the 75-Day Interval. Among these unbelievers will be people who received the Mark of the Beast and survived through the Trib-period. They won't be able to partake of the wedding feast, nor receive a passport into the Millennium. Perhaps, their judgment happens during, or shortly after the Marriage Supper of the Lamb.

These unbelievers are the subject of the chapter entitled, "*The Slaughter of the Goat Gentiles*," and they will be sent to Hades for the duration of the Millennium. (STRIKE THREE)!!!

At this point, you might be asking the following two questions:

1. How do we know the *Marriage Supper of the Lamb* happens on earth rather than in heaven?

2. If the Matthew 22:1-14 wedding parable relates to the Marriage Supper of the Lamb, then how can it include *both bad and good* people as guests?

These are good questions that are answered in an upcoming chapter entitled, "*The Marriage Supper of the Lamb*."

Thus, in conclusion, if the OT and Tribulation saints represent the blessed guests that attend the Marriage Supper of the Lamb, then they must be resurrected prior to the feast. If the wedding feast happens on or around the same time that the Faithful Jewish Remnant returns from exile back into Israel, then it will likely also include this remnant among the guests. Imagine a banquet hall full of guests that might include the OT Saints, Tribulation Saints and the Faithful Jewish Remnant, that are all assembled together with Jesus Christ and His Bride the Church, to celebrate the Marriage Supper of the Lamb. If this is the case, then what a *party this will be*!

The Resurrection of the OT and Tribulation Saints Includes Gentiles

When it comes to the OT Saints, the Jews don't have an exclusive hold upon this title. There were also many Gentiles identified in the Old Testament who believed in God. Likewise, there are many Gentiles included in the Tribulation Saints.

Revelation 7:9 points out that there is *"a great multitude"* of martyrs during the Trib-period, *"which no one could number, of all nations, tribes, peoples, and tongues."* The fact that they come from *"all nations"* means that they are made up of both Jews and Gentiles.

A few examples of OT Saints are provided below. A more exhaustive list can be found in an online article by Charlie Trimm entitled, *"Non-Israelite Followers of YHWH in the Old Testament."*[20] Any quotes that are *italicized* and notated by *"quotation marks"* came from this article.

- **Melchizedek:** he was apparently a Gentile. "Then Melchizedek king of Salem brought out bread and wine; he *was* the priest of God Most High." (Gen. 14:18)

- *"**Egyptians** (Exodus 1-15): The Egyptians are called to "know that I am YHWH" throughout the plague narrative, but it seems that this does not mean conversion."*

- *"**Rahab** (Joshua 2): The Canaanite prostitute."*

- **Ruth**: was a Moabitess according to Ruth 1:5. In Matthew 1:5, she was listed eleventh out of forty in the lineage of Jesus Christ.

- **Job**: he was apparently a Gentile contemporary of Abraham. In Job 1:1 we are told that Job "was blameless and upright, and one who feared God."

- **The Queen of Sheba**: She is the subject of 1 Kings 10:1-13. We are told in Matthew 12:42, "The queen of the South will rise up in the judgment with this generation and condemn it, for she came from the ends of the earth to hear the wisdom of Solomon; and indeed a greater than Solomon *is* here." This foretells that the Queen of Sheba will "rise up" at some later date in order to judge the wicked generation of religious leaders at the time of Christ's First Coming. This implies that she will be resurrected.

- **The Ninevites**: at the time of Jonah the Ninevites repented and found favor with God. This account is found in Jonah 3:5-10. This doesn't mean that all Ninevites from the past will resurrect, but like the Queen of Sheba, these specific Ninevites will also "rise up in the judgment."

  "The men of Nineveh will rise up in the judgment with this generation and condemn it, because they repented at the preaching of Jonah; and indeed a greater than Jonah *is* here." (Matthew 12:41)

- **King Cyrus of Persia**: King Cyrus is one of the most celebrated kings to this day in Iran, which was ancient Persia. He will likely also be among the resurrected OT Saints. In the verse below, King Cyrus publicly declared that "the Lord God of Israel (He is God)."

"Who is among you of all His people? May his God be with him, and let him go up to Jerusalem which is in Judah, and build the house of the Lord God of Israel (He is God), which is in Jerusalem." (Ezra 1:3)

In conclusion, some historical Gentile kings, peoples and individuals will resurrect as OT Saints. Those identified in the bullet points above are merely a sampling of what will likely be a multitude of Gentiles from the past that are appropriately considered Old Testament Saints.

Thus, the resurrection of the OT and Tribulation Saints, the family reunions of the returning Faithful Jewish Remnant and the celebration of the Marriage Supper of the Lamb, which could happen all around the same time, will be a GRAND KICK-OFF START TO THE MILLENNIUM!

But, what about those unbelievers that received the Mark of the Beast and somehow managed to survive through the judgments of the Trib-period? What is their destiny? Read on…

7

Introduction to the Judgment of the Nations

"I was watching in the night visions, And behold, *One* like the Son of Man, (*Jesus Christ the Son of God*), Coming with the clouds of heaven! He, (*Jesus the Son*), came to the Ancient of Days, (*God the Father*), And they brought Him, (*Jesus*), near before Him, (*God*). Then to Him, (*Jesus*), was given dominion and glory and a (*Millennial*) kingdom, That all peoples, nations, and languages should serve Him, (*Jesus Christ*). His dominion *is* an everlasting dominion, Which shall not pass away, And His, (*Messianic*), kingdom *the one* Which shall not be destroyed." (Daniel 7:13-14, NKJV; emphasis added)

In this opening passage, the prophet Daniel describes his futuristic vision into the Messianic Kingdom. What Daniel witnessed was a meeting between God the Father, referred to as the Ancient of Days, with His only begotten Son Jesus Christ. During this meeting God gives Jesus dominion over the kingdom, *which shall not be destroyed*. Since the inhabitants of this kingdom, "*which shall not pass away*," are "*all peoples*" then it's safe to say that this kingdom will exist upon the earth.

Since the referenced kingdom won't be *destroyed* or *pass away*, then it won't be established on this present planet under its current conditions because this earth has an expiration date.

> "But the day of the Lord will come as a thief in
> the night, in which the heavens will pass away
> with a great noise, and the elements will melt
> with fervent heat; both the earth and the works
> that are in it will be burned up. Therefore, since
> all these things will be dissolved, what manner *of*
> *persons* ought you to be in holy conduct and
> godliness, looking for and hastening the coming
> of the day of God, because of which the heavens
> will be dissolved, being on fire, and the elements
> will melt with fervent heat?" (2 Peter 3:10-12)

The apostle Peter points out that this present earth *"and the*
works that are in it will be burned up." The Seven Seal, Seven
Trumpet and Seven Bowl Judgments in the book of Revelation
devastate the planet. Rivers, streams and oceans are turned into
blood in Rev. 8:8-11; 16:3-4. Scorching heat and global wildfires
destroy much of the world's vegetation as per Rev. 8:7: 16:8-
9. Great earthquakes shake the earth and humongous hailstones
pummel the planet causing cities to crumble, mountains to
topple and islands to dislodge from their foundations according
to Rev. 16:17-21. Peter declares that ultimately, the earth will be
burned up.

That's the bad news for the planet, but the good news is
that a new earth, which won't be *destroyed* or *pass away* replaces
the old one. According to the verses below, there will still be
an earth existing in the universe, it's not going away, but it will
receive a facelift.

> *"One* generation passes away, and *another*
> generation comes; But the earth abides forever."
> (Ecclesiastes 1:4)

> "Nevertheless we, according to His promise,
> look for new heavens and a new earth in which
> righteousness dwells." (2 Peter 3:13)

"For behold, I create new heavens and a new earth; And the former shall not be remembered or come to mind." (Isaiah 65:17)

""For as the new heavens and the new earth Which I will make shall remain before Me," says the Lord, "So shall your descendants and your name remain." (Isaiah 66:22)

Therefore, the kingdom identified in Daniel's futuristic vision appears to allude to the Messianic Kingdom that exists in the Millennium. The kingdom is filled with "*all peoples*" from the "*nations*" that spoke in different "*languages.*" These peoples from the nations are the subjects of this and the next two chapters.

The Resurrected Tribulation Saints Go Into the Kingdom

It's clear from the following passages written in the book of Revelation that the Tribulation Saints, who include saved Jews and Gentiles killed during the Trib-period, will resurrect and serve Christ in the Millennium.

"After these things I looked, and behold, a great multitude which no one could number, of all nations, tribes, peoples, and tongues, standing before the throne and before the Lamb, clothed with white robes, with palm branches in their hands." (Rev. 7:9)

"And I said to him, "Sir, you know." So he said to me, "These are the ones who come out of the great tribulation, and washed their robes and made them white in the blood of the Lamb. Therefore they are before the throne of God, and serve Him day and night in His temple. And He who sits on the throne will dwell among them."" (Rev. 7:14-15)

> "And I saw thrones, and they sat on them, and judgment was committed to them. Then *I saw* the souls of those who had been beheaded for their witness to Jesus and for the word of God, who had not worshiped the beast or his image, and had not received *his* mark on their foreheads or on their hands. And they lived and reigned with Christ for a thousand years." (Rev. 20:4)

These above verses indicate that a "*great multitude*" that comes out "*of all nations, tribes, peoples, and tongues,*" will live and reign "*with Christ for a thousand years.*" Do these resurrected Tribulation Saints represent the entirety of the "*all peoples*" from the "*nations*" that spoke in different "*languages*" identified in Daniel's vision, or will there also be living Gentiles who are saved that survive the Trib-period included in this mix?

Will Living Gentile Believers Who Survive the Trib-Period Enter the Millennium?

Interestingly, in the midst of authoring this chapter, I received an email that is related to this very topic from a ministry partner named Bill Williams. Bill has been teaching Bible prophecy for about forty years and recently, while teaching his class at Christ Place Church in Gainesville, Georgia, his group raised the relevant questions below.

> "Will there be living believers (who didn't take the Mark), other than the Jews, at the beginning of the Millennium? Will ALL of the believers who don't take the Mark be killed before the Millennium begins? So, are the living/saved Jews, including the 144,000, the only living people who go into the Millennium? It may very well be a situation where NO non-Jewish living people go into the Millennium!"

To be clear, these questions are NOT asking if there will be believing Gentiles living during the Millennium, rather will there be LIVING believing Gentiles who are saved that survive the seven years of tribulation that enter into this period. This excludes the Gentiles within the martyred Tribulation Saints because they do not survive alive through the Trib-period.

Along these lines, the inquiry arises as to whether or not there will even be any surviving believing Gentiles available to enter into the Messianic Kingdom, or will they all be killed prior. This curiosity is predicated upon the thinking that a believer will not take the Mark of the Beast and by refusing to do so, runs the risk of being beheaded as per Rev. 20:4. Thus, the question is posed, "*Will ALL of the believers who don't take the Mark be killed before the Millennium begins?*"

The other point of interest is about the "*living/saved Jews*" that enter the kingdom. This would include the believing Faithful Jewish Remnant, who were the subject of the previous chapter, and the 144,000 Jewish evangelists in Rev. 7:1-8 and Rev. 14:1-5. Since we are not told anywhere in the Scriptures that they died, we can presume that they are living/saved Jews also.

On a sidenote, some teach that non-believing Jews who survive through the Trib-period without taking the Mark of the Beast will somehow get a pass to enter the Millennium in a condition of unbelief merely because they are Jews. This seems to be wishful thinking that is not supported scripturally. To the contrary, Ezekiel 36:25-28; 37:21-28, Hosea 5:15, Zechariah 12:10-14 and elsewhere, seem to refute this thinking. This includes the quote below.

"And so all, (*not some of*), Israel will be saved, as it is written: "The Deliverer will come out of Zion, And He will turn away ungodliness from Jacob." (Romans 11:26, NKJV; emphasis added)

Lastly, remember that Jesus Christ at His First Coming didn't give the religious leaders of Israel a pass on the basis of their Hebrew heritage, rather He called them a brood of evil speaking vipers in Matthew 12:34. He said their father was not Jehovah, but the Devil in John 8:44 and He forewarned them that their generation would be condemned in the judgment as per Matthew 12:41-42.

The closing sentence presented from Bill William's class above is: "*It may very well be a situation where NO non-Jewish living people go into the Millennium!*" To clarify, a non-Jewish person is a Gentile. This assessment seems to be refuted by the details concerning the judgment of the Sheep and Goat Gentiles in Matthew 25:31-46.

This judgment identifies LIVING Gentiles at the beginning of the Millennium and those classified as Sheep appear to be believers. The Sheep and Goat Gentile Judgment will be covered in the upcoming chapters entitled, "*The Salvation of the Sheep Gentiles*" and "*The Slaughter of the Goat Gentiles*."

The next chapter will point out that the Sheep Gentiles represent LIVING believers on the earth at the beginning of the Millennium. Thus, the answers to the church group questions posed above appear to be:

1. YES, there will be living believers (who didn't take the Mark), other than the Jews, at the beginning of the Millennium.

2. NO, not all of the believers who don't take the Mark are killed before the Millennium begins.

3. NO, the living/saved Jews, including the 144,000, are not the only living people who go into the Millennium.

4. NO, it is not likely a situation that no non-Jewish living people go into the Millennium.

The Three Categories of Gentiles that Survive the Tribulation Period

As we are soon to discover in the subsequent two chapters, the Gentiles in Matthew 25:31-46 somehow manage to make it through the perilous events and judgments that happen during the Trib-period. Although the Sheep and Goat Judgment will ultimately narrow the field down to only two categories, there will likely be three spiritual groupings of surviving Gentiles that exist on the earth just prior to the Sheep and Goat Judgment.

These three groups are; *Group 1,* those who are already saved, *Group 2,* some who still need to be saved and *Group 3,* those who can't be saved.

Before identifying the characteristics of each group, it's important to recognize that the world population after the Trib-period will be vastly smaller than it is presently. As of February 21, 2021, the world population is estimated at 7.8 billion people. By the end of the Trib-period the following prophecies will have happened in a rapid succession, which will significantly lower this estimate. These predicted events that will lessen the global population are:

1.   The Rapture: we are not told how many true believers disappear, but there are an estimated 2.4 billion Christians, who include Catholics, Protestants, Evangelicals, etc. Let's hope at least *500 million* are taken in the Rapture. I have no idea, only the Lord knows how many of the 2.4 billion so-called Christians are actually true believers.

On an alarming sidenote, my guestimate of *500 million* could be substantially less according to a Christian Post article that came out on March 31, 2020. The story headline reads:

"Record low number of Americans hold biblical worldview, survey says."

"Only 6 percent of Americans possess a biblical worldview, according to a new survey."[21]

It's important to note that the United States hosts the largest Christian population in the world. There are about 205 million Christians in America. If only 6% possess a biblical worldview, then there will likely be millions of American Christians that get left behind.

2. The Second and Third Seal Judgments: these judgments speak of world wars, famines and pestilences in Revelation 6:3-6. We don't know how many are killed, starved or diseased, but let's estimate *100 million* on the low side.

3. The Fourth Seal Judgment: some believe that this judgment could kill another one-fourth of the earth because they interpret the passage below to mean Death and Hades kills one-fourth of the earth.

    "When He opened the fourth seal, I heard the voice of the fourth living creature saying, "Come and see." So I looked, and behold, a pale horse. And the name of him who sat on it was Death, and Hades followed with him. And power was given to them over a fourth of the earth, to kill with sword, with hunger, with death, and by the beasts of the earth." (Rev. 6:7-8)

However, when this passage is compared to the verses quoted below with the Sixth Trumpet Judgment, we see that it doesn't specifically say that Death and Hades kills one-fourth of mankind. What it does say, is that Death and Hades have power, or authority in some translations, *"over one-fourth of the earth to kill."* In my estimation, Death and Hades will possess global control *over one-fourth* of the earth's population.

Taking into consideration the population decreases after #1 and #2, let's estimate one-fourth of mankind at this future time to be around *1.8 billion*. If Death and Hades orders *1.8 billion* of their subjects to go out on a killing spree, how many might die as a result of this crusade? Let's estimate that *1.8 billion* get killed.

4. The 6th Trumpet Judgment: The verses below clearly state that one-third of mankind gets killed. Let's remove another *1.8 billion*.

    "So the four angels, who had been prepared for the hour and day and month and year, were released to kill a third of mankind. Now the number of the army of the horsemen *was* two hundred million; I heard the number of them. And thus I saw the horses in the vision: those who sat on them had breastplates of fiery red, hyacinth blue, and sulfur yellow; and the heads of the horses *were* like the heads of lions; and out of their mouths came fire, smoke, and brimstone. By these three *plagues* a third of mankind was killed—by the fire and the smoke and the brimstone which came out of their mouths." (Rev. 9:15-18)

Pull out your calculators: (7,800,000,000 – 500,000,000 – 100,000,000 – 1,800,000,000 – 1,800,000,000 = 3,600,000,000), or 3.6 billion people.

These speculative numbers don't necessarily include the untold many Tribulation Saints that get beheaded for refusing to take the Mark of the Beast, so let's say that by the end of the Trib-period, there may only be about 3.2 billion people left on the planet. Some of these people will be Jews, but the vast majority will be Gentiles and among them, they will likely fall into one of the three spiritual categories below.

Group 1: those who are already saved. These individuals received Jesus Christ as their Savior sometime after the Rapture of the Church. Additionally, they refused to take the Mark of the Beast when it was offered at the midpoint of the Trib-period. By rejecting the Mark of the Beast, they put themselves into survival mode because they became unable to buy and sell in the cashless global economy detailed in Rev. 13:15-17. Moreover, they subjected themselves to potentially being beheaded by the Antichrist's authorities as per Rev. 20:4. In essence, their existence depended upon their ability to hide and survive outside of the global government's guidelines and controls.

Group 2: some who still need to be saved. These peoples, like *Group 1*, also refused to take the Mark of the Beast. In so doing, they also found themselves as outcasts of the global government and cashless society of the Antichrist. The supposition behind the existence of this group is predicated upon the likelihood that they rejected the Mark of the Beast, because for some reason they thought it was a bad idea.

Remember that one of the first things that happens to those who receive the Mark of the Beast in *Group 3* is that they break out in *foul and loathsome sores* as part of the plague from the First Bowl Judgment.

> "So the first went and poured out his bowl upon
> the earth, and a foul and loathsome sore came
> upon the men who had the mark of the beast and
> those who worshiped his image." (Rev. 16:2)

Perhaps these worldwide *loathsome sore* breakouts served as a deterrent to some for receiving the Mark, or maybe it was because some in *Group 2* didn't trust the Big Brother authoritarian Antichrist's government. Whatever the reason(s), it seems likely that there will be a *Group 2* in existence after the Trib-period. However, these peoples will need to follow the lead of *Group 1* and receive Jesus Christ as their Savior in order to receive a passport into the Messianic Kingdom. And, as the next chapter will point out, they must do this before the Sheep and Goat Judgment takes place.

The question arises, "Can people in *Group 2* still get saved after Christ has returned during the 75-Day Interval or will it be too late?" Salvation requires faith according to Ephesians 2:8 which says, "*For by grace you have been saved through faith, and that not of yourselves; it is the gift of God.*" When Christ returns, obtains victory at Armageddon, rescues the Jewish Remnant and sits upon His throne in Jerusalem, it doesn't seem like it would require much faith to know that Jesus is the Messiah. *Group 2* members will be able to see Him in His glory.

For the three reasons below, I believe the answer is YES, these fence-sitting survivors of *Group 2* can still receive Christ and get saved.

FIRST, multitudes saw Jesus Christ at the First Coming and were getting saved while He healed the sick, performed miracles and walked among them. In John 20:29, Jesus told Thomas, "*Jesus said to him, "Thomas, because you have seen Me, you have believed. Blessed are those who have not seen and yet have believed.""*

This implies that even though it's obvious that Jesus is the Messiah, someone still has to believe in Him. In the case of "Doubting Thomas" he had to see to believe that Jesus Christ was resurrected. In the case of *Group 2* they can see Him and believe that He, as the Messiah, has not only resurrected, but has returned.

SECOND, In the Millennium when Jesus Christ is dwelling upon the earth, people that are born in the Millennium will still need to receive Him as their Messiah. According to the verse below, it seems obvious that a person will have up to 100 years to receive Christ to be forgiven of the curse of sin.

> "No more shall an infant from there *live but a
> few* days, Nor an old man who has not fulfilled
> his days; For the child shall die one hundred years
> old, But the sinner *being* one hundred years old
> shall be accursed." (Isaiah 65:20)

These Millennials will be able to see Christ in His glory, but still need to exercise their free choice to receive Him or live in rebellion.

THIRD, It is the heart of God that none should perish, but that all should be saved and receive eternal life.

> "For God so loved the world that He gave His
> only begotten Son, that whoever believes in Him
> should not perish but have everlasting life." (John
> 3:16)

Group 3: those marked by the Beast who can't be saved. These people opted to receive the Mark of the Beast and in so doing rendered themselves unredeemable, which means they all:

- became worshippers of the Antichrist (Rev. 13:15),

- rejected Jesus Christ,

- were enabled to buy and sell in the global cashless economy (Rev. 13:16-17),

- subjected themselves to the outpouring of God's wrath, which included the foul and loathsome sores. This wrath is explained in the passage below.

> "Then a third angel followed them, saying with
> a loud voice, "If anyone worships the beast and
> his image, and receives *his* mark on his forehead
> or on his hand, he himself shall also drink of the

wine of the wrath of God, which is poured out full strength into the cup of His indignation. He shall be tormented with fire and brimstone in the presence of the holy angels and in the presence of the Lamb. And the smoke of their torment ascends forever and ever; and they have no rest day or night, who worship the beast and his image, and whoever receives the mark of his name."" (Rev. 14:9-11)

By receiving the Mark of the Beast they consciously forfeited their opportunity to be saved. In *The FINAL Prophecies* book, I explain how and why this forfeiture occurs.

No matter which of the three groupings these surviving Gentiles fall under, if they are adults at the time, they will all have likely witnessed the following powerful prophetic events displayed in the images below.

The Prophecies of the First 3 ½ Years of the Tribulation Period

Tribulation Prophecies of the First Half

- Signs And Lying Wonders
- Harlot Religion Of "Mystery Babylon"
- 144,000 Hebrew Evangelists
- Worldwide Christian Revival
- Christian Martyrdom By The Harlot
- Third Jewish Temple
- The Two Witnesses
- Seal Judgments
- Trumpet Judgments
- Unholy Harlot And Antichrist Alliance
- The Ten Kings

Second Half of the Trib-Period "Great Tribulation"

| False Confirmed | Covenant | 3.5 Years 1260 Days 42 Months | Midpoint | 3.5 Years 1260 Days 42 Months |

The Prophecies at the Midpoint of the Tribulation Period

First Half of the Trib-Period	• War In Heaven – Satan Cast To Earth • Death And Resurrection Of Antichrist • Desolation Of Harlot • Death Of The Two Witnesses • 7th Trumpet Sounds The 3rd Woe • Abomination Of Desolation • The False Prophet • (666) Image And Mark Of The Beast • Persecution Of Jews	Second Half of the Trib-Period "Great Tribulation"
3.5 Years 1260 Days 42 Months	*Midpoint*	3.5 Years 1260 Days 42 Months

The Prophecies of the Last 3 ½ Years of the Tribulation Period

	Midpoint Endpoint	
First Half of the Trib-Period	• The "Woman In The Wilderness" • The 7 Bowl Judgments • The 8 Stages Of Armageddon Campaign 1. *The Antichrist Assembles His Allies* 2. *The Destruction Of Commercial Babylon* 3. *The Fall Of Jerusalem* 4. *The Antichrist Armies At Petra (Jordan)* 5. *The National Regeneration Of Israel* 6. *The Second Coming Of Jesus Christ* 7. *The Battle At The Valley Of Jehoshaphat* 8. *Christ's Ascent Up The Mount Of Olives*	75 Day Interval
3.5 Years 1260 Days 42 Months	3.5 Years ◄——— 1260 Days ———► 42 Months	

The Prophecies in the Seventy-Five Day Interval Period

Midpoint	Endpoint	
First Half of the Trib-Period	*Second Half of the Trib-Period*	• Antichrist & False Prophet Cast Into Lake Of Fire • Satan Bound For 1000 Years Into Bottomless Pit • Sheep And Goat Gentile Judgment • The First Resurrection • The Resurrection Of Old Testament Saints • The Resurrection Of The Tribulation Saints • The Marriage Supper Of The Lamb
3.5 Years 1260 Days 42 Months	3.5 Years 1260 Days 42 Months	◄———— 75 Day Interval ————►

Conclusion

In summary, the Millennium will be a kingdom *which shall not be destroyed, nor shall it ever pass away.* Jesus Christ will be given an everlasting dominion over this Messianic Kingdom. It will be initially populated by a crop of living Jews and Gentiles who survive through the Trib-period. These peoples will all be believers that come out from severely reduced populations from all the nations. The next few chapters will explain which Gentiles make the cut and which ones don't!

8

The Salvation of the Sheep Gentiles

(Chapter includes a biblical commentary on Matthew 25:31-40)

It appears that during the final days of the 75-Day Interval Period that Jesus Christ renders His crucial decision as to which Trib-period Gentile survivors are going to be granted entry into His Messianic Kingdom.

> "Blessed *is* he who waits, and comes to the one thousand three hundred and thirty-five, (*1335*), days." (Daniel 12:12, NKJV; emphasis added)

> "Then the King, (*Jesus Christ*), will say to those on His right hand, 'Come, you blessed of My Father, inherit the (*Millennial*) kingdom prepared for you from the foundation of the world.'" (Matthew 25:34, NKJV; emphasis added)

The 1335th day alluded to by Daniel is the final day of the 75-Day Interval. All of those Gentiles positioned at the right hand of Christ on that fateful date will be blessed to inherit the Messianic Kingdom. Who are these fortunate individuals and how did they obtain their VIP seat at the prestigious right hand of Jesus Christ? Did they win the lottery or buy a high-priced ticket to the award-winning event? The answers are explained in the passage below.

> "When the Son of Man comes in His glory, and all the holy angels with Him, then He will sit on

the throne of His glory. All the nations will be gathered before Him, and He will separate them one from another, as a shepherd divides *his* sheep from the goats. And He will set the sheep on His right hand, but the goats on the left. Then the King will say to those on His right hand, 'Come, you blessed of My Father, inherit the kingdom prepared for you from the foundation of the world: for I was hungry and you gave Me food; I was thirsty and you gave Me drink; I was a stranger and you took Me in; I *was* naked and you clothed Me; I was sick and you visited Me; I was in prison and you came to Me.' "Then the righteous will answer Him, saying, 'Lord, when did we see You hungry and feed *You,* or thirsty and give *You* drink? When did we see You a stranger and take *You* in, or naked and clothe *You?* Or when did we see You sick, or in prison, and come to You?' And the King will answer and say to them, 'Assuredly, I say to you, inasmuch as you did *it* to one of the least of these My brethren, you did *it* to Me.'" (Matthew 25:31-40)

This passage points out that several specific acts of kindness earned these individuals the right to be placed at the right hand of Jesus Christ, the *"Son of Man"*. Jesus informed these sheep *"inasmuch as you did it to one of the least of these My brethren, you did it to Me."*

What exactly did they do, when did they do it, why did they do what they did, and who specifically are the brethren they helped? These and several other questions will be answered in this chapter. The upcoming chapter entitled, *"The Slaughter of the Goat Gentiles"* will discuss who gets positioned on the left side of Christ. Their plight is part of Matthew 25:41-46 and according to Matthew 25:46, *"these* (goats) *will go away into everlasting punishment, but the righteous* (sheep) *into eternal life."*

What follows is my biblical commentary on Matthew 25:31-40.

The Second Coming of Christ

> "When the Son of Man comes in His glory, and
> all the holy angels with Him, then He will sit on
> the throne of His glory." (Matthew 25:31)

The *Son of Man* is a title of Jesus Christ. The Matthew 24
passage below declares that when the *Son of Man comes* to the earth
at His Second Coming, He comes with power and great glory.
When Jesus Christ returns, He is accompanied by all *the holy angels*.
This happens immediately after the seven-years of tribulation.

> "Immediately after the, *(seven years of)*,
> tribulation of those days the sun will be
> darkened, and the moon will not give its light;
> the stars will fall from heaven, and the powers
> of the heavens will be shaken. Then the sign
> of the Son of Man will appear in heaven, and
> then all the tribes of the earth will mourn, and
> they will see the Son of Man coming on the
> clouds of heaven with power and great glory.
> And He will send His angels with a great sound
> of a trumpet, and they will gather together
> His elect from the four winds, from one end
> of heaven to the other." (Matthew 24:29-31,
> NKJV; emphasis added)

Upon returning to earth, Jesus Christ:

1. Defeats the world armies that are assembled with the
    Antichrist at Armageddon (Rev. 19:21, Zechariah 14:3),

2. Casts the Antichrist and False Prophet into the Lake of
    Fire while they are still alive (Rev. 19:20),

3. Rescues the Faithful Jewish Remnant from Edom, which is in Southern Jordan (Isaiah 63:1-6),

4. Returns the Jewish Remnant back to Israel (Zechariah 14:10-11),

5. Makes His victory ascent to the Mount of Olives (Zechariah 12:10-14 and 14:4),

6. "*Then He will sit on the throne of His glory,*" which will be set up in Jerusalem (Matthew 25:31).

"At that time Jerusalem shall be called The Throne of the Lord, and all the nations shall be gathered to it, to the name of the Lord, to Jerusalem. No more shall they follow the dictates of their evil hearts." (Jeremiah 3:17)

The Gathering of the Gentile Nations to Jerusalem

> "All the nations will be gathered before Him, and He will separate them one from another, as a shepherd divides *his* sheep from the goats. And He will set the sheep on His right hand, but the goats on the left." (Matthew 25:32-33)

Jeremiah 3:12 quoted above stated that, "*Jerusalem shall be called the Throne of the Lord, and all the nations shall be gathered to it.*" This is also the "*throne of His glory*" in Matthew 25:31. In Matthew 25:32, we are told that once Jesus Christ is seated upon His throne of glory in Jerusalem, "*all the nations will be gathered before Him.*"

This is not a resurrection event because the goats represent unsaved Gentiles. It was already pointed out that they "*will go away into everlasting punishment.* Thus, this means that these nations, which are comprised of saved sheep and unsaved goats, represent Gentiles who have survived through the Trib-period.

Once this massive crowd is assembled they are sectioned off into two quadrants. The selection process is made by Jesus, Who according to John 10:11-18, holds the title of being the "Good Shepherd." Possessing this skillset, Jesus is able to discern the characteristics of each Gentile and is qualified to determine what category they belong to. The Sheep are sectioned off on "His right hand," which from the biblical perspective is a position of honor. In contrast, the goats are segregated "on the left," which represents a place of dishonor.

Several questions arise at this point in the Matthew 25 prophecy.

1. Are nations or individuals being divided into two groups?

2. How many nations or individuals are involved?

3. How do they get to Jerusalem from their foreign locations?

4. Who gathers them to Jerusalem?

5. What role might the holy angels, who come to the earth with Christ, have in this process?

Are nations or individuals being gathered and divided into two groups?

The Greek word for nations is "*ethnos*." It can be translated as nation, nations, tribe, Gentiles, people or heathen. Whenever the word is used it usually deals with non-Jews. According to the New American Standard Hebrew and Greek Dictionaries, it is used in the Bible 95 times to identify Gentiles or people, and 67 times to represent a nation or nations.

It seems likely that individuals, rather than nations, are being set apart at this judgment. Below is a quote along these lines from The Bible Knowledge Commentary: New Testament by John Walvoord and Roy B. Zuck.

> *"It's important to note that Christ will not judge the Gentile nations en masse as nations, but as individuals. The word "nations" in v. 32 is neuter in the Gk. while "them" is masculine, referring to individual persons. There will not be "sheep nations" and "goat nations," but "sheep" separated from the "goats" in every nation. While it is true that God has judged entire nations for mistreating the Jews (Egypt, Babylon, etc.), the truth here is that individuals within the nations will be judged, and only those who have evidenced faith in Christ by their love for the "brethren" will enter into the kingdom. They will have life eternal; the others will go away into eternal punishment."*

Observe that this quote says, *"and only those who have evidenced faith in Christ by their love for the "brethren" will enter into the kingdom."* This is an important acknowledgment. It implies that the acts of kindness done by the Sheep Gentiles are not randomly performed, but will be motivated by their faith in Christ. In other words, these are saved sheep.

How many nations or individuals are involved?

The last chapter guesstimated there could be about 3.2 billion people that survive through the Trib-period. The large majority of these survivors will be Gentiles. Is it reasonable to think that this many people are going to assemble within the final days of the 75-Day Interval Period at Jerusalem?

The largest religious gathering in recorded history was the Kumbh Mela 2013 pilgrimage in Prayagraj, India. This crowd was estimated to be about 120 million.[22] These Hindu worshippers gathered over 55 days to take a ritual bath where the Ganges and Yamuna Rivers meet. Most of these sojourners originated from inside India, but the multitude of Sheep and Goats are gathered from the world nations.

Planning food, travel and accommodations for billions of people would seem to be a logistical nightmare. Also, verses found in Jeremiah 25:33 and elsewhere points out that, *"And at that day the slain of the Lord shall be from one end of the earth even to the other end of the earth."* This implies that not all Gentiles come to Jerusalem, but that many are slaughtered in their homelands. This worldwide disaster that will go from nation to nation will be discussed further in the chapter entitled, *"The Slaughter of the Goat Gentiles."*

Therefore, it is more likely that large delegations from the nations are gathered together in Jerusalem, rather than every last surviving Gentile on the planet. What about people who are handicapped in remote parts of the world who are unable to travel, will they be flown across the continents to Jerusalem?

The following is a pertinent quote from William McDonald from the Believer's Bible Commentary. McDonald suggests that these Gentiles are "representatives" or "individual classes."

> *"The word ethne, translated "nations" in this passage, can equally well be translated "Gentiles." Some believe the passage describes the judgment of individual Gentiles. Whether nations or individuals, there is the problem of how such a vast horde could be gathered before the Lord in Palestine. Perhaps it is best to think of representatives of the nations or individual classes assembled for judgment."*[23]

How are the Gentiles gathered to Jerusalem from their foreign locations?

It seems obvious from Matthew 25:32 that there will be a large assembly of Gentiles at Jerusalem. Whether it's in the millions or billions, either way these attendees have to assemble into Israel in a very quick span of time. How will they travel? Obviously, they can't board the *"Slow Boat to China"* as the old adage goes.

Presently, the preferred method of long-distance travel is by airplane. Is it possible that on judgment day the Ben Gurion airport, which is 28 miles NW of Jerusalem, will be bombarded with non-stop international arrivals? This beckons the question, will there still be any airplanes left in the world after the Trib-period? What about automobiles, the Internet, smart phones and GPS tracking capabilities? Will modern technologies and transportation sources make their way into the Millennium?

Why not? I believe the answer is yes to these questions. For example, the passage below declares that a highway will connect Egypt and Assyria and the Egyptians and Assyrians will visit each other and some Egyptians will travel this route to serve the Assyrians. A highway is conducive for automotive travel, such as buses and cars.

> "In that day there will be a highway from Egypt to Assyria, and the Assyrian will come into Egypt and the Egyptian into Assyria, and the Egyptians will serve with the Assyrians." (Isaiah 19:23)

It's hard to imagine that an Egyptian will travel approximately 700 miles by camel to get to Assyria. Also, in the Isaiah verse below we are informed that the whole world will be made aware of the knowledge of the Lord. This important information could be conveyed slowly via word-of-mouth transmissions, or instantly through the Internet.

> "They shall not hurt nor destroy in all My holy mountain, For the earth shall be full of the knowledge of the Lord As the waters cover the sea." (Isaiah 11:9)

Remember, that among the masses that make it into the Millennium, there will be those familiar with the creation, utilization and maintenance of modern technologies. Technology will have become deeply integrated into their daily lives. Why would they opt for a horse and buggy when they know how to manufacture, drive and maintain a car?

Who gathers them to Jerusalem?

Matthew 25:32 informs that, "All the nations will be gathered before Him…" How is that going to happen? Is Jesus Christ going to step away from His "Throne of Glory," leave Jerusalem and go door knocking from household to household? This is not likely!

However, some intelligent beings will need to act as travel agents in order to assemble these masses, because if not, there will be many goats that will refuse the invitation. The last thing the goats will want to do, especially if they bare the Mark of the Beast, is stand before Jesus Christ at the Sheep and Goat Judgment.

But they or their representatives must attend! They can't opt out for fear of their fate! The time clock is ticking. It's the last days of the 75-Day Interval and the Millennium must begin on schedule!

What role might the holy angels play in this process?

Is it possible that the holy angels that come with Jesus Christ are involved in gathering the Gentiles? According to Hebrews 1:14 these holy angels were ministering spirits sent forth to minister for those who will inherit salvation. Luke 15:10 states that these good angels rejoiced when a sinner repented and got saved. If they were offered the opportunity to gather together the Sheep, would the holy angels refuse the offer?

"The Slaughter of the Goat Gentiles" chapter will explore Matthew 13:47-50, 2 Thessalonians 1:6-10, Revelation 14:19 and other Scriptures to see if angels are involved in gathering Gentiles for this final judgment scenario.

The Sheep Gentiles Are Saved

"Then the King, (*Jesus Christ*), will say to those (*Sheep Gentiles*) on His (*honorable*) right hand (*side*), 'Come, you blessed of, (*God*), My Father, inherit the kingdom prepared for you from the foundation of the world." (Matthew 25:34)

These Sheep Gentiles are blessed of God the Heavenly Father. This implies that they are saved and as such, they have become enabled to be blessed. The prior quote from The Bible Knowledge Commentary: New Testament said, "*only those who have evidenced faith in Christ by their love for the "brethren" will enter into the kingdom. They will have life eternal.*"

Some more quotes about the Sheep Gentiles that are taken from this same source elaborate further upon this crucial point.

"*These acts of kindness are not good works that save them (Eph. 2:8-9); they are proof of their faith in the message and their love for Christ.*"... "*His,* (A Sheep Gentile's), *works will not save him; but his works will reveal that he is redeemed.*"... "*The kingdom will begin on earth with only saved individuals in physical bodies constituting the earthly kingdom as the King's subjects.*"

The Sheep Gentiles Acts of Kindness Help the Brethren of Christ

"For I was hungry and you gave Me food; I was thirsty and you gave Me drink; I was a stranger and you took Me in; I was naked and you clothed Me; I was sick and you visited Me; I was in prison and you came to Me.' "Then the righteous will answer Him, saying, 'Lord, when did we see You

hungry and feed You, or thirsty and give You
drink? When did we see You a stranger and take
You in, or naked and clothe You? Or when did we
see You sick, or in prison, and come to You?' And
the King will answer and say to them, 'Assuredly,
I say to you, inasmuch as you did it to one of the
least of these My brethren, you did it to Me.'"
(Matthew 25:35-40)

This passage reveals the acts of kindness performed by the
Sheep Gentiles. They helped Christ's brethren. It's humbling to
realize the sequential order of the six needs that the sheep helped
the brethren with.

1.   Hunger – *"For I was hungry and you gave Me food;"*

2.   Thirst – *"I was thirsty and you gave Me drink;"*

3.   Homelessness – *"I was a stranger and you took Me in;"*

4.   Nakedness – *"I was naked and you clothed Me;"*

5.   Sickness – *"I was sick and you visited Me;"*

6.   Imprisonment – *"I was in prison and you came to Me."*

Considering these needs likely arose primarily in the last 3 ½
years of the Trib-period, when neither the sheep nor the brethren
could buy or sell in the global economy, it makes sense why Christ
sequenced them in the order that He did.

We can deduce that the sheep never took the Mark of the
Beast, otherwise Jesus Christ wouldn't say to them in Matthew
25:34, *"Come, you blessed of My Father."* According to Revelation
14:9-10, people that take the Mark of the Beast receive God's
wrath, rather than His blessings. Likewise, Jesus wouldn't call
the brethren, *"My brethren,"* if they received the Mark, because

in order to receive the Mark they would have had to reject Jesus Christ in order to worship His counterfeit, the Antichrist.

Hunger and Thirst

The first things the brethren experience is hunger and thirst. There are a couple of reasons these conditions develop.

A.   If you can't buy and sell in the marketplace, then you are forced to find your own food and water. Have you ever been forced to do that?

B.   Moreover, food and water are already scarce at the time due to the fact that some of the Trumpet and Bowl Judgments have adversely resulted in burned up vegetation (Rev. 8:7), which hurts farming, and embittered drinking waters (Rev. 8:10-11) and bloodied fresh water sources like major rivers and streams up (Rev. 16:4). These judgments will have also harmed the fishing industry because much of the Seas have been turned to blood resulting in the death of many edible sea creatures (Rev. 8:8-9 and 16:3).

Homelessness

When the refrigerators are emptied and the pantry shelves cleaned out, people will find themselves hungry and thirsty. This could cause many unprepared families to abandon their homes in search of food and water. Not bearing the Mark of the Beast, these people may have to *beg, borrow*, but hopefully not *steal* for their basic staples for survival.

Some may have to travel out of the area to sustain their existence. They may seek and find hidden communes that are set up by others who are facing the same dilemma. This survival scenario could lead to homelessness.

Also, unmarked people will undoubtedly become labeled as dissidents. Many of them may be forced to flee from their homes and go into hiding. This is because Christians who refuse the Mark of the Beast run the risk of getting beheaded as per Rev. 20:4. Happening simultaneously, Jews are forced into exile because the Antichrist is executing a campaign of Jewish genocide at the time in Zechariah 13:8.

Nakedness

Those who are homeless, especially if they had to flee, probably abandoned their homes with only the "*clothes on their back.*" To be without a home is to be without a closet and a change of clothes. Wearing the same clothing for a prolonged period, with no water to do laundry, leads quickly to dirty and torn garments. This scenario could cause nakedness.

Additionally, harsh winters create the need for additional clothing to stay warm. Perhaps some of the Sheep Gentiles will pass out blankets, long sleeve shirts, sweaters and jackets to the brethren in addition to basic clothing.

Sickness

Improper diet, nakedness, stress filled lives and poor hygiene resulting from a lack of clean waters to bathe in, will undoubtedly cause many to become ill. Making matters worse, basic medicines will likely be high in demand and hard to find. Also, these sickly can't fill their vital prescriptions at the pharmacy unless they have the Mark of the Beast.

Jesus said, "*I was sick and you visited Me.*" Notice that He didn't say, "*I was sick and you healed me.*" Some of the visiting sheep could have empty medicine chests as well. In such cases, the best they can accomplish is to visit, comfort and pray over the infirmed.

Imprisonment

After starving of hunger and thirst, living on the run in ripped up rags, and contracting an illness, a person will likely become vulnerable and unable to resist arrest. In this scenario a person is in real trouble because incarceration could likely lead to execution. Jesus said, "*I was in prison and you came to Me.*" Wow, that's going to take a lot of guts on behalf of the visiting Sheep Gentile who dares to set foot in a jailhouse or penitentiary. They may as well put on a set of handcuffs and turn themselves in as fugitives from the law.

Are the Sheep Gentiles Promoting Social Justice?

Before identifying the brethren in Matthew 25:35-40, let's clear up some current confusion as to whether or not the Sheep Gentiles are crusading for social justice. A large growing number of Christian leaders and pastors, along with many influential politicians in government, like to use this passage of Scripture to campaign against social injustice among the poor and oppressed in society.

One example of a politician exploiting this passage in Matthew 25, is a quote below from Nancy Pelosi, the US Speaker of the House of Representatives.

"Nancy Pelosi exploits the Bible, well-known parable of Jesus to advocate for prisoner release" (The Blaze-4/27/20)[24]

"House Speaker Nancy Pelosi (D-Calif.) wants the release of federal prisoners during the coronavirus outbreak — and she is using the Bible to make her case…MSNBC host Joy Reid asked Pelosi on Sunday whether releasing prisoners will be a part of future COVID-19 relief legislation. In response, Pelosi cited a well-known biblical parable.

"In our caucus, we are very devoted to the Gospel of Matthew," Pelosi responded before quoting the allegory. "'When I was hungry, you fed me. When I was homeless, you sheltered me. When I was in prison, you visited me,' and so this for us is part of our value system," she said."

As this chapter has aptly pointed out, the Sheep Gentiles are undergoing a last days crisis that deals with their salvation and survival during the Trib-period. This apocalyptic scenario has nothing to do with social injustice. The hard cold reality is that the global government of the Antichrist will be forcing people to worship him and conform to the dictates of his authoritarian regime. The concept of social injustice won't even be part of the political conversation at that time. The Blaze article concludes with this similar acknowledgment below.

"The parable, found in Matthew 25, tells about the separation of sheep and goats at the end of time. Traditionally, the parable is interpreted to mean that the people whom Jesus refers to as "sheep" are true Christians who receive "eternal life" and those whom he refers to as "goats" are people who will receive "eternal punishment." The parable is often invoked by those advocating social justice to demonstrate the significance that Jesus placed on carrying out justice for vulnerable and marginalized people."

Identifying the Brethren of Jesus Christ

"While He (*Jesus Christ*) was still talking to the multitudes, behold, His mother (*Mary*) and (*His biological*) brothers stood outside, seeking to speak with Him. Then one said to Him, "Look, Your mother and Your brothers are standing outside, seeking to speak with You." But He answered and said to the one who told Him, "Who is My mother and who are My brothers?" And He stretched out His hand toward His disciples and said, "Here are My mother and My brothers! For whoever does the will of My Father in heaven is My brother and sister and mother." (Matthew 12:46-50, NKJV; emphasis added)

Some believe in a *Jewish Brethren* view, which teaches that because Jesus was a Jew, *His brethren* in Matthew 25:40 are the Jews. Others, hold to the possibility of a *Disciples Brethren* view, which teaches that *His brethren* are represented by the passage above that states, "*whoever does the will of My Father in heaven is My brother.*" The *Disciples Brethren* interpretation would include both Jews and Gentiles.

The Jewish Brethren View

Below are quotes from three respected Bible teachers who believe that the biological kinfolk of Jesus Christ, the Jews, are identified as "His brethren" in Matthew 25:40.

> "*In this judgment, all the Gentiles will be divided into two camps: the pro-Semitic sheep camp or the anti-Semitic goat camp... The pro-Semites are those who will provide help for Jesus' brethren the Jews, during the Great Tribulation, a time when it will be very dangerous to do so.*" (Dr. Arnold Fruchtenbaum)[25]

> "*The expression "these brothers" must refer to a third group that is neither sheep nor goats. The only possible group would be Jews, physical brothers of the Lord. In view of the distress in the Tribulation period, it is clear that any believing Jew will have a difficult time surviving.*" (John Walvoord and Roy B. Zuck)[26]

> "*Note the three groups of people in this scene: (1) the sheep, (2) the goats, and (3) those whom Christ calls "My brethren" (v. 40). "My brethren" are the*

believing Jews who witness for Christ during the Tribulation period. Since they would be enemies of the Antichrist, yet sealed and protected by God, they would suffer great persecution. They would not be able to buy or sell, and thus would be hungry. They would flee from their homes (Matt. 24:15-21) and would need places to stay. Without jobs and without the mark of the beast (Rev. 13:17), they could not secure clothing and would be naked. Many would be cast into prison... Many Gentiles during this period will believe the message of the Jewish missionaries (Matt. 24:14; Rev. 7:9-17). They will then show love and mercy to these suffering Jews, by feeding, clothing, and visiting them in prison, etc." (Warren Wiersbe)[27]

These quotes all acknowledge that the Jews will be experiencing another period of severe persecution during the Great Tribulation period. Reminiscent to Hitler's attempt to exterminate the Jews during WWII, the Antichrist will be perpetrating an even worse holocaust in the last 3 ½ years of the Trib-period.

In 1939, the core Jewish population reached its historical peak of 17 million. Because of the Holocaust, the number had been reduced to 11 million by the end of 1945.[28] Hitler eliminated about 6 million Jews, but Zechariah 13:8 says that two thirds of the Jews in the land will be cut off. Presumably, when this happens even more than 6 million Jews will be killed.

If the Jewish Brethren view is correct, then it seems likely that pro-Semite historical figures like Oskar Schindler will rise up amongst the Sheep Gentiles. Schindler was credited for saving about 1200 Jews during the Nazi Holocaust. If the Jewish Brethren view turns out to be correct, then imagine their jubilee when they reunite with the pro-Semites that fed, clothed, sheltered and comforted them in the time of their deepest distress.

The Disciples Brethren View

In Matthew 12:49-50 Jesus Christ, *"stretched out His hand toward His disciples and said, "Here are My mother and My brothers! For whoever does the will of My Father in heaven is My brother and sister and mother."*

With this action and accompanying acknowledgment, Jesus drew attention away from His biological kinship and shifted the focus upon His spiritual family. In essence, He called the disciples His brothers. This promotes the possibility of a *Disciples Brethren* view. Below is a quote about this alternative perspective.

> *"These commentators say that this is a judgment on the Gentiles who have survived the tribulation, and that the judgment will be based on their treatment of the Jews, called Christ's "brothers" (25:40). But another view is that the scene describes a personal, public, final judgment on men, according to the treatment they have given to Christ—and consequently pertains to men within the Christian faith."* (New Commentary on the Whole Bible: New Testament)

The Disciples Brethren view *"pertains to men within the Christian faith."* This would include all saved men and women, whether they are Jews or Gentiles. During the Great Tribulation both categories will have brethren in need of food, clothing, shelter and comfort. In fact, there will likely be many more Gentiles in need than Jews at the time; not because the Gentiles are more needy, rather they will seemingly be far more numerous.

The Potential Problems with Both Views

Although both views have merits, they also have some potential problems. The main foreseeable problem with the *Disciples Brethren* teaching is that there are only three groups listed in Matthew 25:31-

40. They are the Sheep, the Goats and the Brethren. The Sheep are saved living Gentiles, the Goats are unsaved living Gentiles and the Brethren are saved Jews and maybe Gentiles.

The problem arises in the format of this question: If the saved Gentiles are already categorized as sheep, then how could they also be classified as Christ's brethren?

One possible explanation is that the saved Sheep living Gentiles, at some point extended help to the Tribulation Saints who later died during the Trib-period. Jesus didn't specify that all of His brethren who received Gentile assistance survived through the Trib-period. He simply stated that they were hungry, thirsty, homeless, naked, sick and imprisoned during the Trib-period. These harsh conditions could have resulted in the deaths of some of Christ's disciples brethren.

The potential problems with the Jewish Brethren view are below.

The first glaring problem is how does a sheep Gentile find a believing Jew to help out during the Trib-period? Two thirds of the Jews are going to be killed and approximately one-third of the surviving Jews are going into exile in the mountains of Petra, Jordan. Do Gentiles need to travel to Jordan to find a Jew that's hungry, thirsty, homeless, naked, sickly or imprisoned?

Granted, some Jews will still be living within the world nations, but they aren't likely going to be flaunting their yarmulkes in public squares. World Jews will likely be hiding in isolation for fear of persecution. Furthermore, how is a blind, wheelchair-bound, or otherwise handicapped sheep Gentile, who is living in a remote region of the world, going to track down a nearby Jew in need?

Is this another reason why the sheep Gentiles ask three times in Matthew 25:37-39, *"When did we see You?"* I realize this question is taken out of context and somewhat factitious, but there is a possibility during the Trib-period, that some sheep Gentiles won't even cross paths with a believing Jew, let alone help one. Conversely, a sheep Gentile wouldn't need to search high and low to find a disciple brethren of Christ in need. These brethren will be spread throughout the nations.

What about those sheep Gentiles, who are also starving and in need themselves? Lacking in their own resources, how are they going to extend a helping hand to a needy Jew?

This poses another problem with the Jewish Brethren view. Does a sheep Gentile receive any rewards for helping another Gentile disciple, or does that go unnoticed at the Sheep and Goat Judgment?

Summary

In conclusion, the good news is that there will be both Jews and Gentiles that somehow survive through the perils of the Trib-period. The bad news is that many of them will experience hunger, thirst, nakedness, homelessness, sickness and imprisonment. These conditions will worsen dramatically day by day during the last 3 ½ years of the Great Tribulation.

How long do you think you could personally survive under these harsh circumstances? A week, month or year? Do you think you could fight, bite and scratch your way through the entire 3 ½ years?

In 1906, Alfred Henry Lewis stated, "*There are only nine meals between mankind and anarchy.*" Food, water and gas shortages that were experienced in the aftermath of Hurricane Katrina proved that Lewis was correct. Studies done at that time found that most households only stock their pantries with about three days of food and drink, and if electricity shuts down, food in the refrigerators and freezers spoils quickly.

After just a few days most families have to fend for themselves. Unfortunately, they soon discover that their neighborhood grocery stores have been looted and left with empty shelves. If they're lucky, they might be able to find some store or restaurant where they can still buy a meal.

That's the potential hard-luck story now, but in the Trib-period, they will need to sell their souls to the Devil by receiving the Mark of the Beast, just to buy and sell. If someone is starving, they become desperate, vulnerable and susceptible to taking the Mark of the Beast. Millions and maybe billions will make this fatal mistake. Would you be among them?

The GREAT NEWS is that YOU DON'T HAVE TO BE! If the Rapture hasn't happened by the time you're reading this chapter, then you can RECEIVE JESUS CHRIST RIGHT NOW! Yes, people will get saved after the Rapture, but WHY WAIT?

BE SMART! Why risk the chance of surviving through the treachery of the Trib-period. Mankind is existing at the end of the last days prophetic timeline.

ACT NOW! Take a knee, fold your hands, bow your head, repent and receive JESUS CHRIST as LORD and SAVIOR!

"But what does it say? "The word is near you, in your mouth and in your heart" (that is, the word of faith which we preach): that if you confess with your mouth the Lord Jesus and believe in your heart that God has raised Him from the dead, YOU WILL BE SAVED. For with the heart one believes unto righteousness, and with the mouth confession is made unto salvation. For the Scripture says, "WHOEVER BELIEVES ON HIM WILL NOT BE PUT TO SHAME." For there is no distinction between Jew and Greek, (*Gentile*), for the same Lord over all is rich to all who call upon Him. For "WHOEVER CALLS ON THE NAME OF THE LORD SHALL BE SAVED." (Romans 10:9-13, NKJV; EMPHASIS ADDED)

9

The Marriage Supper of the Lamb

This chapter was alluded to in the prior one entitled, "*The Resurrections in the Millennium*," and as such, it is intended to serve as an extension of that chapter. It will primarily address the questions below.

1. What is the Marriage Supper of the Lamb?

2. When is the *Marriage Supper of the Lamb*?

3. How do we determine the location of the *Marriage Supper of the Lamb*?

4. Who are the guests in attendance of the *Marriage Supper of the Lamb*?

1. What is the *Marriage Supper of the Lamb*?

In a nutshell, the *Marriage Supper of the Lamb* is the celebratory event that officially concludes the courtship of Jesus Christ and the Church. In essence, it is likened to the glorious reception that ensues after a couple has concluded their engagement period, exchanged their rings, taken their vows at the altar, been pronounced man and wife and performed their ceremonial wedding kiss.

The prophetic significance of this climactic event can best be explained through the traditional Jewish Wedding model that is summarized below.

The Jewish Wedding Model

Since Jesus Christ in His humanity was born as a Jew and the Church is considered to be His Bride, as per Revelation 19:7-9, Ephesians 5:22-33 and elsewhere, the Jewish Wedding Model serves as a guide for better understanding what's being said in Revelation 19:7-9 below.

> *"Let us be glad and rejoice and give Him glory, for the marriage of the Lamb has come, and His wife has made herself ready." And to her it was granted to be arrayed in fine linen, clean and bright, for the fine linen is the righteous acts of the saints. Then he said to me, "Write: 'Blessed are those who are called to the marriage supper of the Lamb!' " And he said to me, "These are the true sayings of God.""* (Revelation 19:7-9)

The Traditional Jewish Wedding Model consisted of the six primary stages below.

1. *Betrothal* – The groom negotiated a fair price (mohar) for his bride. In the case of believers, the price was paid by Jesus Christ's precious sacrificial blood upon the cross for the sins of believers.

2. *Separation* – The engagement period was actually a time of separation usually lasting about 12 months. While the bride-to-be stayed home, the groom returned to his father's house to make preparations for their future lives together. This gave the bride time to prepare her trousseau, and the groom to construct a place for the two of them to live happily ever after. Presently, Christ and the bride are

separated. He is in heaven while she is on earth preparing her wedding garments, which according to Revelation 19:8 are her righteous acts.

3. *Preparation* – The groom utilized the separation period to return to his father's house to construct the couple's new home on the premises. John 14:1-4 informs that Christ is preparing mansions in heaven for believers.

4. *Fetching* – At the appropriate time after the construction was completed, the groom came to fetch his bride. Although the bride knew the time would come, she didn't necessarily know precisely when. This is the case with believers today; they know Christ is coming but don't know the day or hour. Also, the groom's arrival was usually accompanied by the best man and several friends. When the party arrived to fetch the bride there was often a shout from the friends to announce the groom had arrived. 1 Thessalonians 4:16 declares there will be a shout announcing Christ's return from His friend the archangel.

5. *Consummation* – Once fetched, the two returned to the groom's father›s house where they were secluded in a bridal chamber. While inside the chamber they consummated their marriage by entering into physical union for the first time. They remained secluded in the chamber, usually for about seven days, (*The Wedding Week*), while the wedding guests enjoyed the celebrations occurring simultaneously at the groom's father's house. This will be the similar case with Christ and his believers. Together they will be secluded somewhere in heaven consummating their union, while the seven-years of tribulation takes place on earth. The seven-days seem to represent these seven years of tribulation.

These first five phases above completes Rev. 19:7-8 "*"Let us be glad and rejoice and give Him glory, for the marriage of the Lamb has come, and His wife has made herself ready." And to her it was granted to be arrayed in fine linen, clean and bright, for the fine linen is the righteous acts of the saints."*

Thus, *the marriage of the Lamb* takes place in heaven where *His wife has made herself ready.*

Below are two helpful explanatory quotes from qualified sources about the Wedding Week, whereby the marriage is officially consummated. By simple comparison, the conclusion of the Wedding Week could be likened to when the pastor says, *"you may now kiss the bride,"* after which, the groom lifts the bridal veil and performs the official kiss that finalizes the wedding ceremony.

> *"During the seven days of the wedding feast, the bride and groom remained hidden in the bridal chamber (Cf. Genesis 29:21-23, 27-28) for the seven days of the huppah. Afterwards, the groom came out of hiding, bringing his bride with him, but with her veil removed so that everyone could see her."* (Chuck Missler – January 1, 2003)[29]

Note, that Missler alludes to the *wedding feast* that happens when *the bride and groom remained hidden in the bridal chamber for seven days.* Missler is seemingly referencing the celebrations and feastings taking place when the bride and groom are consummating their marriage behind closed doors, rather than *the Marriage Supper of the Lamb* that follows, whereby the bride and groom are both present.

> *"Before entering the huppah the bridegroom had to recite the seven nuptial benedictions... Outside the huppah (in former times inside) the groomsmen and bridesmaids stood as guards awaiting the good tidings that the union had been happily consummated with reference to Deut. xxii. 17..., while the people indulged in dancing, singing, and*

> *especially in praises of the bride (comp. John iii. 29; Matt. xxv. 1-13). The bride had to remain in the huppah for seven days, as long as the wedding festivities lasted (Judges xiv. 15); hence the name of these festivities, "the seven days of her" or "of the huppah"".. (Kaufman Kohler – abbreviated from the Jewish Encyclopedia)*[30]

6. *Celebration* – After the seven days had elapsed, the groom brought his bride out of the chamber to greet the wedding guests and partake of the marriage supper celebration. This will be the case after the Tribulation Period, the Marriage Supper of the Lamb will happen and then Christ will reign in His messianic kingdom and his bride will co-reign faithfully by His side.

2.   When is the *Marriage Supper of the Lamb*?

The celebration of phase six fulfills Rev. 19:9, which says. *"Then he said to me, "Write: 'Blessed are those who are called to the marriage supper of the Lamb!'" And he said to me, "These are the true sayings of God."*

The timing of the *Marriage Supper of the Lamb* is after the wedding is consummated during the seven-day wedding week. Prophetically speaking, these seven-days could represent the Seven-Year Trib-period, which is followed by the 75-Day Interval period. Thus, the *Marriage Supper* seemingly transpires during this interval period.

3.   How do we determine the location of the *Marriage Supper of the Lamb*?

Some Bible prophecy teachers, such as Dr. Tim LaHaye and Dr. David Reagan believe that the Marriage Supper takes place in heaven.

> *"The marriage of the Lamb must take place in heaven, for in Revelation 19:11, after the marriage of the lamb and the marriage supper of the Lamb, we find the Lord Jesus coming in what we call "the Glorious Appearing" to set up His kingdom. For this reason we must conclude that the marriage and the supper have occurred in heaven. Their location in Revelation 19 shows these events to have taken place at the end of the Tribulation, just before the millennial reign of Christ on the earth."* (Dr. Tim LaHaye)[31]

Dr. LaHaye states, *"we must conclude that the marriage and the supper have occurred in heaven."* In the quote below, Dr. Reagan says, *"this event is clearly pictured as being held in Heaven."*

> *"I have been surprised in recent years to discover that several well known Bible prophecy experts whom I highly respect have started teaching that the Marriage Feast of the Lamb, which is recorded in Revelation 19:7-9, will be held on earth after the return of Jesus — despite the fact that this event is clearly pictured as being held in Heaven before the Second Coming."* (Dr. David Reagan)[32]

The Reagan quote is interesting in that it goes on to list a few passages below, which appear to imply that the marriage supper, feast or banquet actually takes place on the earth.

> *"Their argument seems to be based primarily on a statement in Luke 22:28-30 where Jesus promises believers that they will "eat and drink at My table in My kingdom…" This statement certainly leaves the impression that the feast will be held after the Lord returns and establishes His kingdom here on this earth. Additionally, some point to Luke 13:28-30 where Jesus says that the saved will one*

day "come from east and west, and from north and south, and will recline at the table in the kingdom of God." They conclude their argument by pointing to Isaiah 25:6, which is a Millennial setting and which refers to a "lavish banquet for all peoples on this mountain" — referring to Mount Zion in Jerusalem (Isaiah 24:23)." (Dr. David Reagan)[33]

Other prophecy experts, such as Dr. Arnold Fruchtenbaum, Dr. Ron Rhodes, Dr. Thomas Ice, John MacArthur and Tony Garland teach that the Marriage Supper of the Lamb takes place on the earth. Below are a few select quotes from some of them.

"Revelation 19:9 says, "Blessed are those who are invited to the marriage supper of the Lamb." This passage clearly has a forward look anticipating a future time. It cannot refer to anyone in heaven since the church (the bride) is the only redeemed entity in heaven. However, after the second coming when believers from other ages will be resurrected (Dan. 12:2) along with tribulation saints, both mortal and resurrected ones (Rev. 20:4), these will be the invited guest who will be guests at this celebration supper. I believe that the marriage supper will be during the first part of the millennial reign of Christ. Fruchtenbaum says: Hence, the "many" who are bidden to attend the marriage feast on earth are all the Old Testament saints and the Tribulation saints resurrected after the Second Coming. While the marriage ceremony will take place in Heaven just before the Second Coming, the marriage feast will take place on earth after the Second Coming. In fact, it would seem that the marriage feast is what begins the Millennium or the Messianic Kingdom; the Church's co-reigning with the Messiah will start with a tremendous marriage feast." (Dr. Thomas Ice)[34]

Thomas Ice acknowledges that, *"the marriage ceremony will take place in Heaven just before the Second Coming, the marriage feast will take place on earth after the Second Coming."* This distinction is important to note. As explained prior in the Jewish Wedding Model, the marriage ceremony and the marriage feast are two separate events.

> *"Then, when the Lord Jesus comes back at the end of the time of tribulation to set up His Kingdom, the glorified, resurrected, exalted church comes back and is now presented to those on earth. And there is the glorious manifestation of the children of God made known, not only to heavenly beings but to those who are still alive on the earth who go into the Kingdom. So the presentation of the bride can take place from the rapture to the return of Christ and the establishment of His Kingdom. First they're presented in heaven, then they're presented on earth. And then the culminating thing is the final supper and the ceremony and the consummation of the marriage. We find that final marriage supper, I think, really played out in the millennial Kingdom. It's when glorified saints and saints still alive on earth all come together, all recognizing the glorious bride of Christ, all joining in on the festivities and the celebration, and that's the final supper."* (John F. MacArthur)[35]

John MacArthur advocates for an earthly location of the marriage supper when he says, *"we find that final marriage supper, I think, really played out in the millennial Kingdom. It's when glorified saints and saints still alive on earth all come together."*

> (Revelation 19:7-9) *"The backdrop to this imagery is rooted in Hebrew weddings. There were three phases: 1) the marriage was legally consummated by the parents of the bride and groom; 2) the*

bridegroom came to claim his bride; and 3) there was a marriage supper, which was a feast lasting several days... All three of these phases are seen in Christ's relationship to the church, or bride of Christ... The Bridegroom (Jesus Christ) comes to claim His bride at the Rapture, at which time He takes His bride to heaven, the Father's house (John 14:1-3), with the actual marriage taking place in heaven sometime after the Rapture, prior to the Second Coming (Revelation 19:11-16); and the marriage supper of the Lamb, which apparently takes place on earth at the beginning of the millennial kingdom. That this will be an earthly feast... seems to correspond to the illustrations of weddings in Scripture (see Matthew 22:1-14; 25:1-13)." (Dr. Ron Rhodes)[36]

In line with the Ice, Fruchtenbaum, MacArthur and Rhodes quotes above, and what's said in these verses, Luke 22:28-30, Luke 13:28-30 and Isaiah 25:6, I believe that the *Marriage Supper of the Lamb* takes place on earth. There is another reason that I believe supports this conclusion expressed below.

4.   Who are the guests in attendance of the *Marriage Supper of the Lamb*?

In the related chapter entitled, *"The Resurrections in the Millennium,"* I point out that the resurrected Old Testament and Tribulation Saints will likely be among the guests at the *Marriage Supper of the Lamb.* Along these lines, Dr. Arnold Fruchtenbaum says,

"The fourth stage of the Jewish wedding system is the marriage feast which lasted seven days... The Old Testament and Tribulation saints make up the friends of the bridegroom. Now that they have been resurrected, the wedding feast can take place."[37]

Fruchtenbaum seems to suggest that the *marriage feast* happens when the bride and groom are hidden in the bridal chamber during the seven-day consummation period. After which, he appears to imply that the *wedding feast* that follows is the Marriage Supper of the Lamb.

I emailed Dr. Fruchtenbaum to clarify his point in the quote above and he replied in an email on 3/26/21 with the following comments.

"Dear Bill Salus,... In response to your email of March 12, 2021, my position is that the wedding ceremony will occur in Heaven just before the actual Second Coming and the wedding feast (Marriage Supper of the Lamb) *will occur at the inauguration of the Messianic Kingdom,* (At the onset of the Millennium)... *Yours for the salvation of Israel,.. Arnold G. Fruchtenbaum."*

The general consensus, even among some who believe the marriage supper takes place in heaven, is that these resurrected Old Testament and Tribulation Saints will be among the guests at this celebratory banquet.

Additionally, there is another interesting point to consider that seemingly:

1.   Places the Marriage Supper of the Lamb on the earth,

2.   Lists some survivors of the Trib-period among the guests of this feast.

These helpful details are found in the marriage parable of Matthew 22:1-14. Since this parable is explained in the related *"The Resurrections in the Millennium"* chapter, I will only highlight a few points in this chapter. The verse from the parable below says that the wedding hall gets filled with invitees and among them include *"both bad and good"* guests.

> "So those servants went out into the highways and gathered together all whom they found, both bad and good. And the wedding hall was filled with guests." (Matthew 22:10)

This detail places the location of the wedding hall, which is where the marriage supper is hosted, somewhere that bad beings still exist. The following passage from the same parable reinforces this conclusion.

> "But when the king came in to see the guests, he saw a man there who did not have on a wedding garment. So he said to him, 'Friend, how did you come in here without a wedding garment?' And he was speechless. Then the king said to the servants, 'Bind him hand and foot, take him away, and cast him into outer darkness; there will be weeping and gnashing of teeth.'" (Matthew 22:11-13)

Among the bad guests is some being that needs to be bound hand and foot, removed from the wedding hall and cast into Hell. Considering that the marriage supper won't happen until sometime after the Trib-period ends, and I place it during the Seventy-Five Day Interval Period, this implies that this unwelcome visitor and these bad guests in the hall can't be from heaven.

This is because three and one-half years prior, at the midpoint of the Trib-period, Satan and his bad angels get cast out of heaven.

> "And war broke out in heaven: Michael and his angels fought with the dragon; and the dragon and his angels fought, but they did not prevail, nor was a place found for them in heaven any longer. So the great dragon was cast out, that serpent of old, called the Devil and Satan, who deceives the whole world; he was cast to the earth, and his angels were cast out with him." (Revelation 12:7-9)

With the casting out of all of these bad angels, heaven is rid of all bad beings. If the wedding hall is located in heaven, then this marriage parable can't apply to the Marriage Supper of the Lamb. However, if the banquet takes place on earth, this parable provides an important detail as to what's happening in the world when this wedding feast occurs.

Matthew 22:11 informs, *"But when the king came in to see the guests, he saw a man there who did not have on a wedding garment."* Since the King, representing God the Father of the Groom Jesus Christ, has arrived to see the guests, this means that the timing of His visit is when the marriage supper is taking place. The unwelcome guest who is not properly dressed, alongside the bad invitees crowding into the wedding hall, possibly represents unbelievers still alive on the earth at the time the wedding feast is occurring.

If this is the case, then this infers the following about the *Marriage Supper of the Lamb*:

- It transpires after the Second Coming of Jesus Christ,

- It takes place on the earth and not in heaven,

- It occurs before the Sheep and Goat Judgment of Matthew 25:31-46 is fulfilled,

- It happens during the Seventy-Five Day Interval Period.

10

The Slaughter of the Goat Gentiles

A prior chapter herded up the saved Sheep Gentiles and pointed out how their faith in Christ led them to extend helping hands to His suffering brethren during the Trib-period. As a result, they were awarded access into the Millennium.

Walking side by side with their Messianic Kingdom passports in hand, some of them are among the captives set free that are heading home to witness, and possibly play an active part in, the restoration of their national fortunes. A few examples are below.

Iran: "'But it shall come to pass in the latter days: I will bring back the captives of Elam,' (*West Central Iran*), says the Lord." (Jeremiah 49:39, NKJV; emphasis added)

Northern Jordan: ""But afterward I will restore The fortunes of the sons of Ammon," (*Amman, Jordan*), Declares the Lord." (Jer. 49:6, NASB; emphasis added)

Central Jordan: ""Yet I will restore the fortunes of Moab In the latter days," declares the Lord." (Jer. 48:47, NASB)

Egypt and Assyria: "In that day, (*in the Millennium*), shall there be a highway out of Egypt to Assyria, and the Assyrian shall come into Egypt, and the Egyptian into Assyria; and the Egyptians shall worship with the Assyrians... In that day shall Israel be the third with Egypt and with Assyria, a blessing in the midst of the earth; for that Jehovah of hosts hath blessed them, saying, Blessed be Egypt my people, and Assyria the work of my hands, and Israel mine inheritance." (Isaiah 19:23-25, ASV; emphasis added)

These Middle Eastern nations will have surviving remnants, who were dispersed out of their homelands sometime prior to, or in the midst of, the Trib-period. The believers among the returning Iranian, Jordanian, Egyptian and Assyrian exiles will be doubly excited because, not only are they entering into the Millennium, but they are returning to their historic homelands. Their gripping stories are further developed in the upcoming chapter entitled, *"The Gentiles in the Millennial Kingdom."*

The Indictment of the Goat Gentiles

Now it's time to corral the unsaved Goat Gentiles. These undesirables will mostly include those who rejected Christ, tormented His brethren in the Trib-period, accepted the Antichrist and received the Mark of the Beast. For these misdeeds, their punishment will be death and deportation to Hell.

"And these will go away into everlasting punishment..." (Matthew 25:46a)

The Sheep Gentiles were the subject of commentary on Matthew 25:31-40 in a prior chapter entitled, *The Salvation of the Sheep Gentiles.* The Goat Gentiles are alluded to in Matthew 25:31-33 and 41-46 below.

"When the Son of Man comes in His glory, and all the holy angels with Him, then He will sit on the throne of His glory. All the nations will be gathered before Him, and He will separate them one from another, as a shepherd divides *his* sheep from the goats.And He will set the sheep on His right hand, but the goats on the left." (Matt. 25:31-33)

"Then He will also say to those (*Goat Gentiles*) on the left hand, 'Depart from Me, you cursed, into the everlasting fire (*in Hell*) prepared for the devil and his angels: for I was hungry and you gave Me no food; I was thirsty and you gave Me no drink; I was a stranger and you did not take Me in, naked and you did not clothe Me, sick and in prison and you did not visit Me.' "Then they also will answer Him, saying, 'Lord, when did we see You hungry or thirsty or a stranger or naked or sick or in prison, and did not minister to You?' Then He will answer them, saying, 'Assuredly, I say to you, inasmuch as you did not do it to one of the least of these, you did not do it to Me.' And these (*Goat Gentiles*) will go away into everlasting punishment, but the righteous (*Sheep Gentiles*) into eternal life." (Matt. 25:41-46, NKJV; emphasis added)

These passages point out the stark differences between the kindness shown to Christ's brethren by the Sheep Gentiles in Matthew 25:37-40, and the mistreatment of those brethren by the Goat Gentiles. In the Trib-period, when Christ's brethren were hungry, thirsty, homeless, naked, sick or imprisoned, the sheep stood steadfast by their side. Conversely, the goats abandoned these most important people, which was akin to compounding their sufferings.

Let's put this indictment of the Goat Gentiles into perspective. In the Trib-period, the goats will represent the *HAVES*, whereas the brethren of Christ will be the *HAVE-NOTS*. Presumably, most all of the *"goats"* will become worshippers of the Antichrist and recipients of the Mark of the Beast, which enables them to buy and sell as per Revelation 13:16-17.

On the other hand, the *"brethren"* will be worshippers of Christ, non-recipients of the Mark of the Beast and therefore be unable to buy and sell in the mainstream marketplace. In large part, this is likely the root cause of their hunger, thirst, homelessness, nakedness and sickness.

Moreover, the goats are going to be the *HUNTERS* and the brethren the *HUNTED*. A Jewish brethren/believer of Christ will live under the constant threat of being killed during the genocidal campaign of the Antichrist. Similarly, a Christian Gentile believer in Jesus is headed toward the chopping block if he or she gets caught by the authorities. Zechariah 13:8 points out that two-thirds of the Jews will be exterminated somehow and Revelation 20:4 informs that believers are subjected to beheadings.

In addition to physical hardships, it can be anticipated that the believing brethren will also have to grapple with mental torment and spiritual betrayal within the neighboring goat communities. It is likely that many goats will be family members, dear friends or close neighbors with the brethren. Despite the pleadings of the brethren, these goat dear ones will at some point alienate themselves when they reject Christ and receive the Antichrist. This will dishearten the brethren who will be more concerned about the souls of their loved ones, rather than their sandwiches.

(WARNING: the rest of this chapter is not for the faint of heart)!

The final act of the 75-Day Interval is as the chapter title suggests, a bloody mess. Millions if not billions of unsaved goats have to *"go away into everlasting punishment"* as per Matthew 25:46. This is not a temporary "timeout," rather it is a permanent checkout!

The Millennial Kingdom is not a place that will be characterized by *everlasting punishment,* but Hell is! And, unlike the Lake of Fire, where in Rev. 19:20 the Antichrist and False Prophet are cast into while still breathing, nobody enters into Hell alive!

Death deals with the material departure of a being from its earthly body and Hell, which is Hades in the Greek, is concerned with the immaterial aspect of a person after death, which is their soul. Presently, when someone dies their soul gets detached from its human body and is delivered to its destination, which is either Heaven if they're saved or Hades if they're not.

The Two Phases of the Goat's Everlasting Punishment

Phase one of the everlasting punishment of the goats begins in Hades and lasts for one-thousand years until they appear at the White Throne Judgment prophesied below.

> "Then, (*at the end of the Millennium*), I saw a great white throne and Him who sat on it, from whose face the earth and the heaven fled away. And there was found no place for them. And I saw the (*unsaved*) dead (*throughout time*) small and great, (*including the Goat Gentiles*), standing before God, and books were opened. And another book was opened, which is *the Book* of Life. And the dead, (*including the goats*), were judged according to their works, (*like taking the Mark of the Beast*), by the things which were written in the books. The sea gave up the dead who were in it, and Death and Hades delivered up the dead, (*including the goats*), who were in them. And they were

judged, each one according to his works." (Rev.
20:11-13, NKJV; emphasis added)

The Goat Gentiles are among the dead that will stand before
God at the White Throne Judgment. Each of them will be judged
according to his (or hers) *works*, such as taking the Mark of the
Beast, which rendered them unsavable, Anti-Semitism of Christ's
Brethren in the Trib-period and likely a whole laundry list of other
sinful and lawless deeds.

Phase two of the castigation of the goats is getting cast into
the Lake of Fire. Remember that *everlasting punishment* means no
time off for good behavior after their 1000-year stint in Hades, but
equates to torment throughout eternity.

> "Then Death and Hades were cast into the lake
> of fire. This is the second death. And anyone not
> found written in the Book of Life, (*including the
> Goat Gentiles*), was cast into the lake of fire." (Rev.
> 20:14-15, NKJV; emphasis added)

Without going into a lengthy theological explanation of what
the "*second death*" is, simply put, it represents the permanent
departure of a soul from the presence of its Maker. The White
Throne Judgment is commonly called the Second Resurrection
and it serves as the prerequisite for a *second death*.

So, the story of the goats goes something like this. They die,
their souls go to Hell for 1000-years and then they return alive at
the Second Resurrection to face God. The inference that they are
literally resurrected is found in the passage below.

> "And I saw thrones, (*the Raptured Church*) and
> they sat on them, and judgment was committed
> to them. Then *I saw* the souls of those who had
> been beheaded, (*Tribulation Saints*), for their
> witness to Jesus and for the word of God, who

> had not worshiped the beast or his image, and
> had not received *his* mark on their foreheads or
> on their hands. And they lived and reigned with
> Christ for a thousand years. But the rest of the
> dead, (*including the Goat Gentiles*), did not LIVE
> AGAIN until the thousand years (*Millennium*)
> were finished. This *is* the first resurrection." (Rev.
> 20:4-5, NKJV; emphasis added)

The Raptured Church and the Old Testament and Tribulation
Saints are involved in the "First Resurrection," but *the rest of the
dead* do not *LIVE AGAIN* until the "Second Resurrection" takes
place after the Millennium ends. The Second Resurrection must
occur so that the Philippians foretelling below can be accomplished.

> "Therefore God, (*the heavenly Father*), also has
> highly exalted Him, (*Jesus Christ*), and given
> Him the name which is above every name, that
> at the name of Jesus every knee should bow, of
> those in heaven, and of those on earth, and of
> those under the earth, (*in Hell*), and *that* every
> tongue should confess that Jesus Christ *is* Lord,
> to the glory of God the Father." (Philippians 2:9-
> 11, NKJV; emphasis added)

At the Second Resurrection, alive again with physical bodies,
the goats will all need to drop down to their knees at the White
Throne Judgment and make a public proclamation that, "*Jesus
Christ is Lord!*" This is not an altar call that can save them, rather it
is an admission of guilt that clearly condemns them.

Are the Villains Wanted Dead or Alive?

If the goats are cast alive into the Lake of Fire, they will follow
in the same failed footsteps of their predecessors, the Antichrist
and False Prophet. These two world leaders were cast alive into the
lake of Fire.

"Then the beast, (*the Antichrist*), was captured, and with him the false prophet who worked signs in his presence, by which he deceived those who received the mark of the beast and those who worshiped his image. These two were cast alive into the lake of fire burning with brimstone." (Revelation 19:20, NKJV; emphasis added)

Thus it's possible, that just as nobody gets into Hell unless they're dead, then conversely, no one gets cast into the Lake of Fire unless they are alive. Rev. 20:13 points out that Hades forfeits its dead. Rev. 20:14 informs that subsequently Hades is relocated into the Lake of Fire. Lastly, Rev. 20:15 declares that all the unsaved people, who would include the goats, get cast into the Lake of Fire also.

Therefore, the first death of an unbeliever is physical. It kills the body, but not the soul. The soul proceeds into Hades from the point of death and remains tormented there in the awakened soul-state throughout the duration of the Millennium. In Hades, the soul appears to be cognizant of its dreadful surroundings. This can be understood through the parable of Lazarus and the Rich Man in Luke 19:16-31. A portion of that informative passage is quoted below.

> "So it was that (*Lazarus*) the beggar died, and was carried by the angels to Abraham's bosom. The rich man also died and was buried. And being in torments in Hades, he lifted up his eyes and saw Abraham afar off, and Lazarus in his (*heavenly*) bosom. "Then he, (*the rich man*), cried and said, 'Father Abraham, have mercy on me, and send Lazarus that he may dip the tip of his finger in water and cool my tongue; for I am tormented in this flame. But Abraham said (*to the rich man*), 'Son, remember that in your lifetime you received your good things, and likewise Lazarus evil things; but now he is comforted and you are

tormented. And besides all this, between us and you there is a great gulf fixed, so that those who want to pass from here to you cannot, nor can those from there pass to us."'" (Luke 19:22-26, NKJV; emphasis added)

The rich man was tormented by a flame in Hades and lacked water to cool his tongue. Furthermore, he was stuck behind an impassable great gulf with no ability to depart from his dire straits. He was entirely aware of his depraved condition and deprived location. Thus, it's safe to say that the first death for an unbeliever is HORRIBLE!

That's why it has been wisely said that "*Life on earth is the worst of times for a believer, but the best of times for an unbeliever.*"

For an unbeliever, the first death is only phase one. Phase two is even worse! In order for the unbelieving soul to experience the Second Death after the Millennium, it apparently needs to be suited up in a tangible body once again, which happens at the Second Resurrection. Unlike the first death, the Second Death does not seem to kill the body nor the soul, rather they appear to be attached together and alive when the unbeliever gets cast into the Lake of Fire.

Revelation 19:20 says that the Lake of Fire is filled with burning brimstone. If there was a shortage of cool water in Hades for the rich man, it sounds like there's not a drop to spare in the Lake of Fire either.

The reason it's important for an unbeliever to understand the severity of the eternal depravity they will face, is to alert them that if they are still alive and unmarked by the Beast they can take a knee and confess NOW that Jesus Christ is Lord. This action of repentance, if done sincerely, instantly reclassifies the person from being unsaved to saved and spares them from the aforementioned *everlasting punishment.*

Every Knee and Every Tongue Means Everyone Must Bow and Confess

When the Bible says that *"every knee should bow"* and *"every tongue should confess,"* it alludes to both believers and unbelievers alike. These are not goodwill gestures, but are required actions. All saved people, whether they are Old Testament Saints, Church Age believers, Tribulation Saints or Sheep Gentiles must also take a knee and make this confession.

The Church Age believers turn their personal profession of faith that initially saved them into a public acknowledgment at the Judgment Seat of Christ after the Rapture.

> "But why do you judge your brother? Or why do you show contempt for your brother? For we shall all stand before the judgment seat of Christ. For it is written: *"As* I live, says the Lord, Every knee shall bow to Me, And every tongue shall confess to God."* So then each of us shall give account of himself to God." (Romans 14:10-12)

These believers have physical knees to bow and tongues to confess because they received their resurrected bodies at the time of the Rapture according to 1 Corinthians 15:52 which says, *"in a moment, in the twinkling of an eye, at the last trumpet. For the trumpet will sound, and the dead will be raised incorruptible, and we shall be changed."*

The Old Testament and Tribulation Saints can physically drop to their knees and publicly confess only after they are resurrected and provided with a physical anatomy. Their resurrections seemingly happen during the 75-Day Interval Period. The Sheep Gentiles will likely make their public professions at the time of the Sheep and Goat Judgment. They won't need to be resurrected with physical knees and tongues because they are not dead at the time.

WARNING: No Unsaved People are Allowed into the Millennium

This is the second warning of this chapter. The jaw-dropping information that you are about to read is predicated upon this alert. Only saved sheep are awarded entry into the Millennium, no unsaved goats are allowed. This is why all Trib-period surviving unbelievers, represented by the Goat Gentiles, have to *go away into everlasting punishment.*

Just to clarify, sin will exist in the Millennium, but unsaved goats are not the root of that evil. In the verse below, the prophet Isaiah acknowledges that there will be sinners present in the Messianic Kingdom.

> "No more shall an infant from there *live but a few* days, Nor an old man who has not fulfilled his days; For the child shall die one hundred years old, But the sinner *being* one hundred years old shall be accursed." (Isaiah 65:20)

The good news is that there won't be abortions or infant mortality in the Millennium because the child won't die until it has reached the ripe old age of one-hundred. However, that child is born with a sin nature, but the great news is that he or she can receive Christ as their Savior and avoid being *accursed* further during their one-hundred-year life span.

However, if they reject Christ and die in an unsaved state, then their soul likely detaches itself from their body and goes to Hell. Then, at the Second Resurrection, they are made alive again, judged at the White Throne and then cast into the Lake of Fire along with the goats and all other unbelievers throughout history.

The logical question to ask and answer at this juncture is, *"how does sin creep into the Messianic Kingdom if no unsaved goats are allowed into the Millennium to propagate it?"*

Adding complexity to this mysterious sin scenario, is that Satan is chained up in the Abyss and unable to tempt and deceive people as per Rev. 20:1-3. Thus, the sinner in the Millennium can't use the classic old excuse that, *"the Devil made me do it."*

The only logical reason that sin exists during the Millennium, appears to be because the saved Sheep Gentiles bring their baggage in with them. I'm not alluding to their travel luggage, which by this time they may no longer possess, but rather their sin natures that they were born with. When people get saved, they don't instantly become sinless, rather they are forgiven and with the help of the Holy Spirit and their renewed conscience, they hopefully begin to sin less and less.

It can be anticipated that the desires for power, greed, lust and the other garden variety temptations that are common to man will still flare up from time to time among the sheep in the Millennium. Through the generations the sin natures of the sheep will be passed on naturally through their genealogies.

The big difference between now and then, is that Satan will be gone into the Abyss (Rev. 20:3), Christ will be seated upon His Jerusalem throne (Jer. 3:17), and the whole world will be filled with the knowledge of the Lord (Isaiah 11:9). These facts will make it easier to recognize that Jesus Christ is Lord.

The Egypt and Magog Examples of Sin in the Millennium

Another evidence of unbelievers that are born in the Millennium appears to be found in the passage pertaining to Egypt below.

> "And it shall come to pass *that* everyone who is left of all the nations which came against Jerusalem shall go up from year to year to worship the King, the Lord of hosts, and to keep the Feast of

Tabernacles. And it shall be *that* whichever of the families of the earth do not come up to Jerusalem to worship the King, the Lord of hosts, on them there will be no rain. (*For example*), If the family of Egypt will not come up and enter in, they *shall have* no *rain;* they shall receive the plague with which the Lord strikes the nations who do not come up to keep the Feast of Tabernacles. This shall be the punishment of Egypt and the punishment of all the nations that do not come up to keep the Feast of Tabernacles." (Zechariah 14:16-19; NKJV; emphasis added)

Zechariah warns about the plague of no rain that strikes all the nations that don't make the required annual pilgrimage to Jerusalem. This passage seemingly informs there will be families of the earth that for some reason choose not to make the trip, "*to worship the King, the Lord of hosts, and to keep the Feast of Tabernacles.*"

Presumably one of their reasons for not making the voyage could be that they don't believe that Jesus is the King and Lord of Hosts, *i.e.* they are unbelievers. This forewarning to Egypt points out that, just as is the case presently, in the Millennium people are granted free will to either obey or disobey God.

One more example of unbelievers exercising their free choice to oppose God in the Messianic Kingdom is confirmed in the Satanic rebellion described in the verses below. Shortly after the Millennium has ended, a multitude *whose number is as the sand and sea,* are deceived by Satan. Because they are unbelievers they are vulnerable to the Devil's deception.

"Now when the thousand years have expired, Satan will be released from his prison and will go out to deceive the nations which are in the four corners of the earth, Gog and Magog, to gather them together to battle, whose number *is* as the sand of the sea. They went up on the breadth of the earth and surrounded the camp of the saints and the beloved city. And fire came down from God out of heaven and devoured them." (Rev. 20:7-9)

Some people attempt to connect this Gog of Magog invasion with the prophecy of Ezekiel 38, but these are two separate scenarios. The differences will be pointed out in a forthcoming chapter entitled, "*The Magog Invasion in the Aftermath of the Millennium.*"

The Gathering of the Goat Gentiles

Before the goats can *go away to everlasting punishment*, they are going to be gathered. The Matthew 25 passage below explains how the process works.

> "When the Son of Man comes in His glory, and all the holy angels with Him, then He will sit on the throne of His glory. All the nations will be gathered before Him, and He will separate them one from another, as a shepherd divides *his* sheep from the goats. And He will set the sheep on His right hand, but the goats on the left." (Matthew 25:31-33).

Prior chapters have established the likelihood that:

- The nations identified above, represent individual Gentiles within the nations, rather than the entire national populous,

- Delegations, representatives or individual classes are gathered, rather than every individual Gentile,

- Assembling this large of a gathering may, in part, be assigned to *all the holy angels* who come with Jesus Christ at His Second Coming.

Affirming the angelic role in the gathering of the Gentiles, John Walvoord and Roy Zuck in *The Bible Knowledge Commentary: New Testament* state,

> "Christ's coming will be with His powerful angels; His heavenly servants will be with Him to carry out His bidding."[38]… "*At His second coming, the angels will gather the wicked and throw them into judgment* (Matt. 13:40-42; 49-50; 2 Thes. 1:7-10)."[39]

Below are a few more passages that seem to suggest that these *holy angels* may participate in the gathering of, and the judgment upon, the Goat Gentiles. The first two are provided by Jesus Christ in parables about the kingdom of heaven.

Concerning all of these parables provided by Christ in Matthew 13:1-52, Dr. Andy Woods identifies them as "*Kingdom Mysteries.*" Woods points out the following in his book entitled, "*The Coming Kingdom.*"[40]

> "*Israel's rejection of the kingdom offer (Matt. 12:24) led to the kingdom's postponement. Consequently, Christ began to explain the spiritual conditions that would now prevail during the kingdom's absence. This interim program includes His revelation of the kingdom mysteries (Matt. 13) and the church (Matt. 16:18)…The first aspect of this interim phase is the kingdom mysteries (Matt:13:1-52). These represent the course of events to be experienced by the kingdom's heirs or the "sons of the kingdom" (13:38)" between Israel's rejection and future acceptance of the kingdom offer. Thus, these mysteries cover the time period between Israel's formal rejection of the kingdom and the Second Advent (13:40-42, 49-50).*"[41]

Dr. Woods states that the parables are intended to cover the *"spiritual conditions"* on earth, that would *"prevail during the kingdom's absence."* The kingdom's absence ends when Christ returns in the Second Coming and ushers in His Millennial Kingdom. Andy Woods is therefore correct when he says, *"Thus, these mysteries cover the time period between Israel's formal rejection of the kingdom and the Second Advent."*

In other words, some of these parables continue on beyond the Church Age and on through to the end of the age. To confirm this Woods specifically cites Matthew 13:40-42, 49-50, which deal with the parables of the *"tares"* and the *"dragnet."*

The Parable of the Tares Explained

Jesus Christ issues *"The Parable of the Wheat and the Tares"* in Matthew 13:24-30 and then He interprets the parable's meaning to his disciples in the passage below.

> "Then Jesus sent the multitude away and went into the house. And His disciples came to Him, saying, "Explain to us the parable of the tares of the field." He answered and said to them: "He who sows the good seed is the Son of Man. The field is the world, the good seeds are the sons of the kingdom, but the tares are the sons of the wicked one. The enemy who sowed them is the devil, the harvest is the end of the age, and the reapers are the angels. Therefore as the tares are gathered and burned in the fire, so it will be at the end of this age. The Son of Man will send out His angels, and they will gather out of His kingdom all things that offend, and those who practice lawlessness, and will cast them into the furnace of fire. There will be wailing and gnashing of teeth. Then the righteous will shine forth as the sun in the kingdom of their Father. He who has ears to hear, let him hear!" (Matthew 13:36-43)

Christ says that the tares represent the sons of the devil, *i.e.* the wicked one. These tares represent *all things that offend* and *practice lawlessness*. At *the end of the age,* the *reapers* will gather them together and *cast them into the furnace of fire.* The reapers are the angels. Christ *will send out His angels* to weed out and eliminate these tares.

The harvest in this parable seems to occur when Christ returns at *the end of the age,* which is when the Goat Gentiles are gathered for judgment in Matthew 25:31-33, 41-46. According to 2 Thessalonians 2:7-9, *lawlessness* currently has a lid of restraint placed upon it. However, after the Rapture this hindrance is removed and according to Matthew 24:9-12, the *practice* of, or ultimate manifestation of *lawlessness* will abound during the Trib-period.

It appears that the tares in this parable represent the goats that are sentenced to *everlasting punishment.* The reapers would then be the holy angels that come with Christ in Matthew 25:31. This parable implies that the holy angels are more than spectators, but play a crucial role in gathering the Sheep and Goat Gentiles for the Matthew 25:31-46 judgments.

After the goats are cast into the furnace of fire, Jesus Christ says, "*Then the righteous will shine forth as the sun in the kingdom of their Father. He who has ears to hear, let him hear!*"

Apparently, what Christ declares is, that if you have an ear, then hear this, no unsaved Goat Gentiles will enter the Millennium, but only *the righteous will shine forth as the sun in the kingdom of their Father.*

The Dragnet Parable

> "Again, the kingdom of heaven is like a dragnet
> that was cast into the sea and gathered some of
> every kind, which, when it was full, they drew

> to shore; and they sat down and gathered the good into vessels, but threw the bad away. So it will be at the end of the age. The angels will come forth, separate the wicked from among the just, and cast them into the furnace of fire. There will be wailing and gnashing of teeth." (Matthew 13:47-50)

These verses suggest that at the *end of the age* the *angels* will cast a *dragnet* into the *sea*. The sea can serve as a biblical typology that represents the Gentiles or Gentile nations. The net becomes full, which implies that it contains all of the Gentiles. The catch includes both *good* and *just* Gentiles along with *bad* and *wicked* ones. The *good* and *just* would likely represent the saved sheep and the *bad* and *wicked* could allude to the unsaved goats.

After gathering all the Gentiles the angels come forth to, "*separate the wicked from among the just, and cast them into the furnace of fire. There will be wailing and gnashing of teeth.*" The furnace of fire with wailing and gnashing of teeth is apparently associated with the conditions inside of Hell.

In this dragnet parable the implication is that the angels are employed to gather all the Gentiles, and weed out the unbelievers and then make them *go away into everlasting punishment.*

Thus far, this all sounds just and fair and cut and dry, but what about the possibility that among the sheep and goat Gentiles, there exist unbelieving spouses, children, parents, grandparents, neighbors and co-workers or people within their closest spheres of influence? This thought was introduced at the beginning of the chapter.

How will the sheep respond when they witness these related goats receive *everlasting punishment*? The answer seems to be summed in the two passages below.

> *Passage #1:* "The righteous shall rejoice when he sees the vengeance; He shall wash his feet in the blood of the wicked, So that men will say, "Surely *there is* a reward for the righteous; Surely He is God who judges in the earth." (Psalm 58:10-11)

First note that the *righteous*, which is what the Sheep Gentiles are called in Matthew 25:37 and 46, will apparently witness the severe punishment of their goat counterparts. A *righteous* sheep *shall rejoice when he sees the vengeance* of God executed upon the *wicked* goats. Although a saved sheep might have mixed emotions at the time, he or she will *surely* recognize that *there is a reward for the righteous.* They will understand the significance of the verse below.

"And these (*wicked goats*) will go away into everlasting punishment, but the righteous (*sheep*) into eternal life, (*commencing with a passport into the Millennium*)." (Matthew 25:46, NKJV; emphasis added)

> *Passage #2:* "Since it is a righteous thing with God to repay with tribulation those who trouble you, and to give you who are troubled rest with us when the Lord Jesus is revealed from heaven with His mighty angels, in flaming fire taking vengeance on those who do not know God, and on those who do not obey the gospel of our Lord Jesus Christ. These shall be punished with everlasting destruction from the presence of the Lord and from the glory of His power, when He comes, in that Day, to be glorified in His saints and to be admired among all those who believe, because our testimony among you was believed." (2 Thessalonians 1:6-10)

This judgment *is a righteous thing with God*, and whether or not the goats are family or friends with the sheep, they "*do not obey the gospel of our Lord Jesus Christ.*" Most all of these goats will bear the Mark of the Beast. Pledging their allegiance to the Antichrist and receiving his Mark, they decided not to stand in solidarity with their sheep family members or friends, and as such, they will have to, *"be punished with everlasting destruction from the presence of the Lord."*

This judgment happens, *"when the Lord Jesus is revealed from heaven with His mighty angels, in flaming fire taking vengeance on those who do not know God."* This seems to be another section in scripture that places the *mighty angels* on location at the scene of the Sheep and Goat Judgment.

The parables of the tares and dragnet employed the angels to gather the Gentiles, separate them, and cast the goats into the *furnace of fire.* 2 Thessalonians 1:6-10 places these apparently same mighty angels on location when the goats are, *"punished with everlasting destruction."* These angels fingerprints appear to show up in all of these passages.

The Roles of the Angelic Host in Revelation 14

Revelation 14 provides a sequential order of end times events that enlist the services of many angels, apparently including the holy angels that come with Christ at the time of His Second Advent. The angel action begins in Rev. 14:6-7 with Angel #1, that proclaims the everlasting gospel. This seemingly happens in the first 3 ½ years of the Trib-period.

Then following Angel #1, Angel #2 heralds, *"Babylon is fallen, is fallen, that great city, because she has made all nations drink of the wine of the wrath of her fornication,"* (Rev. 14:8).

This angel appears to be acknowledging that the Harlot world religion of Revelation 17 has just been desolated, under the commands of the Antichrist, by the Ten Kings in Rev. 17:16-17. This prophecy finds fulfillment around the midpoint of the Trib-period.

Now we turn our attention to Angel #3. This angel is warning against taking the Mark of the Beast, which only becomes available after "*Babylon is fallen, is fallen,*" i.e. the Harlot world religion is desolated. Angel #3 clearly declares that the *holy angels* are present with Christ when the people who take the Mark of the Beast receive their final punishment.

> "Then a third angel followed them, saying with a loud voice, "If anyone worships the beast and his image, and receives his mark on his forehead or on his hand, he himself shall also drink of the wine of the wrath of God, which is poured out full strength into the cup of His indignation. He shall be tormented with fire and brimstone in the *presence of the holy angels* and in the presence of the Lamb. And the smoke of their torment ascends forever and ever; and they have no rest day or night, who worship the beast and his image, and whoever receives the mark of his name." (Rev. 14:9-11, NKJV; emphasis added)

Angel #3 boldly proclaims that everyone who worships the beast and his image, and receives his mark on his forehead or on his hand will:

- Experience, (*drink the wine of*), the wrath of God,

- Be tormented with fire and brimstone in the presence of both Christ and His holy angels,

- Suffer torment forever and ever,

- Have no rest day or night.

These warnings have a specific application for the Goat Gentiles that bear the Mark of the Beast. They will be tormented in the *presence of the holy angels* that return with Jesus Christ at

His Second Coming. The proclamations of Angel #3 present another example of the holy angels being present at the time of the judgment of the Goat Gentiles.

The Angel with the Sharp Sickle of Revelation 14:17-20

One last passage that involves the angels in a gathering role deserves and honorable mention.

> "Then another angel came out of the temple which is in heaven, he also having a sharp sickle. And another angel came out from the altar, who had power over fire, and he cried with a loud cry to him who had the sharp sickle, saying, "Thrust in your sharp sickle and gather the clusters of the vine of the earth, for her grapes are fully ripe." So the angel thrust his sickle into the earth and gathered the vine of the earth, and threw it into the great winepress of the wrath of God. And the winepress was trampled outside the city, and blood came out of the winepress, up to the horses' bridles, for one thousand six hundred furlongs." (Revelation 14:17-20)

(CAVEAT: Before sharing my thoughts about the possible interpretation of this passage, it's important to note that most commentators teach that these verses connect this sharp sickle with Christ's victory at Armageddon and not necessarily any angelic involvement in gathering the goats for judgment. Moreover, I was unable to find any commentaries that advocate what I'm about to share. So, I could be wrong and that's why I submit Rev.14:17-20 and my related comments that follow, only as an honorable mention).

Revelation 14:17-20 introduces two more angels, let's call them Angels #5 and #6. Angel #5 comes out of the temple with a sharp sickle. Angel #5 is instructed by Angel #6 to, *"thrust in your sharp sickle and gather the clusters of the vine of the earth, for her grapes are fully ripe."*

The second sickle requires Angel #5 to *gather the clusters of the vine of the earth.* The clusters of grapes could represent the Goat Gentiles. Angel #5 is commanded *to thrust his sickle into the earth and gather the vine of the earth.* The inference seems to be a global gathering of clusters of grapes, possibly the goats, that are spread throughout the earth.

Angel #5 follows his marching orders and *thrust his sickle into the earth and gathered the vine of the earth, and threw it into the great winepress of the wrath of God.*

This Angel #5 action seems to connect with Rev. 14:9-10, whereby Angel #3, in Rev. 14:9-11, had stated that everyone who worships the Antichrist and possesses the Mark of the Beast will *"drink of the wine of the wrath of God."* Thus, Angel #5 may be charged with the responsibility to gather the unsaved Goat Gentiles throughout *the earth* and throw them into the *great winepress* so that they are *forced to drink the wine of the wrath of God.*

If the sharp sickle in the hands of Angel #5 represents the gathering of the goats that leads to their slaughter, this would be the second slaughter of the Gentiles. The first massacre dealt with the rebellious armies of the Gentiles at Armageddon in Rev. 16:16 and 19:17-21 and the second bloodbath would involve the unsaved civilians, i.e. the "Goat Gentiles." Remember that not every unsaved Gentile is a soldier that will be killed at Armageddon, many will be civilians.

To call this potential second slaughter a bloodbath is an understatement according to the next verse.

> "And the winepress was trampled outside the city, and blood came out of the winepress, up to the horses' bridles, for one thousand six hundred furlongs, (*approximately 200 miles*)." (Revelation 17:20, NKJV; emphasis added)

Please be reminded, that this specific verse is commonly taught to represent the bloodshed of the first massacre of the armies of Armageddon, and it may allude to that. However, this judgment takes place *outside of the city*, probably Jerusalem, which is approximately 80 miles south of Mount Megiddo where the armies of Armageddon get destroyed.

So, this slaughter possibly occurs at a different location and involves a different group of people, who are probably the unsaved civilians, or otherwise referred to as the Goat Gentiles in Matthew 25:41-46. The judgment that leads to the slaughter of the unsaved civilians, which would include all those who took the "Mark of the Beast, appears to happen in the Valley of Jehoshaphat, which is also known as the Valley of Decision.

> "I will also gather all nations, And bring them down to the Valley of Jehoshaphat; And I will enter into judgment with them there On account of My people, My heritage Israel, Whom they have scattered among the nations; They have also divided up My land." (Joel 3:2)

> "Let the nations be wakened, and come up to the Valley of Jehoshaphat; For there I will sit to judge all the surrounding nations. Put in the sickle, for the harvest is ripe. Come, go down; For the winepress is full, The vats overflow— For their wickedness *is* great." Multitudes, multitudes in the valley of decision! For the day of the Lord *is* near in the valley of decision." (Joel 3:12-14)

The location of the Valley of Jehoshaphat is debatable. Some think it gets created when the Mount of Olives, which faces Jerusalem, gets geographically divided at the time of the Victory Ascent of Jesus Christ to the Mount of Olives in Zechariah 14:4 below.

"And in that day His feet will stand on the Mount of Olives, Which faces Jerusalem on the east. And the Mount of Olives shall be split in two, From east to west, *Making* a very large valley; Half of the mountain shall move toward the north And half of it toward the south."

Others suggest it could be the modern-day Kidron Valley. Christian tradition generally holds to this view. See the quote and image below.

"Christian tradition made this identification at least as early as the 4th cent. a.d., perhaps beginning with the Bordeaux Pilgrim's account. Both Eusebius and Jerome refer to the Valley of Jehoshaphat in the Onamasticon, though Eusebius calls it the Valley of Hinnom, while Jerome expressly speaks of the Kidron Valley, and uses the Joel 3:2, 12 reference."[42]

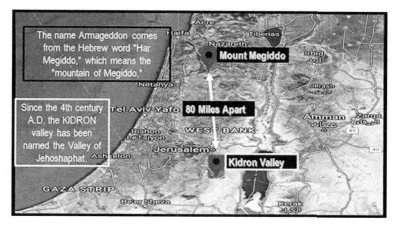

According to Matthew 25:31-32, the gathering of the Gentiles takes place when Christ is seated upon the throne of His glory, which according to Jeremiah 3:17 is going to be located in the city of Jerusalem. It seems feasible that the second sickle with Angel #5

gathers the goats to Jerusalem for a severe trampling by the *holy angels* outside of the *holy city*.

The Global Slaughter of the Goat Gentiles

The first slaughter of the armies at Armageddon and the subsequent massacre around Jerusalem are indeed gory scenes, but the judgment of the goat civilians seemingly spreads throughout the globe. Passages like the ones below suggest that the slaughter of the goats is not confined to the outskirts of Jerusalem.

> "The earth dries up *and* crumbles away, the mainland dries out *and* crumbles away, the exalted of the people of the earth dwindle. The earth is also defiled by its inhabitants, for they violated laws, altered statutes, *and* broke the everlasting covenant. Therefore, a curse devours the earth, and those who live on it suffer for their guilt. Therefore, the inhabitants of the earth decrease in number, and few people are left." (Isaiah 24:4-6, NASB)

> "For so it will be in the midst of the earth among the peoples, As the shaking of an olive tree, As the gleanings when the grape harvest is over." (Isaiah 24:13, NASB)

In these two passages, Isaiah foretells that when the *curse* of the judgment of the unsaved Gentiles *devours the earth* that, "*Therefore, the inhabitants of the earth decrease in number, and few people are left.*" He says the people have "*broke the everlasting covenant.*" This mistake was likely made by the masses when the unsaved Gentiles rejected Christ and received the Antichrist.

The prophecy points out that the judgment is global. It finds fulfillment "*in the midst of the earth among the peoples.*" Isaiah uses the imagery of *the gleanings when the grape harvest is over*, which coincidentally resembles when Angel #5 was told to, "*Thrust in your sharp sickle and gather the clusters of the vine of the earth, for her grapes are fully ripe."*

> "For behold, the Lord will come with fire And with His chariots, like a whirlwind, To render His anger with fury, And His rebuke with flames of fire. For by fire and by His sword The Lord will judge all flesh; And the slain of the Lord shall be many." (Isaiah 66:15-16)

Above, Isaiah informs that *the Lord will judge all flesh*, not just the armies at Armageddon, and that *the slain of the Lord shall be many.*

In the next passage Isaiah states that on the new earth, which is restored for the Millennium, all peoples will make pilgrimages to worship the Lord. As these worshippers make their way to pay tribute to the Lord, they will *look upon the corpses* of the unsaved Gentiles who had been slaughtered. This seems to suggest that the skeletal remains of the unsaved that get killed in the goat judgment will be visible throughout various parts of the world.

> "For as the new heavens and the new earth Which I will make shall remain before Me," says the Lord, "So shall your descendants and your name remain. And it shall come to pass *That* from one New Moon to another, And from one Sabbath to another, All flesh shall come to worship before Me," says the Lord. "And they shall go forth and look Upon the corpses of the men Who have transgressed against Me. For their worm does not die, And their fire is not quenched. They shall be an abhorrence to all flesh." (Isaiah 66:22-24)

One last related quote comes from Jeremiah's vivid account of the worldwide slaughter of the unsaved Gentiles in the passage below.

"Therefore prophesy against them all these words, and say to them: 'The Lord will roar from on high, And utter His voice from His holy habitation; He will roar mightily against His fold. He will give a shout, as those who tread *the grapes, (possibly the holy angels)* Against all the inhabitants of the earth. A noise will come to the ends of the earth— For the Lord has a controversy with the nations; He will plead His case with all flesh. He will give those *who are* wicked *(goats)* to the sword,' says the Lord." Thus says the Lord of hosts: "Behold, disaster shall go forth *(globally)* From nation to nation, And a great whirlwind shall be raised up From the farthest parts of the earth. And at that day the slain of the Lord shall be from *one* end of the earth even to the *other* end of the earth. They shall not be lamented, or gathered, or buried; they shall become refuse on the ground." (Jeremiah 25:30-33, NKJV; emphasis added)

Jeremiah paints a graphic global picture of complete judgment:

- Against all the inhabitants of the earth,

- A noise will come to the ends of the earth,

- The Lord has a controversy with the nations,

- He will plead His case with all flesh,

- Disaster shall go forth from nation to nation,

- A great whirlwind shall be raised up From the farthest parts of the earth,

- The slain of the Lord shall be from one end of the earth even to the other end of the earth.

These Isaiah and Jeremiah passages make it clear that the wholesale slaughter of the unsaved Goat Gentiles is worldwide and comprehensive. In other words, no unsaved Gentile, no matter what remote part of the world they live in, will be alive to enter into the Millennium.

The following two-part quote from Bible prophecy expert John MacArthur provides an appropriate close to this chapter and an excellent summation of the judgment of the Goat Gentiles.

> Part 1: *"So at the end of the tribulation time you have saved and unsaved people, from all over the globe, who have survived the judgment of God and the holocaust of Antichrist. They have lived through the plagues. They have lived through the disasters, the diseases, the wars, the wrath of Christ and the wrath of Antichrist. They have lived through the judgment on the armies at Armageddon, and there are still multitudes, multitudes left. But all of those who are left, who haven't faced God in death to be judged, will now face Him in His second coming. All the people. The word ethnē means peoples. So either a person faces God in death for judgment or at the second coming of Jesus Christ."*[43]

> Part 2: *"The people then who are allowed to go in,* (to the Millennium), *in physical bodies will be the sheep, the believers. The ones who don't believe will be destroyed on the spot. They will be killed on the spot. There will be instantaneous judgment and the destruction of unbelievers, and then the kingdom will be populated only by the redeemed on the earth and the redeemed that are glorified."*[44]

11

The Gentiles in the Millennial Kingdom

The slaughtering of the goats paved the way for the saved sheep Gentiles along with the surviving faithful Jewish Remnant to fulfill the prophecy below.

> "Blessed *is* he who waits, and comes to the one thousand three hundred and thirty-five days." (Daniel 12:12)

The seventy-fifth day of the Seventy-Five Day Interval period has passed; the goats are gone and from this chapter forward the first day of the Millennium begins. The earth needs restoration and the "*Blessed*" who lasted through "*the one thousand three hundred and thirty-five days*" need places to live.

Although some may have had food, drink and a doomsday bunker to hunker down in, many of these survivors experienced hunger, thirst, homelessness, nakedness, sickness and imprisonment. However, that was yesterday and yesterday's gone for them. This is day 1335 and the dawning of a new era and these refugees are returning home.

Several Bible prophecies promise the restored fortunes of the returning captives from Israel, Iran, Jordan, Assyria, Egypt and elsewhere. This chapter is devoted to the happy endings of these and the other Gentiles in the Millennial Kingdom. The bright future for the Jews will be the subject of an upcoming chapter entitled, *"The Jews in the Millennial Kingdom."*

Iran in the Millennium

> "'But it shall come to pass in the latter days: I will bring back the captives of Elam,' says the Lord." (Jeremiah 49:39, NKJV)

> "'But it will come about in the last days That I will restore the fortunes of Elam,' Declares the Lord." (Jeremiah 49:39, NASB)

These two different translations were provided above to point out that the surviving Elamites will be returning to their homelands from exile to restored fortunes. This phraseology also appears for the Jordanians in Jeremiah 48:47 and 49:6. In the original Hebrew language it can mean, to return, restore, refresh, repair, recompense and restitute.[45] The Elamites are returning refreshed and repaired from the Tribulation to be recompensed and restituted in the Millennium.

Elam, which is located in West Central Iran, is among the Middle Eastern territories that will be restored. Thus, at least some land within modern-day Iran will be restored for returning Iranians to inhabit in the Messianic Kingdom.

"Some" is the key term because Iran, as the image below illustrates, includes the regions of ancient Persia and Elam. Elam has a promise of restoration for Iranian re-habitation; however, no equivalent promise is given to Persia in the Bible. Persia is the subject of a latter days prophecy in Ezekiel 38.

> "Persia, Ethiopia, and Libya are with them, all of them *with* shield and helmet." (Ezekiel 38:5)

(In this image, Elam encompasses the darker shaded area bordering the Persian Gulf above the image of the Bushehr Nuclear Reactor)

In Ezekiel 38:1-13, Persia aligns with a powerful coalition of nine populations, including Russia and Turkey, that invades Israel to capture plunder and booty in the end times. This confederacy of belligerents gets destroyed supernaturally by the Lord in the land of Israel in Ezekiel 38:18-39:6. This defeat seems to represent Persia's last stand, or at least the final major battle fought by Iran's military. It is unlikely that what's left of this defeated army will be much of a fighting force in the Battle of Armageddon.

(*This Ezekiel 38 & 39 image locates these populations by their ancient names on a map alongside their probable modern-day equivalents*)

Perhaps there will be a Persia with believing Persians living in the Millennium, but there are no Scriptural promises of returning captives to Persia, nor are there any predictions of restored fortunes for the land of Persia. If Persians exist in Persia during the Millennium, it would be because they and their homeland survived through the Ezekiel 38 battle and the seven years of tribulation.

On the flip side, Elam will be restored and reinhabited. It will need restoration and repopulation because Jeremiah 49:34-39 predicts that:

1.   There will be a disaster in the land (Jer. 49:37),

2.   A dispersion from the land (Jer. 49:36),

3.   And the Lord will set His throne in Elam (Jer. 49:38).

These three scenarios above will necessitate a return and restore campaign in the Millennium. This important rehab operation presents a few questions:

1. How will these exiles be transported from their faraway locations? Will they board a plane, train, bus or boat?

2. How will the restoration of their homelands and fortunes be accomplished? Will the returning captives participate in the rebuilding process, or will the Lord shoulder the full responsibility? According to Amos 9:13-15, it appears that the rebuilding of the ruined cities will involve the returning exiles.

The Destiny of Jordan

Jordan is another Mideast nation that will have returning exiles to restored fortunes. I say fortunes plural because there are two promises of this nature made to Jordan. One is promised to Ammon and the other to Moab. The "Inner Circle Psalm 83" image below illustrates that modern-day Jordan was comprised of three ancient territories named, Ammon, Moab and Edom, all of which are part of the Psalm 83 Arab confederacy.

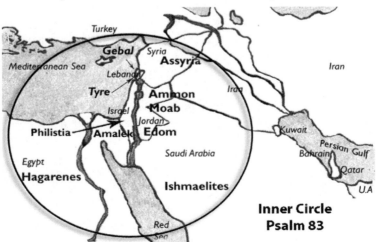

(*Map overlays the Psalm 83:6-8 populations upon their modern-day equivalents*)

Ammon was located in Northern Jordan, Moab sat in Central Jordan and Edom existed in Southern Jordan. According to Joel 3:19 and Isaiah 34:9-10, Edom will not be restored, but will be a desolate wilderness throughout the Millennium. Obadiah 1:18 points out the Edomites, who descended from Esau as per Genesis 36:9, will have no surviving remnant to represent them in the Messianic Kingdom.

> "The house of Jacob, (*the Israeli Defense Forces (IDF)*) shall be a fire, And the house of Joseph, (*the IDF*), a flame; But the house of Esau *shall be* stubble; They shall kindle them and devour them, And no survivor shall *remain* of the house of Esau," For the Lord has spoken." (Obadiah 1:18, NKJV: emphasis added)

To understand the destiny of Jordan, it's important to provide a brief overview of Psalm 83. The details of this prophetic war are explored thoroughly in my *NOW Prophecies* book, which also explains why this prophecy likely finds a Pre-Tribulation fulfillment. As the Psalm 83 image above displayed, Edom, Moab, Ammon, Assyria and Egypt as the Hagarenes, all appear to be part of the Psalm 83 confederacy.

> "For they have consulted together with one consent; They form a confederacy against You: (*the Lord and Israel by association*), The tents of Edom, (*Palestinian Refugees*)[46] and the Ishmaelites; Moab and the Hagrites; (*Hagarenes in some translations*), Gebal Ammon, and Amalek; Philistia with the inhabitants of Tyre; Assyria also has joined with them; They have helped the children of Lot, (*Ammon and Moab*), Selah" (Psalm 83:5-8, NKJV; emphasis added)

These two verses below explain that this confederacy forms to wipe Israel off of the map and all pages of future history. Their motive is to possess the Promised Land of Israel.

> "They have said, "Come, and let us cut them off from *being* a nation, That the name of Israel may be remembered no more."" (Psalm 83:4)

> "Who said, "Let us take for ourselves The pastures of God for a possession." (Psalm 83:12)

This confederacy gets soundly defeated by the Israeli Defense Forces as per, Obadiah 1:18, which was quoted above, Jeremiah 49:2, Zephaniah 2:8-9, Zechariah 12:6, Ezekiel 25:12-14 and several other passages. In the process the Jordanians are either killed, captured or exiled.

The BAD NEWS for Northern and Central Jordan

Presently, Jordan possesses a treaty with Israel. The prophecies that follow will evidence that this peace-pact is paper-thin and will be abandoned as war breaks out between these two nations. Perhaps, as you read this, the treaty may already be, or is on the verge of being eliminated.

> "Therefore behold, the days are coming," says the Lord, "That I will cause to be heard an alarm of war In Rabbah of the Ammonites; (*Amman, the largest city and capital of Jordan*) It shall be a desolate mound, And her villages shall be burned with fire. Then Israel shall take possession of his inheritance," says the Lord. "Wail, O Heshbon, for Ai is plundered! (*Heshbon and Ai were ancient cities located in Ammon*). Cry, you daughters of Rabbah, Gird yourselves with sackcloth! Lament and run to and fro by the walls; For Milcom, (*pagan god of the Ammonites*) shall go into captivity With his priests

and his princes together. Why do you boast in the valleys, Your flowing valley, O backsliding daughter? Who trusted in her treasures, saying, 'Who will come against me?' Behold, I will bring fear upon you," Says the Lord God of hosts, "From all those who are around you; You shall be driven out, (*exiled*) everyone headlong, And no one will gather those who wander off. " (Jeremiah 49:2-5)

The BAD NEWS for Northern Jordanians, is that their capital city will become a "*desolate mound*," many will be exiled, "*shall be driven out, everyone headlong*," and Israel will annex territory therein, "*take possession of his inheritance*." This implies that the IDF conquers Northern Jordan, which seems to happen as a result of the Psalm 83 war. This is further emphasized in the passage below.

"I have heard the reproach of Moab, And the insults of the people of Ammon, With which they have reproached My people, (*Israel*), And made arrogant threats against their borders. Therefore, as I live," Says the Lord of hosts, the God of Israel, "Surely Moab shall be like Sodom, And the people of Ammon like Gomorrah—Overrun with weeds and saltpits, And a perpetual desolation. The residue of My people, (*the IDF*), shall plunder them, And the remnant of My people, (*Israelis*), shall possess them." This they shall have for their pride, Because they have reproached and made arrogant threats Against the people of the Lord of hosts." (Zephaniah 2:8-10, NKJV; emphasis added)

The prophet Zephaniah seems to provide another camera view on the same events in Jeremiah 49:1-6. Except, Zephaniah's portrayal has a wider-angle lens that captures the plundering at, and possession of, both Ammon and Moab. This means that not only Ammon, but also Moab will need restoration and repopulation. This is the BAD NEWS for Central Jordanians.

Observe that both Ammon and Moab are judged for the *"reproachment"* of the Jews and making *"arrogant threats against their borders."* Jeremiah 49:2 informs that these Anti-Semitic actions climax in an *"alarm of war in Rabbah of the Ammonites."* This appears to be a clue to the Psalm 83 connection. As quoted above, Ammon and Moab are enjoined in a war effort to wipe Israel off of the map in order to take possession of Israel.

Central Jordan as Moab is the subject of Jeremiah 48:1-47 and elsewhere. Below is a bullet point summary of events that foretell the future of Moab:

- There will be no more praise in Moab because they have devised an evil plan against Israel. They have said, '*Come, and let us cut her* (Israel) *off as a nation.*' This sounds like the same battle cry of the Arab confederacy in Psalm 83:4, which declared, "*Come, and let us cut them off from being a nation, That the name of Israel may be remembered no more.*" (Jer. 48:2),

- There will be plundering and destruction (Jer. 48:3),

- Moab gets destroyed (Jer. 48:4),

- Moab's pagan god, priests and princes will go into captivity (Jer. 48:7, 46),

- Moabite cities will become desolate (Jer. 48:9),

- Moab's young men will go down to slaughter (Jer. 48:15),

- Moabites will be forced to flee into exile (Jer. 48:19),

- All the cities of the land of Moab will face judgment (Jer. 48:21-24),

- Moab is guilty of exalting himself against the Lord and cursing Israel (Jer. 48:26-27, 42),

- Moab is exceedingly proud and made arrogant threats about Israel's borders (Jer. 48:29 and Zephaniah 2:8-10),

- Over Moab, one shall fly like an eagle and spread his wings over the territory, which could allude to the Israeli Air Force (IAF) (Jer. 48:40),

- Moab will be destroyed by a fire and a flame, which seem to be the same idioms for the IDF used in Obadiah 1:18 representing the house of Jacob (a fire) and the house of Joseph (a flame) (Jer. 48:45),

- Moab will be restored and repopulated in the latter days (Jer. 48:47).

The GREAT NEWS for Northern and Central Jordan

Out with the BAD NEWS, and in with the GREAT NEWS for Northern and Central Jordanians. Those Jordanians:

- That survive through the Psalm 83 war and exilic period that follows,

- Who also survive outside of Jordan through the Seven-Year Trib-period,

- And, with a capital A, receive Jesus Christ as their Savior sometime after the Rapture,

- They get to return as saved Gentiles to their historic homelands at the beginning of the Millennium as per the verses below.

Northern Jordan (Ammon) in the Millennium

""But afterward, (*after Psalm 83 and the Trib-period*),
I will restore The fortunes, (in the Millennium), of

the sons of Ammon," (*Amman, Jordan*), Declares
the Lord." (Jer. 49:6, NASB; emphasis added)

"But afterward I will bring back The captives,
(*exiles and POWs*)[47] of the people of Ammon,"
says the Lord." (Jeremiah 49:6, NKJV;
emphasis added)

Probably about the same time that the believing remnant of
Elamite Iranians get the GREAT NEWS, that they are returning
to Elam, the saved Ammonite Jordanians receive the same blessing
of heading back to their homeland in Northern Jordan.

Some of these returning Jordanian exiles will have likely
experienced the IDF turn their capital city of Amman into a
"*desolate mound.*" Moreover, some of them may have had a change
of their Anti-Semitic hearts during the Trib-period and extended a
helping hand as Sheep Gentiles to the suffering Jewish Brethren of
Christ. What a potential turn of events, that ultimately leads them
back home to dwell in their ancestral lands of restored fortunes
during the Millennium.

Central Jordan (Moab) in the Millennium

""Yet I will restore the fortunes of Moab In the
latter days," declares the Lord." (Jer. 48:47, NASB)

Likely around the same time, the similar GREAT NEWS will
be repeated to the Central Jordanians that they get to "HEAD
HOME." The apparent reasons that these Jordanians, and other
Muslim populations like Elam, Ammon, and Assyria and Egypt
that are about to be discussed, are promised a return to the restored
fortunes of their homelands are because they:

1.   Have converted from Islam to Christianity,

2.   Got saved in the process,

3.   No longer hate the Jews,

4.   Became Sheep Gentiles, at least some of them, as described in Matthew 25:31-40.

Regarding point #1 above, Zephaniah 2:11 points out that when Ammon and Moab are judged and destroyed for reproaching Israel's borders in Zephaniah 2:8-10, that their pagan gods will be famished.

> "The Lord *will be* awesome to them, (*Ammon and Moab*), For He will reduce to nothing all the gods of the earth; *People* shall worship Him, Each one from his place, Indeed all the shores of the nations." (Zephaniah 2:11, NKJV; emphasis added)

Unless things change between now and the destruction of Ammon and Moab, their false religion of Islam and their pagan god Allah will be subjected to this famishing. Allah will lose his Akbar, (his greatness). Ultimately, a remnant of Jordanians will convert from Islam, embrace Christianity, get saved and enter into the Messianic Kingdom.

In the Millennium they will be among the people that worship God, "*each from his place.*" This implies that they will return from exile to their restored homelands and from that location they will praise God. By then, Allah will be long gone!

Assyria in the Millennium

Assyria, like Elam, Ammon and Moab, has BAD and GREAT NEWS in store for its future. Geographically speaking, in the prophecies that follow, Assyria encompasses all of modern-day Syria and parts of Northern Iraq.

On the Psalm 83 map previously displayed in this chapter, Assyria is overlayed on Northern Syria and Northern Iraq. However, this Psalm was written around 1000 BC, but subsequent to that Assyria conquered Aram, which included Damascus in 732 BC. Thus, at that time, Assyria included all of modern-day Syria and parts of Northern Iraq. Presently, Assyria includes Syrians, Iraqis and Kurds.

The prophet Isaiah, who prophesied between 740-701 BC informs that Assyria, likely alluding to Syria and Northern Iraq, will exist in the Millennium as the works of God's hands. The encouraging passage below incorporates Israel, Egypt and Assyria.

> "In that day, (*in the Millennium*), shall there be a highway out of Egypt to Assyria, and the Assyrian shall come into Egypt, and the Egyptian into Assyria; and the Egyptians shall worship with the Assyrians… In that day shall Israel be the third with Egypt and with Assyria, a blessing in the midst of the earth; for that Jehovah of hosts hath blessed them, saying, Blessed be Egypt my people, and Assyria the work of my hands, and Israel mine inheritance." (Isaiah 19:23-25, ASV; emphasis added)

This passage above presents GREAT NEWS for a remnant of surviving Assyrians. Assyria will be *the work of* God's *hands*. However, this workmanship will have by then undergone a severe process of discipline. This progression of crafting Assyria into God's handiwork will involve the following judgment events.

1.   The Destruction of Damascus in Isaiah 17:

    a.   This capital city of Syria will be reduced to rubble (Isaiah 17:1),
    b.   Many Syrian soldiers and civilians will be killed (Jer. 49:26),
    c.   The destruction of Damascus will be caused by the IDF (Isaiah 17:9),

d. Other Syrian cities will be desolated at the time (Isaiah 17:9, Jer. 49:23),

e. The toppling of Damascus will happen overnight (Isaiah 17:14).

2. Assyria's apparent defeat and destruction in Psalm 83. Some of the events just alphabetized above could happen to Assyria as part of the Psalm 83 war:

   a. Assyria helps the *"children of Lot,"* who were Ammon and Moab, in the war "Assyria also has joined with them; They have helped the children of Lot." (Psalm 83:8),

   b. By association, Assyria and Ammon and Moab and all the other Psalm 83 confederates seemingly get defeated by the IDF.

According to Jeremiah 49:24 there will be Syrians who flee from the destruction of Damascus, but there are no promises of returning captives to restored fortunes like with Elam, Ammon and Moab. This could be because some Assyrians don't disperse from their homeland when the fighting takes place. However, Isaiah 19:23-25 above makes it clear that there will be an Assyria in the Millennium.

Egypt in the Millennium

Egypt is the subject of several end times prophecies and although they have some GOOD NEWS to celebrate, they have a triple dose of BAD NEWS to contend with beforehand. Presently, Egypt is the most populated Arab country. It also possesses the strongest military in the Arab world,[48] and like Jordan it has a similar peace treaty with Israel.

According to Bible prophecy, all of the above is destined to change. Egypt will undergo a national collapse that is followed shortly thereafter, by a desolation that forces Egyptians into a forty-year period of exile. In the process their peace pact with the Jewish state disappears.

The GOOD NEWS is that Egypt will have a saved remnant that enters the Millennium, but at that time the restored nation will be ranked among the *"lowliest of kingdoms."*

> "It shall be the lowliest of kingdoms; it shall never again exalt itself above the nations, for I will diminish them so that they will not rule over the nations anymore." (Ezekiel 29:15)

During the Messianic Age, as per Isaiah 19:23-25, Egypt will worship the Lord with the Assyrians, and be *"a blessing in the midst of the earth"* along with Israel and Assyria.

Zechariah 14:16-19 also points out that Egypt will exist in the Millennium. Zechariah's passage reminds Egypt to attend the annual Feast of Tabernacles celebration in Jerusalem or it will be struck by a drought *plague* of *no rain.*

> "If the family of Egypt will not come up and enter in, they *shall have* no *rain;* they shall receive the plague with which the Lord strikes the nations who do not come up to keep the Feast of Tabernacles." (Zechariah 14:18)

The Lord will Strike and Heal Egypt

> "Then the Lord will be known to Egypt, and the Egyptians will know the Lord in that day, and will make sacrifice and offering; yes, they will make a vow to the Lord and perform it. And the Lord will strike Egypt, He will strike and heal it; they will return to the Lord, and He will be entreated by them and heal them." (Isaiah 19:21-22)

This passage above says that "*the Lord will strike Egypt, He will strike and heal it.*" Isaiah uses the word strike two times, which might allude to Egypt's two separate end times judgments.

Strike one, appears to be found in Isaiah 19:1-18, which is explained thoroughly in my book entitled, *The NOW Prophecies.* *Strike two,* seems to be described in Ezekiel 29:1-16 and Daniel 11:42-43. This second judgment is much harsher than the first and it is explained in great detail in my book entitled, *Psalm 83, The Missing Prophecy Revealed.*

The first striking, which is executed by Israel, starts the collapse of Egypt's political, economic and religious systems and the second strike by the Antichrist culminates in the entire desolation of the country.

Egypt's Strike One

Below is a short bullet point summary of Isaiah 19:1-18, which is likely Egypt's strike one:

- Egypt's judgment will be swift. "*Behold, the Lord rides on a swift cloud, And will come into Egypt.*" (Isaiah 19:1b),

- Egypt will experience internal civil strife, which will lead Egypt into a regional, "*kingdom against kingdom,*" conflict (Isaiah 19:2),

- Egypt's religious clerics will lose respect and be overtaken by a cruel dictator (Isaiah 19:3-4),

- Egypt will experience drought-like conditions that adversely affect important rivers and waterways. (Isaiah 19:5-7),

- Egypt's fishing and textile industries collapse and lead to a national unemployment crisis, whereby, " *All who make wages will be troubled of soul.*" (Isaiah 19:8-10),

- Egypt's political system begins to collapse (Isaiah 19:11-13),

- Egypt's economic system begins to collapse (Isaiah 19:14-15).

But why are all of these devastating events above happening inside Egypt?

> "In that day Egypt will be like women, and will be afraid and fear because of the waving of the hand of the Lord of hosts, which He waves over it. And the land of Judah will be a terror to Egypt; everyone who makes mention of it will be afraid in himself, because of the counsel of the Lord of hosts which He has determined against it." (Isaiah 19:16-17)

This passage above connects Egypt's collapse in Isaiah 19:1-15 with circumstances involving *"the land of Judah." "In that day,"* Egypt becomes distraught over something taking place in Israel.

The *"land of Judah will be a terror to Egypt."* Something is taking place in the *land of Judah*, which is located in Southern Israel, which is the closest part of the Jewish state to Egypt's northern border. Perhaps IDF troops are marching, IAF planes are flying, military vehicles are moving and precision-guided missiles are flying in the direction of Egypt.

Commenting on Isaiah 19:16-17, Dr. Arnold Fruchtenbaum writes the following on page 506 of his book entitled, the Footsteps of the Messiah;

> *"Never in ancient history has this been true. Only since 1948, and especially since the 6-day war, have the Egyptian forces evidenced the fear portrayed in this passage. There has been fear and dread of Israel ever since. With Egypt having lost 4 wars against Israel with heavy casualties, the fear*

is deeply rooted. Prophetically, today is still the period of Isaiah 19:16-17."

The next verse suggests that Israel overcomes Egypt in a final conflict, which could be part of Psalm 83. Egypt appears to be identified in Psalm 83 as the Hagarenes. *"The tents of Edom and the Ishmaelites; Moab, and the Hagarenes."* (Psalm 83:6, ASV). Hagar was a main matriarch of Egypt. She was the mother of Ishmael.

> "In that day five cities in the land of Egypt will speak the language of Canaan and swear by the LORD of hosts; one will be called the City of Destruction." (Isaiah 19:18)

Again Isaiah prefaces his prophecy by informing us that *"In that day,"* which seems to represent the same time proximity to when Egypt is terrorized by Israel, that *"five cities in Egypt will speak the language of Canaan,"* which is Hebrew. One of these cities is called *"the City of Destruction."* This seems to imply that Israel wins a war with Egypt and proceeds to annex five cities in Egypt in the aftermath. In commemoration of their victory, Israel may rename one of the captured cities, *"the City of Destruction."*

It appears when the IDF defeats the Egyptian army again, that they will take more Arab territory. They have a precedent for doing this. Acquiring land by conquest has been a historic pattern for Israel. Joshua did it about 3500 years ago, and King David and his son King Solomon also accomplished this about 3000 years ago. In both instances, the land was annexed in the aftermath of Israeli takeovers of the subject Arab territories.

Even in modern history this pattern has repeated itself after the IDF victory in the Six-Day War in June of 1967. At that time Israel nearly tripled its size by taking over the Gaza, West Bank, Golan Heights, East Jerusalem, and the Sinai Peninsula.

Israel can justify land acquisitions of defeated Arab territories because:

1.   Historically, that's what victorious armies have done,

2.   Israel can improve the defensibility of its borders,

3.   These lands belong to the Jews, as heirs to Abraham, Isaac and Jacob. These patriarchs were promised some of the land that lies inside the borders of modern-day Egypt.

> "On the same day the Lord made a covenant with Abram, saying: "To your descendants I have given this land, from the river of Egypt, (*probably the Nile River*), to the great river, the River Euphrates."
> (Genesis 15:18, NKJV; emphasis added)

Egypt's Strike Two

Strike one devastates Egypt, but strike two desolates it. Ezekiel 29:1-7 explains why Egypt will experience the final judgment that desolates the country. Ezekiel 29:3 says that Egypt is prideful and that's problematic, but the final straw that seemingly breaks Egypt's back is found in the passage below.

> "Then all the inhabitants of Egypt Shall know that I *am* the Lord, Because they have been a staff of reed to the house of Israel. When they took hold of you with the hand, You broke and tore all their shoulders; When they leaned on you, You broke and made all their backs quiver."
> (Ezekiel 29:6-7)

Egypt is found guilty of cursing Israel and in so doing the country must be cursed in retaliation, and in the process realize the consequences of their harmful actions. This is all part of the curse-for-curse-in-kind aspect of God's foreign policy to the

Gentiles explained in Genesis 12. This verse below points out that how people treat Abraham and his descendants is how they will be treated by God in return.

> "I will bless those who bless you, And I will curse him who curses you; And in you all the families of the earth shall be blessed." (Genesis 12:3)

The Forty-Year Desolation of Egypt

> "Therefore thus says the Lord God: "Surely I will bring a sword upon you and cut off from you man and beast. And the land of Egypt shall become desolate and waste; then they will know that I *am* the Lord, because he said, 'The River *is* mine, and I have made *it.*' Indeed, therefore, I *am* against you and against your rivers, and I will make the land of Egypt utterly waste and desolate, from Migdol *to* Syene, as far as the border of Ethiopia. Neither foot of man shall pass through it nor foot of beast pass through it, and it shall be uninhabited forty years. I will make the land of Egypt desolate in the midst of the countries *that are* desolate; and among the cities *that are* laid waste, her cities shall be desolate forty years; and I will scatter the Egyptians among the nations and disperse them throughout the countries." (Ezekiel 29:8-12)

God declares that He will bring a sword upon Egypt. The sword is often used as a biblical typology for a military invasion. Thus, Egypt gets invaded and conquered. This invasion could come from Israel as strike one, however for reasons soon to be explained, it probably is instigated by the Antichrist in Daniel 11:42-43 as a second strike upon Egypt.

Isaiah says on behalf of the Lord "*The River is mine, and I have made it,*" which cuts at the heart of Egypt's pride. Ezekiel 29:3 faulted the leader of Egypt for saying that the "*River is my own; I have made it for myself.*" However, God declares through Isaiah, '*I am against you and against your rivers, and I will make the land of Egypt utterly waste and desolate.*'

Isaiah says that when the Egyptians experience their nation become a desolate wasteland, "*then they will know*" that Jehovah God and not Allah, "*is the Lord.*" Isaiah makes it perfectly clear by stating two times, that the desolation of Egypt will last forty-years.

The Forty-Year Dispersion of Egyptians

Ezekiel 29:12 informed that when Egypt gets desolated, the Egyptians will be scattered "*among the nations*" and dispersed "*throughout the countries.*" The passage below explains how long this future Egyptian Diaspora will last.

> "Yet, thus says the Lord God: "At the end of forty years I will gather the Egyptians from the peoples among whom they were scattered. I will bring back the captives of Egypt and cause them to return to the land of Pathros, to the land of their origin, and there they shall be a lowly kingdom. It shall be the lowliest of kingdoms; it shall never again exalt itself above the nations, for I will diminish them so that they will not rule over the nations anymore. No longer shall it be the confidence of the house of Israel, but will remind them of *their* iniquity when they turned to follow them. Then they shall know that I *am* the Lord God."" (Ezekiel 29:13-16)

As the Jews wandered for forty-years in the wilderness after their exodus out of Egypt, the Egyptian exiles will wander among the nations for the same forty-year allotment of time. The

Egyptians who survive through, or are born during, the forty-years of dispersion will be regathered back to Egypt. This implies that Egypt will be restored from its desolate condition.

As stated earlier, the returning remnant of Egyptians will reside in the lowliest of kingdoms. This lowly condition will deter Israel from putting any further confidence in Egypt and remind the Jews to put their trust in the Lord.

These two questions will be answered next.

1.   Who desolates Egypt, is it Israel or the Antichrist?

2.   When does the forty-year desolation of Egypt begin and end?

1.Who desolates Egypt, is it Israel or the Antichrist?

Isaiah 19:1-18 pointed out that Egypt and Israel have a confrontation and apparently Israel prevails. As a result five Egyptian cities implement the Hebrew language. This is not likely a bilingual scenario whereby the defeated Egyptians, who are by then dwelling in a dilapidated economy, find it favorable to learn a second language for job opportunities, rather it's more probable that the Jews capture these five cities and move themselves and their Hebrew language into them.

If this is the case, then Egypt is not desolated for forty-years as a result of the Israel vs Egypt conflict, otherwise there would be no cities existing for Hebrew to be spoken in. The Egyptian desolation is thorough, implying that conditions inside of Egypt are not conducive for anyone, be it an Arabic-speaking Egyptian or a Hebrew-speaking Jew to inhabit.

Furthermore, the IDF conquests over their Arab enemies in Psalm 83 and elsewhere are likely fulfilled before the Trib-period begins. This can be logically deduced by realizing that in the first

3 ½ years of the Trib-period Israel is living at peace and in the second 3 ½ years the Jews are fleeing from the genocidal pursuits of the Antichrist.

Moreover, Egypt has to exist into the Trib-period for the Antichrist to fulfill the Daniel prophecies below.

> "He, (*the Antichrist*), shall stretch out his hand against the countries, and the land of Egypt shall not escape. He shall have power over the treasures of gold and silver, and over all the precious things of Egypt; also the Libyans and Ethiopians *shall follow* at his heels." (Daniel 11:42-43, NKJV; emphasis added)

Daniel predicts that the Antichrist will invade Egypt and capture the country's "*gold and silver*" and "*all the precious things.*" Then he will march across the borders of Libya and Ethiopia and conquer these nations also. It is commonly taught that the Antichrist accomplishes these victories during the Trib-period.

If the IDF desolated Egypt prior, then the Antichrist would have no reason to invade Egypt. However, if Israel defeated Egypt, annexed five cities and began restoring Egypt's economy, then the Antichrist would have two reasons to invade Egypt. First, he can kill the Jews in the five cities, and second he can capture Egypt's gold, silver and precious things.

2.When does the forty-year desolation of Egypt begin and end?

If the deductive reasoning that the Antichrist is the desolater of Egypt is correct, then when does the forty-year time clock begin ticking? The answer would logically be during the Trib-period, and probably in the last 3 ½ years of this timeframe, which appears to be when Daniel 11:42-43 finds fulfillment.

This implies that the desolation of Egypt and dispersion of Egyptians overlaps into the Millennium. This also means that the Egyptians who return to their lowly kingdom of Egypt after forty-years of exile are saved. At some point before the Millennium starts these refugees had to receive Christ or they wouldn't be allowed entry into the Messianic Kingdom.

Even though these Egyptians are returning to the lowliest of kingdoms, they won't likely be an exception to the rule that, NO UNBELIEVERS CAN ENTER THE MILLENNIUM.

The Other Gentile Nations in the Millennium

In addition to Iran, Jordan, Egypt and Assyria, there will be additional Gentile nations that exist during the Millennium. A primary undertaking of these other nations, especially early on in the Millennium, will be to bless Israel.

The return of the Jews into the restored Jewish state will serve as a standard of God's faithfulness. The surviving Jews living in a restored state of Israel, will prove that God kept His unconditional covenant with Abraham, which included fathering a "Chosen People" living in a "Promised Land." The bannering of the Israeli flag in the Millennium will be perceived as God's "*Coat of Arms*" by the Gentile nations.

> "Thus says the Lord God: "Behold, I will lift My hand in an oath to the nations, And set up My standard, (*Israel*), for the peoples; They shall bring your (*Jewish*) sons in *their* arms, And your daughters shall be carried on *their* shoulders; Kings, (*from the international community*) shall be your foster fathers, And their queens your nursing mothers; They shall bow down to you, (*the Jewish state*), with *their* faces to the earth, And lick up the dust of your feet. Then you will know that I *am* the Lord, For they shall not be

ashamed who wait for Me." (Isaiah 49:22-23, NKJV; emphasis added)

Isaiah predicts that kings and queens from the global community will unashamedly bow down to Israel. This indicates that pro-Semitic nations will exist in the Millennium. Many of these political Gentile leaders and their citizens were among the saved sheep of Matthew 25:31-40, who helped Christ's Jewish Brethren through their travails during the Trib-period.

These world leaders will be honored to shoulder the responsibility of facilitating the Aliyah of the surviving sons and daughters back to Israel. At that time, Israel will become a beacon of light that reflects the glory of the Lord.

> "Arise, shine; For your light has come! And the glory of the Lord is risen upon you. For behold, the darkness shall cover the earth, And deep darkness the people; But the Lord will arise over you, And His glory will be seen upon you. The Gentiles shall come to your light, And kings to the brightness of your rising." (Isaiah 60:1-3)

Isaiah contrasts the light of Israel in the Millennium to the deep darkness that overtook the nations during the Trib-period. These Gentiles will see "*the glory of the Lord*" shine upon Israel like a light, after having experienced the "*darkness*" that overtook the earth from the judgments of the Sixth Seal of Rev. 6:12 and Fourth Trumpet in Rev. 8:12. They will also have witnessed the "deep darkness" that came over the world in the Fifth Bowl Judgment of Rev. 16:10. The natural response of these Gentiles will be to pay tribute to Israel.

> "Lift up your eyes all around, and see: They all gather together, they come to you; Your sons shall come from afar, And your daughters shall be nursed at *your* side. Then you shall

see and become radiant, And your heart shall swell with joy; Because the abundance of the sea shall be turned to you, The wealth of the Gentiles shall come to you." (Isaiah 60:4-5, NKJV; emphasis added)

"Therefore your gates shall be open continually; They shall not be shut day or night, That *men* may bring to you the wealth of the Gentiles, And their kings in procession." (Isaiah 60:11)

Isaiah points out above that some of the surviving Jews that return to Israel "*shall come from afar.*" This suggests that Gentile nations outside of the Middle East will exist in the Millennium. These countries will gladly share their wealth with the Jewish state.

"The multitude of camels shall cover your *land,* The dromedaries of Midian and Ephah; All those from Sheba shall come; They shall bring gold and incense, And they shall proclaim the praises of the Lord. All the flocks of Kedar shall be gathered together to you, The rams of Nebaioth shall minister to you; They shall ascend with acceptance on My altar, And I will glorify the house of My glory. "Who *are* these *who* fly like a cloud, And like doves to their roosts? Surely the coastlands shall wait for Me; And the ships of Tarshish *will come* first, To bring your sons from afar, Their silver and their gold with them, To the name of the Lord your God, And to the Holy One of Israel, Because He has glorified you." (Isaiah 60:6-9)

In the passage above, Isaiah identifies some of the nations that will contribute to Israel's economy. In the process we can determine some of the additional Gentile nations that exist in the Millennium.

- *Midian:* would be Northwest Saudi Arabia close to where the Gulf of Aqaba meets the eastern tip of the Red Sea.

- *Ephah:* was a son of Midian, and presumably established himself close to his father.

- *Sheba:* was located in modern-day Southwest Yemen near the joining of the Red Sea with the Arabian Sea.

- *Nebaioth:* may have a connection with the Nabateans, which might identify somewhere between Southern Jordan and Northern Saudi Arabia.

- *Coastlands:* this likely represents some of the more remote parts of the earth that are farther away from Israel.

- *Tarshish:* according to my research, provided in the book entitled, *The NOW Prophecies,* Tarshish seems to represent the United Kingdom. It's important to note in Isaiah 60:9, that Tarshish is among the first countries to bring their wealth to Israel. The "*Merchants of Tarshish*" are listed in Ezekiel 38:13. In that prophecy Tarshish seemingly has commercial interests with Israel that come under threat by the Ezekiel 38 invaders. Thus, commercial relations between Israel and Tarshish will seemingly stand the test of the end times.

- *Lebanon:* is not included in the passage above, but in the same context the country is mentioned in Isaiah 60:13a, which reads, "*The glory of Lebanon shall come to you..*"

Commenting upon Isaiah chapter 60:1-9, The Bible Knowledge Commentary: Old Testament says the following:

> "*This will occur in the Millennium. Though everyone entering the Millennium will be saved, people will be born during that 1,000-year period of time. Many of them will come to salvation because of God's work on Israel's behalf...At the beginning of the Millennium when Israel will be regathered to her land, her sons will come from great distances (cf. v. 9). Also Israel will rejoice because redeemed people from the nations (v. 5; the "sheep" of Matt. 25:31-46) will want to join Israel in her worship in Jerusalem (cf. Zech. 14:16-19). Those people will bring wealth to Israel (cf. Isa. 60:11; 61:6; Hag. 2:7-8; Zech. 14:14).*"[49]

More information about the Gentile nations in the Millennium is provided in the Isaiah 66:18-20 verses below.

> "For I *know* their works and their thoughts. It shall be that I will gather all nations and tongues; and they shall come and see My glory." (Isaiah 66:18)

In the Millennium Israel is the reflection of God's glory as per Isaiah 60:1-2.

> "I will set a sign among them; and those among them who escape I will send to the nations: *to* Tarshish and Pul and Lud, who draw the bow, and Tubal and Javan, *to* the coastlands afar off who have not heard My fame nor seen My glory. And they shall declare My glory among the Gentiles." (Isaiah 66:19)

This verse seems to state that during the Trib-period some Jews will seek refuge in Tarshish, (likely the UK), Pul and Lud, (probably North Africa), and Tubal, (seemingly Turkey), and Javan, (thought to be Greece). These countries, some of which are listed in the Ezekiel 38 prophecy, will ultimately include some saved sheep Gentiles that bless the Jewish Brethren of Christ.

It seems that after God stops the Ezekiel 38 invaders supernaturally in Ezekiel 38:18-39:6, which seems to happen prior to the Trib-period, a majority of these peoples gain a deeper respect for the God of the Jews. Tubal, as Turkey, is listed among the Ezekiel 38 invaders, which means they were mostly Anti-Semitic. However, after getting soundly defeated by the God of the Jews they apparently acquire a different perspective. They become Pro-Semitic, otherwise they wouldn't allow Jewish exiles to escape there.

> "Then they shall bring all your brethren for an offering to the LORD out of all nations, on horses and in chariots and in litters, on mules and on camels, to My holy mountain Jerusalem," says the LORD, "as the children of Israel bring an offering in a clean vessel into the house of the LORD. And I will also take some of them for priests *and* Levites," says the LORD." (Isaiah 66:20-21)

This passage above, in conjunction with Isaiah 66:19, says "*Then they,*" alluding to Tarshish, Pul, Lud, Tubal and Javan, will bring Jews that had been in hiding during the Trib-period in their Gentile nations to "*My holy mountain.*" The holy mountain will be located in Israel as per Isaiah 2:2-3 quoted below. Some of the returning Jews will become priests.

> "And it shall come to pass in the last days, that the mountain of the Lord's house shall be established in the top of the mountains, and shall be exalted above the hills; and all nations shall flow unto it. And many people shall go and say, Come ye, and let us go up to the mountain of the Lord, to the

house of the God of Jacob; and he will teach us of
his ways, and we will walk in his paths: for out of
Zion shall go forth the law, and the word of the
Lord from Jerusalem." (Isaiah 2:2-3)

Isaiah acknowledges in the scripture below, that Assyrians
and Egyptians are among the "*many people*" who "*go up to the
mountain of the Lord*" in the Millennium. Note that in the
verse, Isaiah identifies the Egyptians as "*the outcasts in the land
of Egypt.*" This implies that the Egyptians were exiles for a time,
namely forty years, but upon returning to their homeland in the
Millennium, they and Assyria "*shall worship the Lord in the holy
mount at Jerusalem.*"

> "And it shall come to pass in that day, that the
> great trumpet shall be blown, and they shall
> come which were ready to perish in the land of
> Assyria, and the outcasts in the land of Egypt,
> and shall worship the Lord in the holy mount at
> Jerusalem." (Isaiah 27:13)

Lastly, at least by the end of the Millennium, there are Gentile
nations spanning across the globe, "*the four corners of the earth.*"
Unfortunately at that time, many of them will be deceived by
Satan when he gets loosed from the abyss.

> "Now when the thousand years have expired,
> Satan will be released from his prison and will go
> out to deceive the nations which are in the four
> corners of the earth, Gog and Magog, to gather
> them together to battle, whose number *is* as the
> sand of the sea. They went up on the breadth
> of the earth and surrounded the camp of the
> saints and the beloved city. And fire came down
> from God out of heaven and devoured them."
> (Revelation 20:7-9)

Summary

In the beginning of the Millennium, all of the Gentiles living on the earth will be saved and Pro-Semitic. After the Rapture, the Mideast wars, judgments of the Trib-period and the massive slaughter of the unsaved Goat Gentiles, there will undoubtedly be far fewer Gentiles left on the planet. However, whoever survives all of the above will recognize Israel as a reflection of God's glory and faithfulness. With this understanding the saved Gentiles will embark upon their journey into the Messianic Kingdom.

Life
in the
Millennium

There was no shortage of prophetic information provided for the final generation to navigate through the Trib-period. They needed to know what was coming because survival for Tribulation Saints largely depended upon their ability to understand the pertinent Bible prophecies, anticipate their arrival and be prepared for the events when they happened.

Fast-forwarding from the Trib-period into the Messianic Age, the respected American Christian theologian, Dwight Pentecost, once stated that there is more information in the Bible about the Millennium than any other period in Scripture. In my research about life in the Millennium, I have to agree with Pentecost.

Apparently, the Lord wanted to impart a double dose of good news about the futures of all believers. Whether they be, Pre-Tribulation raptured Church Age believers, surviving Trib-period Sheep Gentiles or Millennial resurrected Old Testament Saints and Tribulation Saints, they all will enjoy what God has planned for them during the 1000-year Messianic Kingdom.

A summary list of the high points of Millennial life is provided below. The following tabulations are not listed in any sequential or prioritized order. During the Millennium there will be:

- A world filled with the knowledge and glory of the Lord – (Psalm 72:19, Isaiah 11:9, Habakkuk 2:14).

- Many kind-hearted people leading righteous upright lives – (Psalm 15:2-5, 24:4).

- No more war – (Isaiah 2:4) According to Revelation 20:7-9, there will be one last major battle spearheaded by Satan, which gets supernaturally defeated by God, but that takes place after the Millennium.

- No remembrance of the bad events that happened on the past earth – (Isaiah 65:16-17).

- Advanced aeronautical methods of air travel and transportation – (Isaiah 60:8).

- A pure singular language – (Zephaniah 3:9).

- A theocratic global government that is ruled with a rod of iron by a just and righteous monarch, (the Messiah), Who maintains world peace – (Isaiah 9:6-7, Psalm 2:7-9, Revelation 2:27, 12:5 and 19:15). This government and its various branches are covered in the chapters entitled, *"The Millennial Government: The Jewish Branch* and *The Millennial Government: The Gentile Branch."*

- Non-predatory animal behavior – (Isaiah 11:6-7, 65:25).

- Children intermingling with dangerous animals and venomous snakes – (Isaiah 11:8-9).

- Instantaneous answers to prayer – (Isaiah 65:24).

- An end of blindness and deafness – (Isaiah 29:18, 35:5).

- Crippled that walk and leap and mute who talk and sing – (Isaiah 35:6).

- Waters gushing from the wilderness and streams flowing in the deserts – (Isaiah 35:6).

- Grain and grapes that grow faster than they can be harvested – (Amos 9:13).

- Plant life flourishing – (Isaiah 35:1, 2, 7).

- Robust construction and farming industries – (Isaiah 65:21).

- Adequate housing supplies – (Isaiah 65:22).

Although some of the above conditions will be more prominent in Israel, it is likely that many of the same conditions will be prevalent throughout the world. However, more specific to Israel there will be:

- Only gladness and rejoicing taking place in Jerusalem and no more crying or weeping – (Isaiah 65:18-19). The only exception will be when the Jews mourn for the Messiah whom they pierced in Zechariah 12:10-14. However, this technically appears to happen prior to the Millennium during the Seventy-Five Day Interval Period.

- Deserts and wilderness areas that are restored to Garden of Eden-like conditions – (Isaiah 51:3, Ezekiel 36:35).

- Vineyards that drip with sweet wine – (Amos 9:13).

- Life in the East Sea, (the Dead Sea) – (Ezekiel 47:1-2, 8-9, Zechariah 14:8).

General Characteristics of the Millennium

This next section will explore some of the general characteristics listed above.

A world filled with the knowledge and glory of the Lord.

> "They shall not hurt nor destroy in all My holy mountain, For the earth shall be full of the knowledge of the Lord As the waters cover the sea." (Isaiah 11:9)

The knowledge of the Lord: Presently, creation serves as one example that testifies to the existence of God.

> "For since the creation of the world His invisible *attributes* are clearly seen, being understood by the things that are made, *even* His eternal power and Godhead, so that they are without excuse." (Romans 1:20)

Even though all people are expected to know that the Lord exists, most refuse to recognize this reality. During the Millennium there will be no getting around the fact that the Lord exists; *"For the earth shall be full of the knowledge of the Lord As the waters cover the sea."* (Isaiah 11:9b)

More important than acknowledging that the Lord exists in the Millennium, will be the ability to learn from His treasure troves of knowledge. A few examples of how, *"the earth shall be full of the knowledge of the Lord,"* in the Millennium are:

1.   All people who enter the Millennium are saved. This means that they will be indwelt by the Holy Spirit and have God's laws written upon their hearts in fulfillment of the New Covenant. As part of the natural course of human interactions, there will be fellowshipping and the spreading of the knowledge of the Lord throughout the world.

> "But this *is* the *(New)* covenant that I will make with the house of Israel after those days, says

the Lord: I will put My law in their minds, and write it on their hearts; and I will be their God, and they shall be My people. No more shall every man teach his neighbor, and every man his brother, saying, 'Know the Lord,' for they all shall know Me, from the least of them to the greatest of them, says the Lord." (Jeremiah 31:33-34)

"Listen to Me, you who know righteousness, You people in whose heart *is* My law." (Isaiah 51:7a)

Although the New Covenant is made with the house of Israel, all believers are grafted into it according to Romans 11:11-31. The means through which God inscribes His law in the minds and upon the hearts of His believers is through the indwelling of the Holy Spirit. He is identified as the Helper in John 14:16-17, 26.

2. In the beginning of the Millennium God will restore the earth to its former Garden of Eden-like glory. This re-creation will help facilitate the spread of the knowledge of God.

Here's how; when God created the heavens and the earth in six days, Adam and Eve were inserted into place at the tail end. They experienced the existence of creation, but probably didn't witness its formation. However, it appears that when the Lord restores the earth after all the devastation of the Trib-period, the saved people alive at the time will get a bird's eye view of the Creator's craftsmanship.

As people intermingle in the Millennium, they should have no shortage of nature's wonderment to share with each other. If the creation presently testifies of God, how much more will the re-creation banner His power and glory?

3. The resurrections of the Old Testament and Tribulation Saints should also be an eye-opener to the inhabitants of the Millennium. Some of these saints, like Noah, Abraham,

Joseph, David, Isaiah, Jeremiah, Ezekiel and Daniel have had past experiences with the Lord in ancient times. Some of us will want to know what they learned from their personal encounters with the Lord, and in turn, they will likely want to hear how their testimonies and prophecies played a positive role in our salvation and sanctification processes.

4.   The global government, which will include the Church Age saints, will be set up in a way to disseminate the knowledge of the Lord throughout the earth. This will be explained in the chapters entitled, "*The Millennial Government: The Jewish Branch* and *The Millennial Government: the Gentile Branch.*"

The Glory of the Lord: In Psalm 72:1-18, David writes about the glory and universality of the Messiah's reign in the Messianic Age. Then he concludes by stating that the glory of the Lord will fill the whole earth.

> "And blessed *be* His glorious name forever! And let the whole earth be filled *with* His glory. Amen and Amen." (Psalm 72:19)

Habakkuk 2:14 also prophesies,

> "For the earth will be filled With the knowledge of the glory of the Lord, As the waters cover the sea."

It's possible that David and Habakkuk are alluding to the observable "Shekinah Glory" of the Lord. This glory was formatted in multiple manifestations in the Old Testament accounts. Below are quotes about this attribute of God's glory from Christianity.com.

> "*Shekinah Glory is a visible manifestation of God on earth, whose presence is portrayed through a natural occurrence. The word Shekinah is a Hebrew name meaning "dwelling" or "one who*

dwells." Shekinah Glory means "He caused to dwell," referring to the divine presence of God… The rabbis used the term Shekinah to describe the following to the Jewish people:

- *The presence of God amongst His people (Exodus 19:16-18; 40:34-38; I Kings 6:13)*

- *The glory of God dwelling in the Temple (2 Chronicles 7:1)*

- *How God dwells in the mountain (Psalm 68.16-18; Joel 3:17)…*

…The divine presence of God on earth is depicted through the following:

- *As a cloud (Exodus 24:16-18; Exodus 33:9; 1 Kings 8:10-13)*

- *As a pillar of smoke and fire (Exodus 13:21-22)*

- *As fire and a burning bush (Zechariah 2:5; Exodus 3:2)"*[50]

Jesus Christ will be primarily reigning from His throne in Jerusalem as per Jeremiah 3:17, but these Old Testament Shekinah references suggest that God's glory might manifest itself through natural occurrences throughout the globe to evidence His presence among people.

No remembrance of the bad events that happened on the past earth.

"So that he who blesses himself in the earth Shall bless himself in the God of truth; And he who swears in the earth Shall swear by the God of truth; Because the former troubles are forgotten,

And because they are hidden from My eyes. "For behold, I create new heavens and a new earth; And the former shall not be remembered or come to mind."" (Isaiah 65:16-17)

Isaiah foretells of the re-creation of *"new heavens and a new earth."* These do not appear to be the same new heaven and new earth of Revelation 21:1, rather they represent a renovation of the existing ones. This restoration is in response to the destructions pointed out in the passages below.

"Lift up your eyes to the heavens, And look on the earth beneath. For the heavens will vanish away like smoke, The earth will grow old like a garment, And those who dwell in it will die in like manner; But My salvation will be forever, And My righteousness will not be abolished." (Isaiah 51:6)

"But the day of the Lord will come as a thief in the night, in which the heavens will pass away with a great noise, and the elements will melt with fervent heat; both the earth and the works that are in it will be burned up. Therefore, since all these things will be dissolved, what manner *of persons* ought you to be in holy conduct and godliness, looking for and hastening the coming of the day of God, because of which the heavens will be dissolved, being on fire, and the elements will melt with fervent heat? Nevertheless we, according to His promise, look for new heavens and a new earth in which righteousness dwells." (2 Peter 3:10-13)

Isaiah states that the present *heavens will vanish away like smoke* and he likens the earth to a *garment* that *will grow old* and be discarded. The apostle Peter, speaking of these same heavens, informs they *will melt with fervent heat* and that *the earth,* along with its *works, will be burned up.*

Painting a more graphic image, Peter states *"heavens will be dissolved, being on fire, and the elements will melt with fervent heat."* Both Isaiah and Peter appear to be referring to the visible atmospheric heavens, which become subjected to several devastating judgments during the Trib-period, such as:

> "I looked when He opened the sixth seal, and behold, there was a great earthquake; and the sun became black as sackcloth of hair, and the moon became like blood. And the stars of heaven fell to the earth, as a fig tree drops its late figs when it is shaken by a mighty wind. Then the sky receded as a scroll when it is rolled up, and every mountain and island was moved out of its place." (Revelation 6:12-14)

> "Then the third angel sounded: And a great star fell from heaven, burning like a torch, and it fell on a third of the rivers and on the springs of water." (Rev. 8:10)

> "Then the fourth angel sounded: And a third of the sun was struck, a third of the moon, and a third of the stars, so that a third of them were darkened. A third of the day did not shine, and likewise the night." (Rev. 8:12)

> "Then the fourth angel poured out his bowl on the sun, and power was given to him to scorch men with fire." (Rev. 16:8)

> "Then the fifth angel poured out his bowl on the throne of the beast, and his kingdom became full of darkness; and they gnawed their tongues because of the pain." (Rev. 16:10)

These and other cosmic convulsions will adversely affect the atmospheric heavens and cause them to *melt with fervent heat* and ultimately *dissolve*. As these disturbances in the skies occur, Isaiah 51:6 instructs mankind to, *"Lift up your eyes to the heavens, And look on the earth beneath."*

Isaiah is specifically speaking to people who are alive during the Trib-period. The prophet is letting them know that they will be eye-witnesses of the passing of the current heavens and earth in fulfillment of Isaiah 51:6 and 2 Peter 3:10-13.

Those who get saved during, and then somehow manage to survive through the Trib-period, will also witness the re-creation of *the new heavens and a new earth* in fulfillment of Isaiah 65:17. These individuals will also become so enamored with the miraculous restoration by God that *the former* things they experienced *shall not be remembered or come to mind*.

This does not likely allude to memory loss from a neuralyzer[51] type device or the destruction of history books, but it implies that the saved Trib-period survivors will be freed from the haunting memories of the past so that they can look forward to a new life in the Millennium.

Below is a helpful quote about this topic from Dr. Arnold Fruchtenbaum.

> "These new heavens and new earth are not to be confused with those of Revelation 21-22. The latter describes the new heavens and new earth of the Eternal Order, while the Isaiah passage describes those of the Messianic Kingdom which will be a renovation of the present heavens and earth. Those of the Revelation are not a renovation, but a brand new order. Hence, for the Millennium, there will be a total renovation of the heavens and the earth. The fact that the

term create is used shows that this renovation will be a miraculous one, possible by God alone."[52]

Advanced aeronautical methods of air transportation and travel.

"Who are these who fly like a cloud, And like doves to their roosts?" (Isaiah 60:8)

This verse seems to suggest that air travel will continue on into the Millennium. The context of this Scripture, as per Isaiah 60:5-6, is the wealth of the Gentiles be transported to Israel during the Messianic Age. Isaiah essentially asks, "*who are these Gentiles that are able to fly like a cloud and know exactly where and how to safely land at their destination, like a dove to its nest?*"

This may imply that these Gentiles are utilizing advanced aeronautical methods of air transportation. Currently, air travel, apart from hot air balloons and gliders, requires engine propulsion, rather than wind energy. The floating cloud and the flying dove rely exclusively on natural energy to travel through the sky.

As per the following passage, which is also found later in Isaiah chapter 60, perhaps millennial aeronautical methods of travel might someday utilize God's light as a source of solar energy for sky transportation. Moreover, maybe this abundance of God-given light explains the enormous amount of human and natural productivity that occurs in the Messianic Kingdom.

"The sun shall no longer be your light by day, Nor for brightness shall the moon give light to you; But the Lord will be to you an everlasting light, And your God your glory. Your sun shall no longer go down, Nor shall your moon withdraw itself; For the Lord will be your everlasting light, And the days of your mourning shall be ended." (Isaiah 60:19-20)

> "Moreover the light of the moon will be as the light of the sun, And the light of the sun will be sevenfold, As the light of seven days, In the day that the Lord binds up the bruise of His people And heals the stroke of their wound." (Isaiah 30:26)

A pure singular language.

> ""Therefore wait for Me," says the Lord, "Until the day I rise up for plunder;
>
> My determination is to gather the nations To My assembly of kingdoms, To pour on them My indignation, All My fierce anger; All the earth shall be devoured With the fire of My jealousy." "For then I will restore to the peoples a pure language, That they all may call on the name of the Lord, To serve Him with one accord."" (Zephaniah 3:8-9)

Some estimates suggest that there are currently 6500 languages spoken around the world. According to Genesis 11, there used to be only one language.

> "Now the whole earth had one language and one speech." (Genesis 11:1)

This was apparently the exclusive language that Adam and Eve, Enoch and Noah all communicated with. Then sometime after the flood of Noah, mankind assembled in Shinar (Babylon) to build a structure that reached into the heavens as an act of rebellion against God.

Some have suggested that the intent of these rebels was to construct a tall enough building to rise above any future floodwaters that God could send again. Apparently, they didn't trust God to honor His promise to never destroy all flesh by a future flood. This covenant was confirmed by the creation of the rainbow.

> "I set My rainbow in the cloud, and it shall be for the sign of the covenant between Me and the earth. It shall be, when I bring a cloud over the earth, that the rainbow shall be seen in the cloud; and I will remember My covenant which *is* between Me and you and every living creature of all flesh; the waters shall never again become a flood to destroy all flesh." (Genesis 9:13-15)

The bottom line was that these belligerents, who had descended from Noah, were attempting to avoid being scattered abroad to repopulate the earth, which was God's post-flood plan for Noah and his descendants.

> "So God blessed Noah and his sons, and said to them: "Be fruitful and multiply, and fill the earth." (Genesis 9:1)

> "And they, (*Noah's rebellious descendants*), said, "Come, let us build ourselves a city, and a tower whose top is in the heavens; let us make a name for ourselves, lest we be scattered abroad over the face of the whole earth." (Genesis 11:4, NKJV; emphasis added)

The following passage points out that this episode is when multiple languages were introduced into the world as a form of judgment against these disobedient descendants.

> "But the Lord came down to see the city and the tower which the sons of men had built. And the Lord said, "Indeed the people *are* one and they all have one language, and this is what they

begin to do; now nothing that they propose
to do will be withheld from them. Come, let
Us go down and there confuse their language,
that they may not understand one another's
speech." (Genesis 11:5-7)

Confusing their language was God's clever way of overriding
their rebellion and getting His will accomplished.

"So the Lord scattered them abroad from
there over the face of all the earth, and they
ceased building the city. Therefore its name is
called Babel, because there the Lord confused
the language of all the earth; and from there
the Lord scattered them abroad over the face of
all the earth." (Genesis 11:8-9)

Zephaniah 3:9 says that in the Millennium, God will "*restore*," or
in some translations, "*turn to*" a singular language so that all peoples,
"*may call on the name of the Lord, To serve Him with one accord.*"

Unfortunately, we are not informed, what the pure language
will be, if it will be the only language spoken in the Millennium
or how people learn to speak it, thus, we can't get a head start
on learning this future language. According to the passage below,
there may still exist other languages in the Millennium.

"Thus says the Lord of hosts: 'In those days ten
men from every language of the nations shall grasp
the sleeve of a Jewish man, saying, "Let us go with
you, for we have heard *that* God *is* with you." ' "
(Zechariah 8:23)

My best guess is that the pure language will be Hebrew and
that it will become instantaneously programmed into our brains at
the beginning of the Millennium.

Non-predatory animal behavior.

> "The wolf also shall dwell with the lamb, The leopard shall lie down with the young goat,
>
> The calf and the young lion and the fatling together; And a little child shall lead them. The cow and the bear shall graze; Their young ones shall lie down together; And the lion shall eat straw like the ox." (Isaiah 11:6-7)
>
> ""The wolf and the lamb shall feed together, The lion shall eat straw like the ox, And dust *shall be* the serpent's food. They shall not hurt nor destroy in all My holy mountain," Says the Lord." (Isaiah 65:25)

Presently, the wolf licks its chops while eating a lamb, the leopard chases down the young goat for dinner and the young lion considers feasting upon a fatling a delicacy. However, in the Millennium, bears will graze on grass, not cows, lions will eat straw alongside oxen and wolves and lambs will share food together from the same trough.

Children intermingling with dangerous animals and venomous snakes.

> "The nursing child shall play by the cobra's hole, And the weaned child shall put his hand in the viper's den. They shall not hurt nor destroy in all My holy mountain, For the earth shall be full of the knowledge of the Lord As the waters cover the sea." (Isaiah 11:8-9).

Isaiah 11:6 said that a wolf, lamb, leopard, goat, cow and a lion will follow a child, not necessarily an adolescent, teenager or young adult. Along these lines, can you imagine a mother instructing her child to go play with these critters or sound the cowbell to round them up for their feeding? Apparently, that time is coming in the Millennium.

How about taking it a step further? Can you envision a young mother breastfeeding her baby and then setting the child down next to a cobra? What about this for a mind-blower? Is it possible that a few months later, after the toddler is weaned off its mother's milk, that mom will let the innocent infant crawl over to a den filled with vipers? I mean, how does a child even find a den of vipers?

Is this sequence of child-rearing intentional? Is it part of a staged training process so that a child can grow into a wise young adult?

Stage One: A newborn to cuddle with a cobra.

Stage Two: A toddler must visit a vipers den.

Stage Three: A preschooler shall lead wild varmints in the wilderness.

It's hard to know, but it sure seems like National Geographic will have an abundance of stories to document in the Millennium.

Instantaneous answers to prayer.

> "It shall come to pass That before they call, I will answer; And while they are still speaking, I will hear." (Isaiah 65:24)

This verse implies that in the Millennium, God will be omnipresent, deeply involved in personal lives and well aware of individual needs. It also evidences that prayer will continue to be an important conduit of communication between God and man.

Lastly, it points out that people will still have specific supplications that rely upon the Lord for remediation. For instance, people will still have a sin nature and they may pray to God for victory over personal temptation(s) or perhaps to intercede for a loved one.

Revelation 1:6 informs that God is grooming the Church to be kings and priests. 1 Peter 2:9 identifies it as a "royal priesthood." An important priestly function is to offer up to God intercessory prayer on behalf of another. Presumably during the Millennium, the Church Age Saints will become the "royal priesthood" that actively intercedes on behalf of the God-fearing.

The next few topics are supported with verses that essentially need little to no commentary because, when interpreted literally, they speak for themselves.

An end of blindness and deafness.

> "In that day the deaf shall hear the words of the book, And the eyes of the blind shall see out of obscurity and out of darkness." (Isaiah 29:18)

> "Then the eyes of the blind shall be opened, And the ears of the deaf shall be unstopped." (Isaiah 35:5).

Crippled that walk and leap and mute who talk and sing.

> "Then the lame shall leap like a deer, And the tongue of the dumb sing." (Isaiah 35:6).

Robust construction and farming industries.

> "They shall build houses and inhabit *them;* They shall plant vineyards and eat their fruit." (Isaiah 65:21)

Adequate housing supplies.

"They shall not build and another inhabit; They shall not plant and another eat; For as the days of a tree, *so shall be* the days of My people, And My elect shall long enjoy the work of their hands." (Isaiah 65:22)

Life in the East Sea, (the Dead Sea).

"And in that day (*in the Millennium*) it shall be *That* living waters shall flow from Jerusalem, Half of them toward the eastern (*modern-day Dead*) sea And half of them toward the western (*Mediterranean*) sea; In both summer and winter it shall occur."(Zechariah 14:8, NKJV; emphasis added)

"Then he said to me: "This water flows toward the eastern (*Dead Sea*) region, goes down into the valley, and enters the sea. *When it* reaches the (*Dead*) sea, *its* waters are healed. And it shall be *that* every living thing that moves, wherever the rivers go, will live. There will be a very great multitude of fish, because these waters go there; for they will be healed, and everything will live wherever the river goes." (Ezekiel 47:8-9, NKJV; emphasis added)

Below are two good quotes from John Walvoord and Roy Zuck's commentary entitled, The Bible Knowledge Commentary: Old Testament. They discuss the Dead Sea's conversion to a life sponsoring sea in the Millennium.

Commentary on Zechariah 14:8:

"*A perennial spring of water (living water as opposed to rainwater) will erupt in Jerusalem dividing its water flow between the eastern sea (the Dead Sea) and the western sea (the Mediterranean). This year-round provision apparently will promote unsurpassed fertility throughout the land (cf. Isa. 27:6; 35:1-3, 6-7; Amos 9:13-14)."*

Commentary on Ezekiel 47:8-9:

"The millennial river will flow toward the eastern region and will go down into the Arabah, where it will enter the Sea. The "Arabah" is the Jordan Valley running south from the Sea of Galilee to the Dead Sea and ultimately to the Gulf of Aqabah. The millennial river will merge with the Jordan River at the northern mouth of the Dead Sea.

As this new river enters the Dead Sea, the water there will become fresh. The Dead Sea, now some six times saltier than the ocean, will become completely salt-free—truly a miracle of God! This now-lifeless body of water will then support life so that where the river flows everything will live. Fishermen will crowd the shores from En Gedi to En Eglaim ... to catch many kinds of fish there. "En Gedi" is a settlement about midway down the western shore of the Dead Sea."

Summary

In conclusion, I'll quote Romans 8:18-25 and insert my comments within this passage.

"For I consider that the sufferings of this present time are not worthy *to be compared* with the glory which shall be revealed in us (*in the Millennium*). For the earnest expectation of the creation, (*including its predatory animals*), eagerly waits for the revealing of the sons of God, (*who will be recognized in the Millennium*). For the creation was subjected to futility, (*at the time of the fall of Adam and Eve*), not willingly, but because of Him who subjected *it* in hope; because the creation itself also will be delivered (*in the Millennium*) from the bondage of corruption into the glorious liberty of the children of God. For we know that the whole creation groans and labors with birth pangs together until now. Not only *that*, but we, (Church Age Saints), also who have the firstfruits of the Spirit, even we ourselves groan within ourselves, eagerly waiting for the adoption, the redemption of our (immortal) body (in the First Resurrection). For we were saved in this hope, but hope that is seen is not hope; for why does one still hope for what he sees? But if we hope for what we do not see, we eagerly wait for *it* with perseverance." (Romans 8:18-25, NKJV; emphasis added)

13

The Jews in the Millennial Kingdom

A previous chapter entitled, *Faithful Jewish Remnant Returns to Israel,* pointed out that there will be a faithful remnant of Jewish believers, who in the following sequence of events will:

- Survive through the Trib-period,

- Return to a restored Israel,

- Enter into the Millennium.

Another chapter called, *The Resurrections in the Millennium*, explained how the Jewish Old Testament Saints and the Jewish Tribulation Saints would resurrect, probably in the 75-Day Interval Period, and dwell together with this surviving remnant. All three groups represent Jewish believers who can legitimately be classified as the biological descendants of Abraham.

How Many Jews will exist in the Millennium?

Before exploring Jewish life during the Millennium, let's attempt to answer the question of how many Jews will exist in the Millennium? Genesis 22:17 declares that Abraham would have as many descendants as *"the stars of the heaven and as the sand which is on the seashore."* As of yet, this prophecy has obviously not been fulfilled. Therefore, this promise will need to find fulfillment within the Messianic Age.

It appears that this vast multitude includes the three above groupings, plus the generations of offspring that spawn through the genealogical loins of the remnant. Being born into believing Jewish families, these progenies will hopefully also grow up to be believers like their parents. We can probably restrict Jewish child-bearing in the Millennium to the remnant because it is not likely that the resurrected saints in their immortal bodies will be birthing any Jewish children.

Thus, the four groups of Jews residing on earth in the Millennium are:

1.   The Faithful Jewish Remnant,

2.   The Offspring of this Jewish Remnant,

3.   The Resurrected Old Testament Jewish Saints,

4.   The Resurrected Jewish Tribulation Saints.

There is no way to predict the Jewish headcount totals of these four groups in the Millennium, but estimating the number of *the stars of the heaven* has already been done. Below is a quote from the European Space Agency website.

> *"Astronomers estimate there are about 100 thousand million stars in the Milky Way alone. Outside that, there are millions upon millions of other galaxies also!"*[53]

Concerning *the sand, which is on the seashore*, Alexa Answers website says that *"Earth's beaches contain roughly 5,000 billion billion-aka, 5 sextillion-grains of sand."*[54]

It's not likely that Abraham will have between *100 thousand million* to *5 sextillion* descendants. The *stars* and *sand* analogies were probably, God's way of informing Abraham that he would be the patriarchal father of a vast multitude.

> "I will make you, (*Abraham*), a great nation; I will bless you And make your name great; And you shall be a blessing." (Genesis 12:2, NKJV; emphasis added)

The verse above points out that Abraham would father a "great nation." The Hebrew word used for "great" is *gadol* or *gadowl*. According to the Strong's Lexicon this term can mean, a distinguished large magnitude of men in number and importance.

Considering that in the Millennium there will be no more war, longer life and much healthier lifestyles, the number of living Jews could, over a period of time, easily reach or probably exceed population totals comparable to that of modern-day China and India.

Using the May 24, 2021, Worldometer global population estimate of 7.9 billion,[55] perhaps it's not far-fetched to suggest that several billion Jews could at some time occupy Israel during the Millennium.

Several billion may seem like too large of a number, but whatever the total of Abraham's descendants comes in at, he's the odds-on favorite to be the father of the most populated nation on the planet during the Millennium. No other nation is promised to possess populations that total *"the stars of the heaven and as the sand which is on the seashore."*

How Large is the Jewish State in the Millennium?

Genesis 15:18 predicts that Israel's national borders will greatly expand in order to handle this vast multitude of Jews. The enlarged territory will span between the river in Egypt, probably the Nile, on to the Euphrates River that courses through modern-day Syria and Iraq. This could include about 300,000 square miles.[56]

This would make Israel in the Millennium comparable in landmass to modern-day Turkey, which is estimated at 300,948 sq. miles.[57] Turkey's population currently totals about 85 million.[58]

If these population and territorial estimates hypothesized above are anywhere near accurate, this implies that the nation of Israel, at some point in the Millennium, could turn out to be the most densely populated country. By comparison, China presently has about 1.4 billion people living on nearly 3.7 million sq. miles and India hosts approximately 1.3 billion inhabitants dwelling on 1.3 million sq. miles.

Putting these details and calculations into prophetic perspective, it's safe to surmise, as per God's Word, that the tiny Israel of today will be vastly larger and much more populated in the Millennium.

Jewish Life in Israel in the Millennium

The impending boom in Jewish population will precipitate the need for more than just enlarged territory, but will also necessitate increased food supplies and adequate housing accommodations. Ruined cities will need to be rebuilt or rezoned for agricultural use.

The Ezekiel verses below promise that when the Lord restores the remnant of Israel, He will beautify the desolated areas in Israel and rebuild and repopulate its ruined cities.

> "Thus says the Lord God: "On the day that I cleanse you from all your iniquities, I will also enable *you* to dwell in the cities, and the ruins shall be rebuilt. The desolate land shall be tilled instead of lying desolate in the sight

of all who pass by. So they will say, 'This land that was desolate has become like the garden of Eden; and the wasted, desolate, and ruined cities *are now* fortified *and* inhabited.' Then the nations which are left all around you shall know that I, the Lord, have rebuilt the ruined places *and* planted what was desolate. I, the Lord, have spoken *it,* and I will do *it.*" 'Thus says the Lord God: "I will also let the house of Israel inquire of Me to do this for them: I will increase their men like a flock. Like a flock *offered as* holy *sacrifices,* like the flock at Jerusalem on its feast days, so shall the ruined cities be filled with flocks of men. Then they shall know that I *am* the Lord." ' " (Ezekiel 36:33-38)

The rebuilding of these cities will become necessary because during the Trib-period the Antichrist's armies will cause ruination within Jerusalem and elsewhere.

"Watch, for the day of the Lord is coming when your possessions will be plundered right in front of you! I will gather all the nations to fight against Jerusalem. The city will be taken, the houses looted, and the women raped. Half the population will be taken into captivity, and the rest will be left among the ruins of the city." (Zech.14:1-2, NLT)

In anticipation of the coming Jewish population boom, the restoration of the cities will likely happen early on in the Millennium. The following passages describe other aspects of the rebuilding process that will accommodate the influx of Jews at that time.

"The time will come," says the Lord, "when the grain and grapes will grow faster than they can be harvested. Then the terraced vineyards on the hills of Israel will drip with sweet wine! I will bring my exiled people of Israel back from distant lands, and they will rebuild their ruined cities and live in them again. They will plant vineyards and gardens; they will eat their crops and drink their wine. I will firmly plant them there in their own land. They will never again be uprooted from the land I have given them," says the Lord your God." (Amos 9:13-15, NLT)

Amos points out that the remnant of Israel, the *"exiled people,"* will take part in the re-jew-vination of the Jewish nation. This alludes to Israel in the Millennium, rather than modern-day Israel. Current Israel is not *"firmly"* planted *"in their own land,"* but will *"be uprooted from the land"* once again when the Antichrist starts his campaign of Jewish genocide at the midpoint of the Trib-period.

A few more important highlights about Israel and the Israelis in the Millennium are listed below. Israel will:

- Be the headquarters of the Messiah's global government – (Jeremiah 3:17),

- Be a highly esteemed nation by the international community – (Isaiah 49:22-23, 65:12-14, Zephaniah 3:20),

- Be a place where international laws are established and world political leaders convene – (Isaiah 2:3, 60:11),

- Capitalize on abundant global resources and become a very wealthy nation – (Isaiah 60:5-11),

- Become a popular destination for tourism and holy pilgrimages – (Isaiah 2:2-4, 60:3-4, Zechariah 14:16),

- Possess farms, dairies and large pastures for flocks – (Jeremiah 31:5, 24, Joel 3:18, Zephaniah 2:6-7, Isaiah 17:2, 30:23-24),

- Experience a tremendous increase of daylight – (Isaiah 30:26, 60:19-20),

- Host the highest mountain in the world – (Isaiah 2:2, Micah 4:1-2),

- Be the location of Jehovah's House on this highest mountain – (Ezekiel 40:1-4, 45:1-8, 48:8-20).

Summary

This chapter has pointed out that there will be an Israel in the Millennium. It will be filled with lots of Jews and some extremely interesting Jewish people, such as Jesus Christ, Abraham, David, Daniel and many other resurrected Jewish saints. The Jewish state will undoubtedly be the happiest and most happening place on earth.

Book your tickets to Israel in advance by receiving Jesus Christ as your personal Lord and Savior today. You will receive abundant life now (John 10:10), eternal life afterward (John 3:16), and a free ticket to Israel in the Millennium. Why wait, don't put off until tomorrow what needs to be done today!

> "For He says: "In an acceptable time I have heard you, And in the day of salvation I have helped you." Behold, now *is* the accepted time; behold, now *is* the day of salvation." (2 Corinthians 6:2)

14

The Millennial Government: The Jewish Branch

"The Messianic Kingdom will be administered through an absolute monarchy with a definite chain of command and lines of authority. The absolute monarch will be the Person of Jesus the Messiah. The delegated authority will be split into two branches: a Jewish branch of government and a Gentile branch, each in turn having a chain of command."[59] (Dr. Arnold Fruchtenbaum)

The monarchy and the Jewish branch of the Millennial government are identified and explained in this chapter. The Gentile branch will be covered in the next chapter entitled, *The Millennial Government: The Gentile Branch.*

The Jewish branch of the Millennial government consists of the monarch, Who is Jesus Christ, and King David, The 12 Apostles, Princes, Judges and Counselors, and Israel.

Messiah the Monarch

"He shall have dominion also from sea to sea, And from the River to the ends of the earth." (Psalm 72:8)

The ruler of the global government in the Millennium will be Jesus Christ, Who is the *"KING OF KINGS AND LORD OF LORDS."* *(Revelation 19:16b)*

"For unto us a Child is born, Unto us a Son is given; And the government will be upon His shoulder. And His name will be called Wonderful, Counselor, Mighty God, Everlasting Father, Prince of Peace. Of the increase of *His* government and peace *There will be* no end, Upon the throne of David and over His kingdom, To order it and establish it with judgment and justice From that time forward, even forever. The zeal of the Lord of hosts will perform this." (Isaiah 9:6-7)

The above passage provides the basis of understanding the monarchy in the Millennium. It starts by acknowledging the First Coming of Jesus Christ, *"a Child is born, Unto us a Son is given."*

"And she, (*the virgin Mary*), brought forth her firstborn Son, (*baby Jesus*), and wrapped Him in swaddling cloths, and laid Him in a manger, because there was no room for them in the inn." (Luke 2:7, NKJV; emphasis added)

"For God so loved the world that He gave His only begotten Son, that whoever believes in Him should not perish but have everlasting life." (John 3:16)

"While he, (*the Apostle Peter*), was still speaking, behold, a bright cloud overshadowed them; and suddenly a voice, (*God's*), came out of the cloud, saying, "This is My beloved Son, (*Jesus Christ*), in whom I am well pleased. Hear Him!" And when the disciples heard *it,* they fell on their

faces and were greatly afraid. But Jesus came
and touched them and said, "Arise, and do not be
afraid." When they had lifted up their eyes, they
saw NO ONE BUT JESUS ONLY." (Matthew
17:5-8, NKJV; EMPHASIS ADDED)

These three passages above clearly identify Jesus Christ as the
Child and only begotten *Son* of God, Whom Isaiah prophesies,
"*the government will be upon His shoulder.*" This significant transfer
of world authority obviously alludes to sometime after the Second
Coming of Christ because the dominant world government in
place at Christ's first advent crucified Him, rather than rested
upon His shoulder.

The Transfer of the Global Government to Christ

"Then the seventh angel sounded: And there were
loud voices in heaven, saying, "The kingdoms of
this world have become *the kingdoms* of our Lord
and of His Christ, and He shall reign forever and
ever!" (Revelation 11:15)

The seventh trumpet sounds unleashing the Seven Bowl
Judgments of Revelation 16. Revelation 15:1 declares that the
completion of God's wrath is delivered through the outpouring
of these final seven judgments. Technically, it appears that the
transference of earthly governmental authority happens prior to
the outpouring of the bowls as per this above verse. However, there
is some major house cleaning on earth that is required to be done
before "*His Christ*" can "*reign forever and ever!*"

The following sequence of events chronicles the future transfer
of the global government upon the shoulder of Jesus Christ. When
Christ returns, He will:

1.   Cast the Antichrist and False Prophet alive into the Lake
     of Fire – (Rev. 19:20),

2. Destroy the rebellious world nations that were aligned with the Antichrist in the battle of Armageddon – (Rev. 19:21),

3. Purge the nations of its unbelievers in the goat judgment – (Matthew 25:41-46),

4. Fulfill the Psalm 2 passage below.

    "I will declare the decree: The Lord (*God*) has said to Me, (*Jesus Christ*), 'You *are* My Son, Today I have begotten You. Ask of Me, and I will give *You* The nations *for* Your inheritance, And the ends of the earth *for* Your possession. You shall break them with a rod of iron; You shall dash them to pieces like a potter's vessel.' " (Psalm 2:7-9, NKJV; emphasis added)

The process of this transfer of political power goes something like this:

1. The global dictator in the Trib-period, the Antichrist, will be eliminated,

2. At the same time, the Antichrist's armies are broken as *with a rod of iron,*

3. Then, the unbelieving goat Gentiles will be dashed into *pieces like a potter's vessel,*

4. In the aftermath Christ will proclaim: "*The Lord has said to Me, 'You are My Son, Today I have begotten You,*"

5. Christ will then ask God to give Him authority over the *nations* as His *inheritance,* and *the ends of the earth for* His *possession.*

This will not be the first time that authority over the global government could have rested upon the shoulder of Jesus Christ. This opportunity was presented to Him by Satan at His First Coming. However, Christ rejected the Devil's valid offer.

> "Again, the devil took Him, (*Jesus Christ*), up on an exceedingly high mountain, and showed Him all the kingdoms of the world and their glory. And he said to Him, "All these things I will give You if You will fall down and worship me." Then Jesus said to him, "Away with you, Satan! For it is written, 'You shall worship the Lord your God, and Him only you shall serve.' " Then the devil left Him, and behold, angels came and ministered to Him." (Matthew 4:8-11, NKJV; emphasis added)

Had Christ accepted this initial offer, He would have had to worship Satan, which means His allegiance would be to the one who, *"was a murderer from the beginning, and does not stand in the truth, because there is no truth in him. When he speaks a lie, he speaks from his own resources, for he is a liar and the father of it."* (John 8:44)

Unlike Jesus Christ, the Antichrist will take the Devil up on his offer of authority over the kingdoms of the world. This seed of the serpent Satan will become the authoritarian world dictator around the Midpoint of the Trib-period. This Beast of Revelation 13:1 will worship Satan, the father of lies, but his tenure as the world's ruler will be short-lived, only three and one-half years.

When Christ returns, He dethrones this evil dictator by casting him alive into the Lake of Fire. The last breath on earth the Antichrist takes will be in the hands of Christ and the last sight he will see is his political replacement, Messiah the Monarch, plunging him into this burning lake.

Christ rejected the Devil's offer because it was not God's will and also the strings attached were foreign to Christ's inherent nature. Satan is a murderer and liar, but Jesus is *"the way, the truth, and the life"* as per John 14:6.

Isaiah 9:6-7 goes on to point out that, *"His name will be called Wonderful, Counselor, Mighty God, Everlasting Father, Prince of Peace."* These are among the attributes that Christ, as the benevolent Monarch in the Millennium, will characterize, and as such, *"of the increase of His government and peace there will be no end."*

The Headquarters of the Global Government in the Millennium

Unlike the governmental seat of Antichrist in Mystery, Babylon, of which the location scholars today debate, there will be no mystery as to where the headquarters of the global government of the Messiah will be set up.

> " "Yet I, (*God*), have set My King (*of Kings and Lord of Lords*) On My holy hill of Zion, (*Jerusalem*)."
> (Psalm 2:6, NKJV; emphasis added)

> "At that time, (*during the Millennium*), Jerusalem shall be called The Throne of the Lord, and all the nations shall be gathered to it, to the name of the Lord, to Jerusalem. No more shall they follow the dictates of their evil hearts." (Jer. 3:17, NKJV; emphasis added)

This Jerusalem location is set up in accordance with the Davidic Covenant. David completed the time of his reign in the ancient city of Jerusalem.

> "David *was* thirty years old when he began to reign, *and* he reigned forty years. In Hebron he reigned over Judah seven years and six months,

and in Jerusalem he reigned thirty-three years over all Israel and Judah." (2 Samuel 5:4-5)

Isaiah 9:7 reiterates, "*Upon the throne of David and over His kingdom, To order it and establish it with judgment and justice From that time forward, even forever. The zeal of the Lord of hosts will perform this.*"

The *Lord of hosts will perform this* in fulfillment of the Davidic Covenant as per below.

> "When your days, (*King David*), are fulfilled and you rest with your, (*patriarchal*) fathers, (*Abraham, Isaac and Jacob*), I will set up your seed, (*Jesus Christ*) after you, who will come from your body, (*lineage*), and I will establish his kingdom, (*during the Millennium*). He shallbuild a house, (*the Millennial Temple*), for My name, and I will establish the throne of his kingdom, (*in Jerusalem*), forever." (2 Samuel 7:12-13, NKJV; emphasis added)

> "In mercy the throne will be established; And One will sit on it in truth, in the tabernacle of David, Judging and seeking justice and hastening righteousness." (Isaiah 16:5)

Messiah the Monarch Rules with a Rod of Iron

Psalm 2:9 begins with, "*You shall break them with a rod of iron.*" The "rod of iron" phraseology shows up four times in the Bible. In Psalm 2:9 the rod of iron is wielded as a weapon to dash the rebellious Gentile nations into pieces. However, the other three uses of this iron rod are for governing purposes in the Millennium.

Because this rod is cast in iron, rather than woven in willows, it implies that Messiah the Monarch will rule the global government with an iron fist. Even though Isaiah 9:6-7 identifies him as the *"Prince of Peace"* and says, *"of the increase of His government and peace there will be no end,"* this peace apparently requires the skillful use of the rod of iron to establish and maintain it throughout the Millennium.

The rod of iron first comes out of its sheath when Jesus Christ rids the world of the Antichrist, his rebellious armies and the unsaved Goat Gentiles. Psalm 2:9 says that the rod of iron is used to *"break them."* The Hebrew word for break is *ra'a'* with a phonetic spelling (*raw-ah*). It can be interpreted *to break the good for nothing into pieces.*[60]

The same rod remains actively in use throughout the Millennium, but to shepherd people rather than break them into pieces. The uses in the following three passages display the rod functioning as an instrument for ruling or shepherding, rather than breaking or dashing. These verses all use the following Greek words for ruling (*poimaino*) with a rod (*rhabdos*) of iron (*sidereos*). These words will be defined following the pertinent passages.

> (*Proof Text #1*) "She bore a male Child who was to rule (*poimaino*) all nations with a rod (*rhabdos*) of iron (*sidereos*). And her Child was caught up to God and His throne." (Rev. 12:5, NKJV; emphasis added)

> (*Proof Text #2*) "Now out of His mouth goes a sharp sword, that with it He should strike the nations. And He Himself will rule (*poimaino*) them with a rod (*rhabdos*) of iron (*sidereos*). He Himself treads the winepress of the fierceness and wrath of Almighty God. And He has on *His* robe and on His thigh a name written: KING OF KINGS AND LORD OF LORDS." (Rev. 19:15-16, NKJV; emphasis added)

(*Proof Text #3*) "And he who overcomes, and keeps My works until the end, to him I will give power over the nations—'He shall rule (*poimaino*) them with a rod (*rhabdos*) of iron (*sidereos*); They shall be dashed to pieces like the potter's vessels'" (Rev. 2:26-27, NKJV; emphasis added)

The Greek words poimaino, rhabdos and sidereos are defined below.[61]

- Poimaino: G4166 to shepherd or pastor.

- Rhabdos: G4464 a stick, wand, rod, scepter, or staff.

- Sidereos: G4603 made of iron.

These three references above to the rod of iron in the book of Revelation point out that the Messiah Monarch will be pastoring the peoples in the Millennium like sheep with a shepherd's staff. However, this specific staff is not the typical standard shepherd issue made of wood, but is a special edition forged in iron.

But why iron, rather than wood? Before answering this, it's helpful to understand the biblical role of a corrective rod. The Hebrew word commonly used for rod in the Old Testament is *shebet*.[62] It is translated as a rod, staff or scepter, but the term also applies to a stick used for punishing and correction. The passages below point out why the rod of correction is important.

"Foolishness *is* bound up in the heart of a child; The rod of correction will drive it far from him." (Proverbs 22:15)

"Do not withhold correction from a child, For *if* you beat him with a rod, he will not die. You shall beat him with a rod, And deliver his soul from hell." (Proverbs 23:13-14)

"The rod and rebuke give wisdom, But a child left *to himself* brings shame to his mother." (Proverbs 29:15)

The disciplinary instructions in these Proverbs passages find application now and should also apply in the Millennium. This is because the mortals who enter into the Millennium will have a sin nature that they will pass on through their offspring.

Proverbs 22:15 pointed out that a child born with a sin nature inherently has *foolishness* bound up in its heart. Proverbs 23:13-14 instructs a parent to correct a foolish child in order to deliver *his soul from hell,* which is where foolishness leads. Proverbs 29:15 warns that a child left to himself remains foolish and as such, behaves shamefully.

Isaiah 65:20 warns that in the Millennium, "*the child shall die one hundred years old, but the sinner being one hundred years old shall be accursed*," which means there is an age of accountability. The one-hundred-year-old unsaved sinner that dies accursed, goes to Hades. This unsaved sinner began as a foolish child in need of the rod of correction in order to deliver his soul from Hell.

"My son, do not despise the chastening of the Lord, Nor be discouraged when you are rebuked by Him; For whom the Lord loves He chastens, And scourges every son whom He receives." If you endure chastening, God deals with you as with sons; for what son is there whom a father does not chasten? But if you are without chastening, of which all have become partakers, then you are illegitimate and not sons." (Hebrews 12:5b-8)

The point of providing all of these disciplinary passages under this section is to qualify the need for the Messiah Monarch to shepherd the global government with a rod of iron in order to maintain world peace. There will not only be individual sin issues, but apparently there will be power struggles among peoples and nations that will require His iron hand for just and righteous deliberations.

> "He shall judge between the nations, And rebuke many people; They shall beat their swords into plowshares, And their spears into pruning hooks; Nation shall not lift up sword against nation, Neither shall they learn war anymore." (Isaiah 2:4)

> "Many nations shall come and say, "Come, and let us go up to the mountain of the Lord, To the house of the God of Jacob; He will teach us His ways, And we shall walk in His paths." For out of Zion the law shall go forth, And the word of the Lord from Jerusalem. He shall judge between many peoples, And rebuke strong nations afar off; They shall beat their swords into plowshares, And their spears into pruning hooks; Nation shall not lift up sword against nation, Neither shall they learn war anymore." (Micah 4:2-3)

These two above passages explain that in the Millennium international disputes will no longer be resolved militarily. This is because at the inception of the Millennium all of the world's existing conventional weapons, which were not destroyed previously in the multiple wars of the last days, will be broken into pieces and then converted into useful farm implements, such as plowshares and pruning hooks.

The Hebrew word for beat is "*kathath*" and it can be translated, to crush by beating with a hammer to the point of being broken into pieces.[63] It alludes to a two-step process, first break down the weapons and then recycle the materials into useful farming tools. Without weapons, conventional wars will no longer be waged rather, the Lord will use His rod of iron to *judge between many peoples, And rebuke strong nations afar off.*

This iron fist policy will be the backbone of Messiah's global government. All of those placed in political power will be required to execute their duties in strict compliance with His laws. This includes all governing Church Saints. Proof text #3 above, which addressed overcomers in the Church, pointed out that *"he who overcomes, and keeps My works until the end, to him I will give power over the nations." 'He shall rule them with a rod of iron.'"* (Rev. 2:26-27)

This is one of the passages that informs the Church Age Saints will be reigning in the Millennium alongside Jesus Christ. Below is a quote from the Bible Knowledge Commentary: New Testament that speaks to this point.

> *"Christ promises believers who are faithful that they will join Him in His millennial rule (Ps. 2:8-9; 2 Tim. 2:12; Rev. 20:4-6). The word in verse 27 translated "rule" poimaino means "to shepherd," indicating that they will not simply be administering justice but will also, like a shepherd using his rod, be dealing with his sheep and protecting them as well... Believers will have authority just as Christ does."*[64]

Lastly, at the end of the Millennium a multitude of unsaved people will rebel against the iron fisted rule of Messiah the Monarch.

> "Now when the thousand years have expired, Satan will be released from his prison and will go out to deceive the nations which are in the four corners of the earth, Gog and Magog, to gather them together to battle, whose number *is* as the sand of the sea. They went up on the breadth of the earth and surrounded the camp of the saints and the beloved city. And fire came down from God out of heaven and devoured them." (Revelation 20:7-9)

Isaiah 2:4 and Micah 4:2-3 said that people in the Millennium would not learn war anymore, but that they allow Jesus Christ to *judge between many peoples, And rebuke strong nations afar off.* Apparently by the end of the Millennium there will be a multitude of unsaved people that are fed up with the iron fisted method of governing and will prefer war.

In summary of this rod of iron section, Messiah the Monarch will govern over a peaceful planet. In fact, *"of the increase of His government and peace there will be no end."* This world peace will be maintained by Messiah Who, with a rod of iron, will judge and rebuke nations and chastens those He loves. In conclusion, why the rod of iron? Because mankind will still have his sin nature in the Millennium.

The Jewish Branch of Government in the Millennium

King David, The 12 Apostles, Princes, Judges and Counselors, and Israel.

King David the Prime Minister of Israel

The governance in Israel flows from top down, starting with Jesus the Messiah as the monarch king over the world, including the Jewish state, then down the political ladder to its second rung, which will be King David. Below are a few passages that pronounce this.

> "'For it shall come to pass in that day,' Says the Lord of hosts, *'That* I will break his, (*the Antichrist's*), yoke from your neck, And will burst your, (*Israel's*), bonds; Foreigners shall no more enslave them, (*the Jews*). But they, (*the Jews*), shall serve the Lord, (*Jesus Christ*), their God, And David their king, Whom I will raise up, (*resurrect and enthrone*), for them." (Jeremiah 30:8-9, NKJV; emphasis added)

"Afterward the children of Israel shall return and seek the Lord their God and David their king. They shall fear the Lord and His goodness in the latter days." (Hosea 3:5)

"I will establish one shepherd over them, and he shall feed, them—My servant David. He shall feed them and be their shepherd. And I, the Lord, will be their God, and My servant David a prince among them; I, the Lord, have spoken." (Ezekiel 34:23-24)

"David My servant *shall be* king over them, and they shall all have one shepherd; they shall also walk in My judgments and observe My statutes, and do them. Then they shall dwell in the land that I have given to Jacob My servant, where your fathers dwelt; and they shall dwell there, they, their children, and their children's children, forever; and My servant David *shall be* their prince forever." (Ezekiel 37:24-25).

This sequence of passages above are relatively self-explanatory.

1. Jesus Christ will eliminate the Antichrist and rid all Anti-Semitism from the planet.

2. Afterwards, the surviving saved Faithful Jewish Remnant will return to Israel to seek the Lord and His servant David.

3. The Lord will "*raise up*" David, along with the resurrection of all the other Old Testament Saints.

4. David will serve, without any term limits of future elections, as Israel's Prime Minister *forever*.

(On a side note, at the time of authoring this chapter on May 30, 2021, Israel has undergone four national elections in two years and is still unable to decide upon a future Prime Minister, or form a coalition government. Ultimately, according to Isaiah 28:14-15, scornful rulers will emerge in Jerusalem and confirm the false covenant of Daniel 9:27, which triggers the Trib-period, a.k.a, the "*Time of Jacob's Trouble*" in Jeremiah 30:7. None of this present political uncertainty and future divisiveness will ever occur in the Millennium).

5.   As Prime Minister, David will uphold the constitution of God's statutes and laws.

6.   Ezekiel 34:23-34 above points out two times that David will shepherd and feed them. This suggests that he will preside over a wealthy nation that provides lots of employment and economic opportunities. It was pointed out earlier in this book that according to Isaiah 60, the abundant wealth of the Gentiles worldwide will pour into Israel in the Millennium.

It's interesting to note that David's son and immediate heir to his throne, King Solomon, was the recipient of abundant resources during his reign. Solomon's accumulated wealth might provide historical hints of the fortunes destined to come to Israel in the Millennium. According to 2 Chron. 1:16-2:16, Solomon conducted international trade with the Egyptians, Hittites, Syrians, Lebanese and more. In fact, the Lord promised Solomon that he would become the world's wealthiest king of all times.

"Wisdom and knowledge *are* granted to you; and I will give you riches and wealth and honor, such as none of the kings have had who *were* before you, nor shall any after you have the like." (2 Chronicles 1:12)

Below is a quote about Solomon's great wealth from an article entitled, "*The Twenty Richest People of All Time.*"

> *"King Solomon of Israel – peak net worth: $2 trillion (£1.42trn) According to the Bible, King Solomon ruled from 970 BC to 931 BC, and during this time he is said to have received 25 tons of gold for each of the 39 years of his reign, which would be worth billions of dollars in 2016."*[65]

I will conclude this section about King David the Prime Minister of Israel with a quote from Ned Bankston one of my researchers for this book series. Ned points out that King David has historically already proven to be an "Able Administrator."

> *"King David was a very able "Administrator" as he handled all the national affairs of Israel while he was their King. It was King David who assembled all the gold, silver and precious stones as per 1 Chronicles 28:11-19. King David, as per 1 Chronicles 29:2-8, also gave to his son, King Solomon, all the written details to build the First Jewish Temple, which is another quality of an able administrator. Thus, King David, as the Prime Minister of Israel, will be well able to support and supply his nation. I think that is well pointed out in Ezekiel 34: 23-24. If all the wealth of the nations is going to be pouring into the nation of Israel, who better than King David to be Israel's "Able Administrator."*

The 12 Apostles

In addition to Jesus Christ sitting upon the reestablished throne of David, the Twelve Apostles will also be seated nearby on their individual thrones. The clue that these twelve thrones will likely be close in proximity to the Messiah's is provided in the passage below.

> "But you are those who have continued with Me in My trials. And I bestow upon you a kingdom, just as My Father bestowed *one* upon

> Me, that you may eat and drink at My table in
> My kingdom, and sit on thrones judging the
> twelve tribes of Israel." (Luke 22:28-30)

The Twelve Apostles will possess VIP passes to dine at the table of Jesus the Messiah. The content of this passage suggests that these dining engagements happen on a frequent basis, which would require that the Twelve Apostles reside and preside close by. When they are not eating and drinking with the Messiah, or performing some other important activities, they are judging the Twelve Tribes of Israel. This is also confirmed in the verse below.

> "So Jesus said to them, "Assuredly I say to you, that
> in the regeneration, when the Son of Man sits on
> the throne of His glory, you who have followed
> Me will also sit on twelve thrones, judging the
> twelve tribes of Israel." (Matthew 19:28)

In the regeneration, which alludes to the renovated earth, the Twelve Apostles will be judging Israel, represented by the Twelve Tribes of Israel. This puts the chain of command over Israel thus far as follows:

The KING OF KINGS: Jesus Christ

Prime Minister: King David

Supreme Court Justices: Peter, James, John, Andrew, Phillip, Bartholomew, Matthew, Thomas, James *the son of Alphaeus*, Thaddaeus, Simon and Paul.

Presently, The Supreme Court in Jerusalem is the highest court of Israel and it consists of 15 Justices and two registrars. In the Millennium, there will apparently only be 12 justices. The fact that the Twelve Apostles will be acting in the capacity of judging the Twelve Tribes implies that, even though Israelis in the Millennium are saved, some tribal disputes will occasionally arise that require the Apostles to intervene.

When the Twelve Apostles are dining with Jesus, they may occasionally discuss some of the more controversial cases that are on their docket. Maybe their table talk will periodically be just conversational, but if the tribe of Judah has a territorial beef with the neighboring tribe of Simeon, then the apostle in charge may seek advice from Jesus the Messiah.

The Princes of Israel

> "Behold, a king will reign in righteousness, And princes will rule with justice." (Isaiah 32:1)

The king in this verse is Jesus the Messiah, and princes will rule in His government. The next passage implies that these are not the Apostles and that these princes are ruling over Israel and not the Gentile nations.

> "The land shall be his possession in Israel; and My princes shall no more oppress My people, but they shall give *the rest of* the land to the house of Israel, according to their tribes." (Ezekiel 45:8)

This verse points out that non-oppressive princes will serve in the land distribution of Israel according to their tribes. Perhaps, these princes will serve as politicians in some sort of a Millennial Knesset. Dr. Arnold Fruchtenbaum points out in his Footsteps of the Messiah book that the resurrected Zerubbabel could be among these princely politicians.

> "*The resurrected Zerubbabel, mentioned in Haggai 2:20-23, will very likely be among these princes...*

*And the word of Jehovah came the second time
unto Haggai in the four and twentieth day of the
month, saying, Speak to Zerubbabel, governor
of Judah, saying, I will shake the heavens and
the earth; and I will overthrow the throne of
kingdoms; and I will destroy the strength of the
kingdoms of the nations; and I will overthrow
the chariots, and those that ride in them; and
the horses and their riders shall come down, every
one by the sword of his brother. In that day, saith
Jehovah of hosts, will I take thee, O Zerubbabel,
my servant, the son of Shealtiel, saith Jehovah,
and will make thee as a signet; for I have chosen
thee, saith Jehovah of hosts.*

*The time of Zerubbabel's exalted position will be
after the shaking of the heavens and the earth (vv.
20-21) and the destruction of the invading armies
(v. 22). Both of these will occur at the Second
Coming."*[66]

Judges and Counselors

"Therefore the Lord says, The Lord of hosts, the
Mighty One of Israel, "Ah, I will rid Myself of
My adversaries, And take vengeance on My
enemies (*at Armageddon*). I will turn My hand
against you, (*unsaved Israel in the Trib-period*),
And thoroughly purge away your dross, And
take away all your alloy. I will restore, (*in the
Millennium*), your *judges* as at the first, And your
counselors as at the beginning. Afterward you shall
be called the city of righteousness, the faithful
city (*of Jerusalem*)." Zion shall be redeemed with
justice, And her penitents with righteousness."
(Isaiah 1:24-27, NKJV; emphasis added)

After the Lord gets rid of the Antichrist and his evil armies, who were responsible for purging away many of the unsaved Jews in a genocidal campaign, (*see Zechariah 13:8*), He will restore judges and counselors to dispense justice. Although these judges and counselors may be involved in statewide activities, the primary context of Isaiah's passage is mostly dealing with Jerusalem.

Israel

The importance of the Messiah ruling with a rod of iron and the succession of command from King David, the 12 Apostles, Princes, Judges and Counselors filtering down to the Jewish state is because Israel will actually have governing responsibilities over the Gentile nations. The passages below point this out.

> "For the Lord your God will bless you just as He promised you; you shall lend to many nations, but you shall not borrow; you shall reign over many nations, but they shall not reign over you." (Deuteronomy 15:6)

This above verse pictures Israel as being a wealthy and self-sufficient nation that is in no need of borrowing. On the contrary, the state of their national economy is such that they can extend credit to Gentile nations in need. It also points out that Israel *"shall reign over many nations."*

The next two verses in Deuteronomy 28 explain that God will position Israel in a dominant position as the head above all the nations.

> "Now it shall come to pass, if you diligently obey the voice of the Lord your God, to observe carefully all His commandments which I command you today, that the Lord your God will set you high above all nations of the earth." (Deuteronomy 28:1)

This promise was conditional when it was made. It required that Israel "*diligently obey the voice of the Lord.*" History tells us that Israel's tendency was to be disobedient, rather than obedient, *to the voice of the Lord*. As such, the Lord had no reason historically to set Israel "*high above all nations of the earth.*"

However, in the Millennium, Israel's ruling elite, the Messiah, King David, the Twelve Apostles etc. will rule over a Jewish state that will *diligently obey the voice of the Lord*. At that time, God can, and apparently will, reward this good national behavior by setting Israel *high above all nations of the earth*. The next verse supports this by positioning Israel as the "*head and not the tail*" of the Millennial government.

> "And the Lord will make you the head and not the tail; you shall be above only, and not be beneath, if you heed the commandments of the Lord your God, which I command you today, and are careful to observe *them.*" (Deuteronomy 28:13)

The last passage below points out that Gentiles will facilitate Jewish Aliyah back into Israel. Also, some Gentiles will find gainful employment in the land of Israel.

> "For the Lord will have mercy on Jacob, and will still choose Israel, and settle them in their own land. The strangers will be joined with them, and they will cling to the house of Jacob. Then people will take them and bring them to their place, and the house of Israel will possess them for servants and maids in the land of the Lord; they will take them captive whose captives they were, and rule over their oppressors." (Isaiah 14:1-2)

Summary

This chapter opened with a quote from Dr. Arnold Fruchtenbaum, so fittingly it will close with another one. I say fittingly, because much of the research for this chapter was collected from his prior scholarly work on this subject. He sums up what the Jewish branch of government will look like in the Millennium.

> "*The chain of command in the Jewish branch of government is from the Messianic King to David, to the Twelve Apostles, to the princes, to the judges and counselors, over all Israel, which will be serving as the head of the Gentiles. The rod of iron that will characterize the rule of the government in the Kingdom will be implemented through various spheres and positions of authority.*"[67]

15

The Millennial Government: The Gentile Branch

n the Millennium, there will be mortal Gentile kings ruling over the Gentile nations. Jesus the Messiah will be the ruler over these earthly kings. These kings will also be serving under the reigning Church Saints and Resurrected Tribulation Saints.

> "And from Jesus Christ, the faithful witness, the firstborn from the dead, and the ruler over the kings of the earth." (Revelation 1:5)

The Church Age Saints Reign with Christ in the Millennium

The Church Age Saints will reign alongside Jesus Christ in the capacity of qualified kings and priests.

> "To Him who loved us and washed us from our sins in His own blood, and has made us kings and priests to His God and Father, to Him *be* glory and dominion forever and ever. Amen." (Revelation 1:6)

> "*This is* a faithful saying: For if we died with *Him,* We shall also live with *Him.*

If we endure, We shall also reign with *Him*. If we deny *Him*, He also will deny us." (2 Timothy 2:11-12)

In the letter to the Church of Thyatira, Jesus Christ pledges to bestow *power over the nations* to the overcoming Church Saints.

"And he who overcomes, and keeps My works until the end, to him I will give power over the nations— 'He shall rule them with a rod of iron; They shall be dashed to pieces like the potter's vessels'" (Revelation 2:26-27)

The passage below emphatically informs two times that Church Age Saints and Resurrected Tribulation Saints will rule under Christ throughout the entire one-thousand years of the Messianic Kingdom.

"And I saw thrones, and they sat on them, and judgment was committed to them. Then *I saw* the souls of those who had been beheaded for their witness to Jesus and for the word of God, who had not worshiped the beast or his image, and had not received *his* mark on their foreheads or on their hands. And they lived and reigned with Christ for a thousand years. But the rest of the dead did not live again until the thousand years were finished. This *is* the first resurrection. Blessed and holy *is* he who has part in the first resurrection. Over such the second death has no power, but they shall be priests of God and of Christ, and shall reign with Him a thousand years." (Revelation 20:4-6)

The Church Age Saints are identified as those who are sitting upon thrones. The sentence goes on to say, "*and judgment was committed to them.*" This implies that the ones seated upon the thrones are authorized to commit judgment within the realm of their allotted *power over the nations.*

However, unlike the NKJV, the ASV translates, *"judgment was given,* (rather than committed), *unto them."* This could be referring to power and authority of those perched upon their thrones to give judgment over the nations, but it could also be alluding to the fact that these individuals were given, or in other words previously underwent, judgment themselves. Dr. Arnold Fruchtenbaum says the following about this subject matter in Revelation 20:4.

> *"In verse four, John describes the saints who are to co-reign with the Messiah. First, there are those to whom judgment has been given. This would be a reference to the Church saints who were raptured at some time preceding the Great Tribulation. The judgment spoken of is that of the Judgment Seat of the Messiah, the judgment of the believer's works. In fact, it is the outcome of this judgment that will determine the position of each Church saint in the Kingdom."*[68]

I think both scenarios could apply.

First, the Bema Seat Judgment of the Church Saints happens. This judgment is described in three places: Romans 14:10-12, 1 Corinthians 3:10, 4:5, and 2 Corinthians 5:1-10. This is not a punishment scenario, rather it is a purification process that results in a reward rendering ceremony.

In Revelation 4:4 we read about the crowns rewarded to the twenty-four elders, who seem to represent the Raptured and subsequently rewarded Church. These crowns are seemingly presented to these elders during the Bema Seat Judgment. In Revelation 4:10 these elders are noted to be casting these crowns in humility before the throne of God.

In the passage below, we see that these elders appear to represent the redeemed Church Age Saints who have graduated into their kingship and priestly roles.

> "And they sang a new song, saying: "You are worthy to take the scroll, And to open its seals; For You were slain, And have redeemed us to God by Your blood Out of every tribe and tongue and people and nation, And have made us kings and priests to our God; And we shall reign on the earth." (Revelation 5:9-10)

This above passage seems to echo what was said in Revelation 1:6, which was quoted above.

> "To Him who loved us, (*Church Age believers*), and washed us from our sins in His, (*Jesus Christ*), own blood, and has made us, (*a.k.a. twenty-four elders*), kings and priests to His God and Father, to Him *be* glory and dominion forever and ever. Amen." (Revelation 1:5c-6, NKJV; emphasis added)

Second, having first been "*given*" to the Bema Seat Judgment, and becoming crowned and enthroned as kings at that time, the Church Age Saints are then qualified to be "*committed*" with ruling *power over the nations.*

The Resurrected Tribulation Saints Reign with Christ in the Millennium

Revelation 20:4 also stated the following:

> "Then *I saw* the souls of those who had been beheaded for their witness to Jesus and for the word of God, who had not worshiped the beast or

> his image, and had not received *his* mark on
> their foreheads or on their hands. And they lived
> and reigned with Christ for a thousand years."

These saints are those who underwent the beheadings of the
Antichrist, which happened in the last three and one-half years
of the Tribulation period. They refused to worship the Antichrist
or receive his mark and for their non-compliance were executed.
There will be other Tribulation Saints who similarly won't comply,
but somehow they escape the beheadings in the Great Tribulation.

This latter group of survivors are not being identified in
Revelation 20:4. They are among the Sheep Gentiles who enter
into the Millennium alive in their existing mortal bodies. The
Tribulation Saints who will be reigning with Jesus Christ are the
immortal resurrected ones.

According to the Revelation 7 passage below, they will reign
in the Millennium, but their primary functions are going to *"be
before the throne of God, and serve Him day and night in His temple."*

> "After these things I (*the Apostle John*) looked, and
> behold, a great multitude (*of Tribulation Saints*)
> which no one could number, of all nations,
> tribes, peoples, and tongues, standing before the
> throne and before the Lamb, clothed with white
> robes, with palm branches in their hands, and
> crying out with a loud voice, saying, *"Salvation
> belongs* to our God who sits on the throne, and to
> the Lamb!" (Revelation 7:9-10, NKJV; emphasis
> added)

> "Then one of the elders answered, saying to me,
> "Who are these arrayed in white robes, and where
> did they come from?" And I said to him, "Sir, you
> know." So he said to me, "These are the ones who
> come out of the great tribulation, and washed

their robes and made them white in the blood of the Lamb. Therefore they are before the throne of God, and serve Him day and night in His temple. And He who sits on the throne will dwell among them. They shall neither hunger anymore nor thirst anymore; the sun shall not strike them, nor any heat; for the Lamb who is in the midst of the throne will shepherd them and lead them to living fountains of waters. And God will wipe away every tear from their eyes." (Revelation 7:13-17)

It is commonly taught that these Saints have been martyred for their faith in Christ during the Tribulation. The Pulpit Commentary points out that even some early Christian theologians, such as, *"Arethas, Bede, De Lyra, consider that the robes are washed of those who have endured martyrdom, and that they are washed in the blood of the Lamb, because it is the blood of his members. Revelation 7:14."*[69]

Thus, it appears that a primary function of the resurrected Tribulation Saints in the Millennium will be to congregate around, *"the throne of God, and serve Him day and night in His temple."*

(*Caveat:* Church Age Saints and resurrected Tribulation Saints are comprised of both Jews and Gentiles. It isn't clear whether the Jewish contingencies within these two groups are called to differing ruling duties than their Gentile counterparts. Moreover, Some Tribulation saints die in the Trib-period and resurrect into the Millennium with new bodies. Some of them remain alive at the end of the Trib-period and enter the Millennium with their existing mortal bodies).

Gentile Kings

The Scriptures below point out that there will be mortal Gentile Kings ruling over their own nations.

> "The kings of Tarshish and of the isles Will bring presents; The kings of Sheba and Seba Will offer gifts. Yes, all kings shall fall down before Him; All nations shall serve Him." (Psalm 72:10-11)

These two Psalm 72 verses above make it clear that "*all kings shall fall down before Him*; (King Jesus), and "*All nations shall serve Him.*" The fact that these world kings fall prostrate before Jesus Christ is an indication of their adoration towards Him. It pictures these kings as desiring to serve and please Jesus the Messiah.

> "Thus says the Lord God: "Behold, I will lift My hand in an oath to the nations, And set up My standard for the peoples; They shall bring your sons in *their* arms, And your daughters shall be carried on *their* shoulders; Kings shall be your foster fathers, And their queens your nursing mothers; They shall bow down to you with *their* faces to the earth, And lick up the dust of your feet. Then you will know that I *am* the Lord, For they shall not be ashamed who wait for Me."" (Isaiah 49:22-23)

One of the important acts of servitude the Gentile Kings will perform for their King Jesus is to facilitate the Aliyah of the Jews back to Israel. When we read that "*Kings shall be your foster fathers, And their queens your nursing mothers,*" it suggests that during the genocidal campaign of the Antichrist in the Trib-period, some Jewish families were scattered into the nations and some children lost their parents in the process. These surviving Jewish sons and daughters will receive the best possible care upon their return to Israel.

> "Arise, shine; For your light has come! And the glory of the Lord is risen upon you. For behold, the darkness shall cover the earth, And deep

darkness the people; But the Lord will arise over you, And His glory will be seen upon you. The Gentiles shall come to your light, And kings to the brightness of your rising." (Isaiah 60:1-3)

"Therefore your gates shall be open continually; They shall not be shut day or night, That *men* may bring to you the wealth of the Gentiles, And their kings in procession." (Isaiah 60:11)

These two Isaiah passages above point out the kings will come in procession, both day and night, bringing their national treasures to the headquarters of King Jesus in Jerusalem.

It's important to note that the Gentile Kings operate in a subservient role to the governing Church Saints and Resurrected Tribulation Saints. Below is another Dr. Arnold Fruchtenbaum quote that explains this.

"These (Gentile) *kings will have their natural bodies while the saints who will be over them will have their spiritual, resurrected, and glorified bodies. While the individual kings will be the supreme rulers over their own nations, they themselves will be under the authority of the Church and* (resurrected) *Tribulation saints."*[70]

16

The Millennial Jerusalem, Temple and Tribal Territories

This chapter will explore the following topics as they apply to the Millennium:

1. The present pre-Millennial Jerusalem,

2. The restored Jerusalem in the Millennium,

3. The rebuilt Fourth Jewish Temple with its sacrificial system,

4. The parameters of the Promised Land.

The Present Pre-Millennial Jerusalem

"Israel welcomes record-breaking 4.55 million tourists in 2019"(Jerusalem Post on 12/29/19)[71]

As the headline illustrates, in the year prior to the COVID 19 outbreak, Israel was a tourism hotspot. But then, as pointed out in the headline below, tourism decreased dramatically as the Jewish State levied stiff restrictions on tourists entering the country.

"Tourist arrivals to Israel decreased by 81.3% in 2020: Ministry" (i24 News on (2/2/21)[72]

Additionally, numerous Israeli businesses were closed down and according to the headline below, this trend is expected to continue.

"Up to 60,000 Israeli businesses may close in 2021 amid COVID-19 fallout: reports" (Times of Israel on 10/22/20)[73]

All of the above has taken its toll on the holy land of Israel and its historic city of Jerusalem. Perhaps the Jewish state and Jerusalem might rebound and again bolster a bustling economy and thriving tourist industry, but according to end times Bible prophecy, Jerusalem is ultimately destined for disaster. The present Jerusalem is going to need a facelift after the following prophesied events happen. The holy city will become:

1.   a cup of trembling to the surrounding Arab nations when they lay a final siege upon it (Zechariah 12:2),

2.   a burdensome stone to the international community as it continues its attempts to divide the city (Zech. 12:3),

3.   trodden over during the first 3 ½ years of the Trib-period by the Gentiles, probably alluding to both the clergy and laity of the Harlot world religion, *a.k.a.,* Mystery Babylon of Rev. 17 (Rev. 11:2),

4.   captured by the Antichrist and his armies at the midpoint of the Trib-period after the Harlot world religion is desolated by the Ten Kings in Rev. 17:16 (Zech. 14:2),

5.   split in two from east to west by an enormous earthquake that carves out a very large valley by moving half of the

mountain toward the north and half of it to the south. This occurs at the time of the Second Coming of Jesus Christ (Zech. 14:4),

6.   reduced to ruins from the above events and need to be rebuilt for the return of the Faithful Jewish Remnant (Ezek. 36:38).

The Restored Jerusalem in the Millennium

The fulfillment of these above events will *firstly*, render the existing Jerusalem unsuitable for the Messiah to establish His throne there. *Secondly*, make it uninhabitable for the returning Jews to live there. *Thirdly*, cause it to be uninviting for the Gentiles to tour there. All three of these are prophesied scenarios expected to find fulfillment in the Millennium. Therefore, Jerusalem will need to be restored.

We catch our first glimpse of the restored Millennial Jerusalem through the visionary eyes of Ezekiel.

> "In the visions of God brought he me into the land
> of Israel, and set me upon a very high mountain,
> by which was as the frame of a city on the south."
> (Ezekiel 40:2, KJV)

Ezekiel appears to get a foretaste of the framework of the Millennial Jerusalem in its early stages. He then devotes most of the content of his last chapters, 40 through 48, to describing the city's restoration. Below are some passages that describe the city's forthcoming renovation.

> "Great *is* the Lord, and greatly to be praised
> In the city of our God, *In* His holy mountain.
> Beautiful in elevation, The joy of the whole earth,
> *Is* Mount Zion *on* the sides of the north, The city
> of the great King." (Psalm 48:1-2)

It will be *beautiful* and elevated on a *mountain* on its *sides of the north*. It will become the *city of our God* and *of the great King*. This has a double meaning. First, the throne of Messiah, *the great King*, will be established there as per Jeremiah 3:17 and second, the glory of Jehovah, *our God*, will reside inside the Millennial Temple according to Ezekiel 44:4.

> "Also He brought me by way of the north gate to the front of the temple; so I looked, and behold, the glory of the Lord filled the house of the Lord; and I fell on my face."

As a result of these two features, the restored Jerusalem in the Millennium will be given a new name entitled, THE LORD *IS* THERE!

> "For Zion's sake I will not hold My peace, And for Jerusalem's sake I will not rest, Until her righteousness goes forth as brightness, And her salvation as a lamp *that* burns. The Gentiles shall see your righteousness, And all kings your glory. *You shall be called by a new name, Which the mouth of the Lord will name.*" (Isaiah 62:1-2, NKJV; emphasis added)

> "And the name of the city from *that* day *shall be:* THE LORD *IS* THERE." (Ezek. 48:35b)

The Millennial Jerusalem will not only be beautiful in elevation, but is going to have certain sections that are built compactly together.

> "Jerusalem is built As a city that is compact together, Where the tribes go up, The tribes of the Lord, To the Testimony of Israel, To give thanks to the name of the Lord." (Psalm 122:3-4)

The Hebrew words used for *"compact together"* can be translated as *"tightly joined together, like tying a magic knot."* The compactly built holy city is well defined in chapters like Ezekiel 45, which explains that a holy district will be set aside for:

- the rebuilt Fourth Temple (Ezek. 45:3),

- housing the Temple priests and Levite ministers (Ezek. 45:5; 48:10),

- the prince King David to have his designated sections (Ezek. 45:7).

The city will have some walls that are built by Gentiles.

> "The sons of foreigners shall build up your walls, And their kings shall minister to you; For in My wrath I struck you, But in My favor I have had mercy on you. Therefore your gates shall be open continually; They shall not be shut day or night, That *men* may bring to you the wealth of the Gentiles, And their kings in procession." (Isaiah 60:10-11)

This above passage says the gates to the city *shall be open continually*. According to Ezekiel 48:30-35 the gates will bear the names of the Twelve Tribes of Israel. Three gates will be located on each of the east, north, south and west walls. According to Revelation 21:12-13 this theme seemingly repeats itself when the NEW JERUSALEM replaces the restored Jerusalem.

The Gates of the Twelve Tribes of Israel

The three *east gates* are named after the tribes of Joseph, Benjamin and Dan.

> "On the east side, four thousand five hundred *cubits*, three gates: one gate for

Joseph, one gate for Benjamin, and one gate for Dan." (Ezek. 48:32)

The three *north gates* are named after Reuben, Judah and Levi.

"The gates of the city shall be named after the tribes of Israel, the three gates northward: one gate for Reuben, one gate for Judah, and one gate for Levi." (Ezek. 48:31)

The three *south gates* are named after Simeon, Issachar and Zebulun.

"On the south side, measuring four thousand five hundred cubits, three gates: one gate for Simeon, one gate for Issachar, and one gate for Zebulun." (Ezek. 48:33)

The three *west gates* are named after Gad, Asher and Naphtali.

"On the west side, four thousand five hundred cubits with their three gates: one gate for Gad, one gate for Asher, and one gate for Naphtali." (Ezek. 48:34)

Four thousand five hundred cubits are approximately 6,750 feet or 1.28 miles. This measurement applies to these four specific walls in the Millennium, but may not be on the same size and scale in the NEW JERUSALEM, which according to Rev. 21:16 is a tremendously larger city.

Although there will be walled areas inside the Millennial Jerusalem that have exit gates named after the Twelve Tribes, there will be many men and livestock residing within the outer city limits in unwalled townships. The Lord, acting as a wall of fire, will personally safeguard these unprotected areas from unwanted intruders.

"Then I raised my eyes and looked, and behold, a man with a measuring line in his hand. So I said, "Where are you going?" And he said to me, "To measure Jerusalem, to see what *is* its width and what *is* its length." And there *was* the angel who talked with me, going out; and another angel was coming out to meet him, who said to him, "Run, speak to this young man, saying: 'Jerusalem shall be inhabited *as* towns without walls, because of the multitude of men and livestock in it. For I,' says the Lord, 'will be a wall of fire all around her, and I will be the glory in her midst.'" (Zech. 2:1-5)

The public streets of the city will be lined with the elderly and also filled with boys and girls playing together. There will be no more fears of bus bombings or terrorist suicide attacks, those days will have passed. It will be a marvelous sight for the spectators to behold.

"Thus says the Lord: 'I will return to Zion, And dwell in the midst of Jerusalem. Jerusalem shall be called the City of Truth, The Mountain of the Lord of hosts, The Holy Mountain.' "Thus says the Lord of hosts: 'Old men and old women shall again sit In the streets of Jerusalem, Each one with his staff in his hand Because of great age. The streets of the city Shall be full of boys and girls Playing in its streets.'" "Thus says the Lord of hosts: 'If it is marvelous in the eyes of the remnant of this people in these days, Will it also be marvelous in My eyes?' Says the Lord of hosts.'" (Zech. 8:3-6)

The Rebuilt Fourth Jewish Temple with its Sacrificial System

Ezekiel 44:4 provided earlier in this chapter acknowledged that there would be a Millennial Temple and that "*the glory of the Lord filled the house of the Lord.*" The image below is a model of this future Temple.

THE MILLENNIAL TEMPLE

A - Altar (Ezek. 43:13-17)

C- 30 Chambers(Ezek. 40:17)

IG- Inner Gates (Ezek. 40:28-37)

KP- Kitchens for Priests (Ezek. 46:19-20)

KS- Kitchens for people's sacrifices (Ezek. 46:21-24)

OG- Outer Gates (Ezek. 40:6-17, 20-27)

PC- Priests Chambers (Ezek. 42:1-14)

TP- Temple Proper (Ezek. 40:48; 41:11, 13-14, 16-26)

WB- West Building (function not explained) (Ezek. 41:12)

"The Spirit lifted me up and brought me into the inner court; and behold, the glory of the Lord filled the temple. Then I heard *Him* speaking to me from the temple, while a man stood beside me. And He said to me, "Son of man, *this is* the place of My throne and the place of the soles of My feet, where I will dwell in the midst of the children of Israel forever." (Ezek. 43:5-7b)

Ezekiel was brought into the *inner court* of the Millennial Temple, which further acknowledges that this holy site is forthcoming. The Temple's measurements and functions are primarily described throughout Ezekiel 40:5-43:37.

There will be sacrifices performed in the Millennial Temple. Ezekiel 43:18, 21, 24, 27 describe some of the burnt offerings and Ezekiel 44:1-46:24 describes the Millennial Priesthood and its sacrificial system. Other verses that speak of Millennial sacrifices are found in, Isaiah 56:6-7; 60:7; Jeremiah 33:18 and Malachi 3:3-4.

There are differences between the future Millennial and former Mosaic systems, which means that the Millennial system is not simply a reinstatement of the Mosaic system. Dr. Arnold Fruchtenbaum explains this fact in the following quote.

"*While there are similarities with the commandments of the Law of Moses, there are also some marked differences. For this reason, the millennial system of priesthood and sacrifice must not be viewed as a reinstitution of the Law of Moses, which ended permanently and forever with the death of the Messiah. During the Messianic Kingdom, a whole new system of law, Kingdom Law, will be instituted.*"[74]

A case in point related to the stark differences between the antiquated Mosaic sacrificial system and the future Millennial sacrificial system is found by comparing Exodus 29:1-37 to Ezekiel 43:18-27.

Mosaic System	Millennial System
Anointed the altar	No anointing of the altar
Seven-days of bullock offering for sin	One-day bullock offering
No goat offerings	Goat offerings for six-days
Blood only on horns of altar	Blood on horns, corners and lower molding
Ram offered every day	Ram and bullock offered every day
Ram offered for priesthood consecration	No ram offered for priesthood only the altar

Also an important distinction is that the Mosaic system had the Ark of the Covenant, whereas according to Jeremiah 3:16 below the Millennial system will not.

> "Then it shall come to pass, when you are multiplied and increased in the land in those days," says the Lord, "that they will say no more, 'The ark of the covenant of the Lord.' It shall not come to mind, nor shall they remember it, nor shall they visit *it,* nor shall it be made anymore."

The Reasons for Millennial Sacrifices

Both the priesthood and sacrificial systems were part of Israel's heritage and they will continue on, although with marked differences, into the Millennium.

The thought of literal sanctioned sacrifices occurring in the Millennium has disturbed some scholars who believe that the Crucifixion of Jesus Christ was the complete and final sacrifice for sin. As such, some attempt to allegorize these sacrifices. However, due to the clear specificity of these offerings, it is better to interpret them literally, but to explain why they will take place well after the Crucifixion.

Concerning this matter, the Bible Knowledge Commentary: Old Testament states the following.

> *"No difficulty exists if one understands the proper function of these sacrifices. First, animal sacrifices never took away human sin; only the sacrifice of Christ can do that (Heb. 10:1-4, 10). In Old Testament times Israelites were saved by grace through faith, and the sacrifices helped restore a believer's fellowship with God. Second, even after the church began, Jewish believers did not hesitate to take part in the temple worship (Acts 2:46; 3:1; 5:42) and even to offer sacrifices (Acts 21:26). They could do this because they viewed the sacrifices as memorials of Christ's death. Levitical sacrifices were connected with Israel's worship of God. When the church supplanted, (not replaced), Israel in God's program (cf. Rom. 11:11-24) a new economy or dispensation began. The Levitical sacrificial system, which looked forward to Christ, was replaced by the Lord's Supper, which looked back to His death and forward to His second coming (1 Cor. 11:24, 26). At Christ's second coming Israel will again assume her place of prominence in God's kingdom program (cf. Rom. 11:25-27). The Lord's Supper will be eliminated because Christ will have returned. It will be replaced by animal sacrifices, which will be memorials or object lessons of the supreme sacrifice made by the Lamb of God. The slaughtering of these animals will be vivid reminders of the Messiah's suffering and death."* (Dr. John Walvoord and Roy B. Zuck; emphasis added by this author)

This above quote emphasizes the commemorative aspect of the Millennial sacrificial system, but there are some functional reasons to consider also. The Millennial sacrifices provide:

1.   A means of restoring fellowship for the Millennial saint. This is especially the case for sacrifices involved with the celebration of some Millennial feasts, which will be discussed later in this chapter.

2.   A ritual cleansing for ritual uncleanness. Dr. Fruchtenbaum explains this below.

> *"Since the Shechinah Glory will be within the Holy of Holies of the Millennial Temple, it would be impossible to approach the Temple compound in a state of ritual impurity and therefore the sacrifices will be for the cleansing of ceremonial uncleanness."*[75]

This thinking is supported by the verse below, which deals with the protection of the purity of the glory of God's presence within the Millennial Temple.

> "Thus says the Lord God: "No foreigner, uncircumcised in heart or uncircumcised in flesh, shall enter My sanctuary, including any foreigner who *is* among the children of Israel." (Ezekiel 44:9)

The spiritual symbolism of circumcision is explained in Romans 4:9-12. This passage points out that Abraham's circumcision served as a seal of the righteousness that he had faith in God. It was an outward act representing a genuine inward faith. Since that time, circumcision became a rite of passage for a male Jew to evidence his Jewishness.

However, the physical act of circumcision in itself does not mean that a Jew has a genuine inward faith in God. In fact, throughout their history most circumcised Jews lacked faith and became stiff-necked toward God. The disciple Stephen, at the time of his Christian martyrdom, stated the following to his religious Jewish executioners.

> "*You* stiff-necked and uncircumcised in heart and ears! You always resist the Holy Spirit; as your fathers *did,* so *do* you." (Acts 7:51)

Stephen's point was that physical circumcision void of its spiritual association is useless, in that it does not please God, but leads toward resistance of His Holy Spirit. Obviously, stiff-necked and uncircumcised in heart types of people, like those that martyred Stephen, will never be allowed anywhere near the presence of God in the Millennium. The apostle Paul sets the record straight in the next verse.

> "On the contrary, a person is a Jew who is one inwardly, and circumcision is of the heart—by the Spirit, not the letter. That man's praise is not from men but from God." (Romans 2:29, HCSB)

Paul informed that the outwardly circumcised Jews who lacked inward circumcised hearts—*by the Spirit*, do not receive their praise from God, but rather receive their praise from men. So when Ezekiel 44:9 proclaims that *no uncircumcised in heart* can enter God's sanctuary, it means two things: *First*, that an uncircumcised heart represents someone who doesn't believe in God and by no means is allowed anywhere near the pure presence of God and *Second*, such unbelieving types of people will exist in the Millennium.

The fact that unbelievers will exist in the Messianic Kingdom has already been well-established in prior chapters. These unbelievers, whether they are Jews or Gentiles, are all considered to have uncircumcised hearts, even though they may have been physically circumcised.

In order for someone to receive a circumcised heart and thereby become pleasing to God, they must become a born-again believer—*by the Spirit,* by receiving Jesus Christ as their Savior. Thus, one of the functional purposes for the Millennial sacrifices is to remind people of their uncleanness and their need to receive Jesus Christ as their means of receiving a circumcised heart.

The Millennial Feasts

It was stated in the upper section that there will be Millennial Feasts and that they and their associated sacrifices will serve as a means of restoring fellowship for the Millennial saint. Ezekiel 45:18-25 is mostly devoted to the Millennial Feasts.

Below is a quote about the Millennial Feasts and related festivals from The Bible Knowledge Commentary: Old Testament.

> "Ezekiel 45:18-25: The festivals where the offerings will be given will include the New Year feast (vv. 18-20), the Passover/ Unleavened Bread feast (vv. 21-24), and the seven-day Feast of Tabernacles (v. 25). The New Year's day celebration, on Nisan 1 (mid-April), will be to purify the sanctuary (v. 18). If someone sins unintentionally, a second purification will be offered on the seventh day of the month (v. 20). This offering and ceremonial cleansing possibly will replace the Day of Atonement (in the seventh month, Lev. 23:26-32). This time of cleansing will be followed by the celebration of the Passover (Ezek. 45:21-24) / Unleavened Bread festival. The Passover will last seven days, during which the people will eat bread made without yeast. The prince will provide the sacrifices for that period (vv. 22-24). The fact that the

prince is to make a sin offering for himself shows that he is not Christ. The third feast will begin in the seventh month on the 15th day. This is the Festival of Tabernacles, also a seven-day celebration (Lev. 23:33-44), the last feast in Israel's yearly calendar."[76]

Millennial references to the Feast of Tabernacles are also provided by Zechariah the prophet.

"And it shall come to pass that everyone who is left of all the nations which came against Jerusalem shall go up from year to year to worship the King, the Lord of hosts, and to keep the Feast of Tabernacles. And it shall be that whichever of the families of the earth do not come up to Jerusalem to worship the King, the Lord of hosts, on them there will be no rain. If the family of Egypt will not come up and enter in, they *shall have* no *rain;* they shall receive the plague with which the Lord strikes the nations who do not come up to keep the Feast of Tabernacles. This shall be the punishment of Egypt and the punishment of all the nations that do not come up to keep the Feast of Tabernacles." (Zechariah 14:16-19)

Among the various Millennial festivals, attending the Feast of Tabernacles is mandatory. Representatives from the nations and the families of the earth must attend this celebration or they will be punished with a plague of no rain. Zechariah singles out Egypt as an example to the other nations of the consequences for absenteeism.

This Feast of Tabernacles, also known as Sukkot, celebrates the reality that in the Millennium God dwells among the peoples. The origins of this feast date back to the time of the Hebrew exodus out of Egyptian captivity, which is likely why Egypt is signaled out by Zechariah. At that historic time, the Lord spoke the following to Moses.

> "And let them make Me a sanctuary, that I may
> dwell among them. According to all that I show
> you, *that is,* the pattern of the tabernacle and the
> pattern of all its furnishings, just so you shall
> make *it.*" (Exodus 25:8-9)

The importance of this feast is that it serves to remind the
nations and families of the earth that GOD DWELLS among
them in the personage of Jesus Christ the Messiah and the glory
of Jehovah in the Millennial Temple. In the beginning of the
Millennium most of the peoples will understand this truth, but
over time their descendants apparently need an annual reminder,
which is what the Feast of Tabernacles is fashioned to do.

Remember, that Isaiah 65:20 points out that sinners will exist
on earth in the Millennium. Ezekiel 44:9 identified these sinners
as unbelievers with uncircumcised hearts. Revelation 20:7-10
informs that at the end of the Millennium these deceived sinners
are spread throughout the entire world and they represent a great
multitude.

Required attendance at the Feast of Tabernacles is for the good
of all peoples. It provides evidence that the Messiah dwells among
them and presents them with the opportunity to receive Him
as their Savior. For those already saved, it reinforces their faith.
However, absenteeism from the event is harmful to the unbelievers
because it deprives them of realizing that there is a God and He
literally dwells among them.

The Parameters of the Promised Land

At various points in Israel's history the Jews possessed some
portions of their Promised Land, which according to Genesis
15:18 extends from the river of Egypt to the Euphrates River.
However, they never held sovereignty over all of this land. In the
Millennium, they will finally take full possession of all this land. It
will be distributed to the Twelve Tribes of Israel.

Ezekiel 47:13-48:29 provides the specific details about the boundaries of the Promised Land and which tribe gets what territory.

- The Northern Border: (Ezekiel 47:15-17) – will extend from the Mediterranean Sea through parts of Lebanon and Syria on through to the Euphrates River. It includes Damascus, which will have been reduced to rubble beforehand as per Isaiah 17:1.

- The Eastern Border: (Ezekiel 47:18) – courses southward down the Euphrates River and ends up at the south side of the Dead Sea via moving westward and incorporating the Golan Heights, portions of Syria and continuing to the Jordan River.

- The Southern Border: (Ezekiel 47:19) – will head south from the Dead Sea and incorporate the Negev and parts of the Sinai all the way to the Brook of Egypt to the point where it meets the Mediterranean Sea.

- The Western Border: (Ezekiel 47:20) – the Mediterranean Sea becomes the western border. Ezekiel 48:1-28 specifies which tribe inherits which territory.

17

Introducing the Aftermath Age

When the Millennium ends, the Aftermath Age begins. The length of this period is not specified, but within this likely short interval of time, many powerful and necessary prophetic events happen. The Aftermath Age serves as the segue between the end of the Millennium and the start of the Eternal Order.

Events in the Aftermath Age

Below is a tabulation of the events that take place during the Aftermath Age. They are sequenced in their likely chronological order.

1. Satan gets released from the Abyss – (Rev. 20:7),

2. Satan deceives the nations – (Rev. 20:8),

3. The Second Magog Invasion occurs – (Rev. 20:8-9),

4. God destroys the Magog Invaders with fire from heaven – (Rev. 20:9),

5. Satan is cast into the Lake of Fire forever – (Rev. 20:10),

(The events #1-#5 are explained in the next chapter entitled, *"The Magog Invasion in the Aftermath of the Millennium"*).

6.   The Millennial heaven and earth flee away from the face of God – (Rev. 20:11),

7.   The Second Resurrection occurs, whereby all of the unsaved return from the dead, (Rev. 20:12-13),

8.   The White Throne Judgment happens, whereby the resurrected unsaved people are judged – (Rev. 20:11-13),

9.   The Second Death takes place, which is when all of the unsaved are cast alive into the Lake of Fire – (Rev. 20:14-15).

(The events #6-#9 are explained in the upcoming two chapters entitled, "*The Great White Throne Judgment*" and "*The Lake of Fire and the Second Death*").

10.   The New Heaven and Earth are created and there will be no more sea – (Rev. 21:1),

11.   The NEW JERUSALEM descends down from heaven to earth – (Rev. 21:2),

(The events #10-#11 are explained in the chapter entitled, "*The Eternal Order and the NEW JERUSALEM*").

18

The Magog Invasion in the Aftermath of the Millennium

EXTRA, EXTRA, READ ALL ABOUT IT! "ANCIENT PROPHECY PREDICTS THE RETURN OF SATAN!"

"3000-year-old biblical prediction declares that the Devil's not done and according to the Millennial Calendar he's returning soon to planet earth to exact his revenge!" (Jerusalem Post- 5/24/3051)

It was the final days of the Millennium and millions around the world awaited the release of Satan from the bottomless pit in fulfillment of a 3000-year-old prophecy. *"Will it really happen,"* some of them wondered?

Large crowds were assembling rapidly around the globe awaiting to see if the righteous Messiah, Who had ruled the planet for 1000 years with a rod of iron, would dare unleash His historic nemesis, the Devil. They had heard the ancient tales of woe that surrounded this serpent of old, but was he really as wicked and powerful as the Bible had portrayed him to be?

> "We know that we are of God, and the whole world lies *under the sway of* the wicked one." (1 John 5:19)

As the crowds grew larger, the radicals became increasingly uneasy sparking riots and looting in the major cities. Then the restless throngs started realizing that, "*in the ancient earth the Devil held sway over the whole planet and when he returns he's going to be mad as HE-double-LL .*" They readied for the inevitable conflict between the Messiah and the fallen angel Lucifer.

Adding more fuel to the fire, were the electronic messages and pocket-size printed tracts that were circulating amongst the masses. These communications informed them of the "*Satan Prophecy*" from the book of Revelation.

> "Now when the thousand years have expired, Satan will be released from his prison, and will go out to deceive the nations which are in the four corners of the earth, Gog and Magog, to gather them together to battle, whose number *is* as the sand of the sea. They went up on the breadth of the earth and surrounded the camp of the saints and the beloved city." (Revelation 20:7-9)

Who was behind the spread of this dangerous information? Why wasn't the Messiah censoring it? Whoever was doing the disseminating, was intentionally inciting the multitudes to riot and prepare for the impending battle at Jerusalem. Their obvious frustration of having been ruled over by a Monarch with a rod of iron was bannering itself on their billboards and protest signs worldwide. All they needed now was a fearless leader who could successfully wage a holy war against Jesus the Monarch on their behalf.

It was going to have to be a spiritual battle that could be fought without conventional weapons because throughout the generations all swords and spears were turned into plowshares.

Neither were the people schooled in warfare, as it was not part of the educational curriculum during the Messianic age. Both sides, the saints versus the ungodly, only had sticks and stones in their weapons arsenals.

Then all of a sudden, Satan was freed and the electronic messages and neon billboards all instantly read "*it's time for, THE SECOND ARMAGEDDON.*"

I took some author liberties in the above section in an attempt to paint a possible picture of what the world may look like in the final days of the Millennium. Revelation 20:7-10 clearly predicts that after the Millennium Satan will be freed from the abyss to lead one final battle against God.

What's astonishing is that in a short order of time the Devil is able to muster up a multitude of rebels, *whose number is as the sand of the sea*, worldwide *from the four corners of the earth*. This implies the following:

1.   While Satan was confined for 1000 years he wasn't repenting, rather he was concocting a plan to turn man once again against God,

2.   By the end of the Millennium, the planet will be heavily populated,

3.   The Devil recognized that this Satan Prophecy of Revelation 20 would find fulfillment and that when it did, there would be throngs of easy to deceive sinners upset with the global government of the Messiah. As per Isaiah 65:20, this last crop of sinners will be under one-hundred years old, which makes them relatively young and healthy according to Millennium standards.

4.   Satan theorized that with so many rebels on his side, he could wage and win a final war with God.

Satan Gets Cast Alive Into the Lake of Fire

Whether you call this final rebellion in the aftermath of the Millennium, *The Second Armageddon, Second Magog Invasion,* or *Sins Last Stand,* it winds up being Satan's final feat. The most important part of the "*Satan Prophecy*" that was excluded from the fictitious storyline above is included below.

> "They went up on the breadth of the earth and surrounded the camp of the saints and the beloved city. And fire came down from God out of heaven and devoured them. The devil, who deceived them, was cast into the lake of fire and brimstone where the beast and the false prophet are. And they will be tormented day and night forever and ever." (Rev. 20:9-10)

There's no Antichrist, False Prophet or Gog of Magog leading this last charge, as they have all been eliminated long before this time. One thousand years prior, the Antichrist and False Prophet were cast alive into the Lake of Fire as per Revelation 19:20.

Some people believe that this final Magog invasion is the same one described in Ezekiel 38, but for reasons provided at the close of this chapter, it doesn't seem likely. The proponents of this teaching think that Gog in Ezekiel 38:2, which alludes to the princely title of the leader of the first Magog invasion, is involved in this final battle.

However, according to Ezekiel 39:11-16, *that* Gog is dead and buried with his hordes in the "Valley of Hamon Gog." That former Gog will resurrect along with all the other unsaved souls for the White Throne Judgment, but that happens in Rev. 20:11-15, which is after this second Magog invasion. Thus, the Gog of Ezekiel 38:2 is incapacitated when this second invasion occurs.

This final Magog conflict is apparently led by Satan. The Devil comes out of the bottomless pit and deceives a multitude of malcontent mortals to wage war against the Messiah and His saints at the "beloved city" of Jerusalem. Notice that Satan doesn't break out of prison, but he is intentionally released.

"Now when the thousand years have expired, Satan will be released from his prison." (Rev. 20:7)

The Devil's release is part of God's plan. The planet finds itself again filled with Christ-rejecting sinners that need to be purged out. Up to this point, the final batch of troublemakers have been operating exclusively out of their own sin natures without the evil sway of Satan. They obviously hate the way Jesus the Messiah is running the global government. Satan is let out to lead a coup against Christ.

Satan and his band of sinners deploy to Jerusalem and when they arrive they surround the camp of the saints. With their sticks held high in their left hands and stones clutched in their right, they are ready to attack the saints. Not realizing they have set themselves up for an ambush, they become an easy target for God to rain down fire from heaven and devour them.

As per Rev. 20:10, this scenario turns out to be Satan's last stand. Watching his final attack fail with the fire from heaven, the Devil is then thrust into the Lake of Fire for a reunion with the Antichrist and the False Prophet.

The Devil's career ends as he is cast into the Lake of Fire, which is his sixth and final address. In the chapter entitled, "The War in Heaven" of my book entitled, *The Final Prophecies*, I identify the six abodes of Satan.

By way of review, the six abodes of Satan are:

1. The First Abode: The Throne of God.

2. The Second Abode: The Mineral Garden of Eden.

(The first two abodes are to be found in Ezekiel 28:11-15).

3.   The Third Abode: The Atmospheric Heavens – (Ephesians 2:2 and 6:12).

4.   The Fourth Abode: The Earth – (Rev. 12:7-12).

5.   The Fifth Abode: The Abyss – (Rev. 20:1-3).

6.   The Sixth Abode: The Lake of Fire – (Rev. 20:7-10).

Although the 1000 years concluded just prior to Satan's release from the Abyss, the Messianic kingdom doesn't come to an end until the Devil's departure. After Satan is bid his final farewell, then Jesus Christ, the Son of God, can deliver all authority and power to God, the Father.

> "Then *comes* the end, when He delivers the kingdom to God the Father, when He puts an end to all rule and all authority and power. For He must reign till He has put all enemies under His feet. The last enemy *that* will be destroyed *is* death. For "He has put all things under His feet." But when He says "all things are put under *Him*," *it is* evident that He who put all things under Him is excepted. Now when all things are made subject to Him, then the Son Himself will also be subject to Him who put all things under Him, that God may be all in all." (1 Corinthians 15:24-28)

The quote below from Dr. Arnold Fruchtenbaum explains how and why the transfer of authority process works.

> *"Ultimately, the power and the authority of the Kingdom must be turned over to God the Father. But this can only occur after every enemy of man*

is abolished and there is no longer any challenge to God's rule, authority and power (v.24). For this very reason, the Messiah must rule until every enemy of man has been placed under subjection (v.25). The last of the enemies of man is not Satan, but death itself (v.26). It should be remembered that death will still exist in the Kingdom. It is only after Satan's final revolt and his confinement in the Lake of Fire that death can be abolished. It is Satan who caused death for man by tempting the first parents. It is only when the originator of death for man is forever confined in his final abode that death can be abolished. And at this point, it will be. With this, the Millennial Kingdom will come to an end. All things will now have been placed in total subjection to the Messiah, and that totality of subjection will now be subjugated to God the Father in order that God may be all in all (vv.27-28)."[77]

The Two Magog Invasions

Some teach that the Magog invasion identified in Ezekiel 38 is the same as the one in Revelation 20:7-10. However, there are several distinct differences between these two biblical predictions. Some of these dissimilarities are provided below.

*   *The battlefields*: Ezek. 39:2; 38:16 takes place on the mountains of Israel, but Rev. 20:9 says the troops surround the camp of the saints and the beloved city of Jerusalem.

*   *The defeats*: Ezek. 38:19-22 predicts a great earthquake, Every man's sword will be against his brother, pestilence and bloodshed, flooding rain, great hailstones, fire, and brimstone. In Rev. 20:9 only fire comes down from God out of heaven.

- *The troops*: Ezek. 38:2-7 identifies a limited group of localized Muslim nations led by Russia that invade from the north. Rev. 20:8 speaks of an international army, whose number is as the sand of the sea, from nations which are in the four quarters of the earth.

- *The weapons of warfare*: Ezek. 39:9-10 says that Israel will be burning the enemies' weapons for seven years. According to Isaiah 2:4 and Micah 4:3, the weapons that use to exist in the old earth have since been destroyed and turned into farm implements, (plowshares and pruning hooks). It hardly seems that Israel will be able to burn weapons that likely no longer exist.

- *The timing of the weapons' burning*: Ezek. 39:9 emphasizes the weapons supply can provide fuel to burn for seven years, but shortly after the Rev. 20:7-10 Magog prophecy concludes, the White Throne Judgment happens and then the Eternal Order starts. It seems unlikely that weapons will be burning in these two aftermath scenarios.

- *The timing of Israel's rebirth vs. the reign of Jesus Christ*: Ezek. 38:8 points out that the Gog of Magog invasion takes place shortly after the Jews are restored to their homeland Israel. Rev. 20:7 says that Satan is loosed after Jesus the Messiah has reigned over the world for 1000 years.

- *The timing of the regathering of Israel*: Ezek. 38:8 points out that the Jews are regathered from the nations to Israel. In the Millennium, there is no hint of an additional Jewish dispersion that would require another regathering. Thus, Rev. 20:7-10 happens over 1000 years after Israel had been regathered.

- *The leaders of the invasions*: Ezek. 38:2-11 says it's Gog of Magog, but in Rev. 20:7-8 it's clearly Satan released from the abyss.

In his book about the Ezekiel 38 prophecy entitled, *Northern Storm Rising*, Dr. Ron Rhodes brings up the additional points below. *Firstly*, Rhodes addresses the likely reason that the apostle John referred to Gog and Magog in Revelation 20:8. *Secondly*, he points out how the chronology between Ezekiel 38-39 and Revelation 20:7-10 is all wrong.

Firstly...

> *"It is likely that the apostle John was simply using the terms Gog and Magog as a shorthand metaphor, kind of like we do today. For example, the word Wall Street in the English language has come to metaphorically refer to the stock market. Likewise, back in New Testament times, terms like Corinthian and Nazarene came to metaphorically refer to people with less-than-desirable qualities. Whether among modern people or people in New Testament times, the hearers of such words immediately draw the right connection and understand what is meant by the use of such terms. Likewise, when John used the terms Gog and Magog in Revelation 20:7- 10, his readers no doubt immediately drew the right connection and understood that this invasion at the end of the millennium would be similar to what Ezekiel described in that a confederation of nations will attack Israel but not succeed. In other words, this was to be a Gog/Magog-like invasion."*

In his quote above, Dr. Rhodes draws our attention to the importance of the Ezekiel 38 Gog of Magog prophecy. It is the marquee event of the latter years that God uses to notify the world:

1. That He exists and is all powerful,

2. That His name is holy,

3. That He keeps His covenants and promises.

Ezekiel 38:18-39:6 prophesies that God supernaturally defeats the Magog invaders and thwarts their plans to destroy Israel and capture its plunder and great booty. Then, Ezekiel 39:7 informs why God intercedes.

> "So I will make My holy name known in the midst of My people Israel, and I will not let them profane My holy name anymore. Then the nations shall know that I am the Lord, the Holy One in Israel." (Ezekiel 39:7)

Through the events of the Gog of Magog invasion of Ezekiel 38, God shows the nations, all of the nations in the world, that "I am the Lord, the Holy One in Israel."

Similarly, in the Gog of Magog-like invasion of Revelation 20:7-10, God will supernaturally stop Satan and his band of sinners, and the results will be made perfectly clear to all the nations throughout the world again that, "I am the Lord, the Holy One in Israel."

Secondly…

> *"The chronology is all wrong. The invasion described by Ezekiel in Ezekiel 38—39 is part of a larger section of Ezekiel's book which deals with the restoration of Israel (chapters 33—39). This is followed by another large section of Ezekiel's book which describes the Jewish millennial temple and the restoration of sacrifices (chapters 40—48). In other words, Ezekiel's invasion is before the millennial kingdom. By contrast, the invasion described in Revelation 20:7-10 takes place at the end of the millennial kingdom, and hence these invasions are separated by a thousand years…. In keeping with the above, the invasion prophesied by Ezekiel is immediately followed by the establishment of the millennial kingdom (Ezekiel 40—48), whereas the invasion prophesied in Revelation 20:7-*

*10 is immediately followed by the establishment of
the eternal state (Revelation 21)."*

Summary of the Second Magog Invasion

Reserved for the Aftermath Age that follows the Millennium
and precedes the Eternal Order is this final Magog rebellion. God
allows Satan and the sinners one last chance to show their true
colors. The Lord had to let rebellion have its due course.

Six thousand years of sin under the influence of the Devil
ended with the defeat of Antichrist at Armageddon, destruction of
the earth, imprisonment of Satan and the Goat Gentile judgment.
One thousand years of mortal sin, without satanic influence
concludes with this final Magog invasion.

It's incredible to think that in the beginning of the Millennium:

- The earth is restored to Garden of Eden-like conditions,

- Everyone is a believer,

- There are no more handicaps, the blind see, the deaf hear
  and the lame leap,

- People live healthier, happier and longer lives,

- There is peace on earth,

- The world is crime-free,

- There are no more threats of war,

- No more social injustice,

- Proof of God's existence is evident in that the Messiah
  reigns on earth,

- Old Testament Saints and Tribulation Saints are resurrected to the astonishment of all the earth-dwellers,

- The animal kingdom lives in peaceful harmony with mankind,

- Satan is bound and unable to influence people through their sin nature,

- For all intents and purposes it's Utopia.

In essence, the conditions present in the Millennium eliminate every possible excuse to deny the existence of God as the Creator. At that time people will no longer be able to legitimately ask the typical questions asked by Atheists and Agnostics today, such as if there's a god:

1. Where's the proof of his existence?

2. How can he allow so much evil to flourish in the world?

3. Why is there so much sickness and poverty in the world?

These are just a few of the detractors tossed about by unbelievers, but even in the Millennium, when proof of God's love, mercy, goodness, longsuffering, wisdom, power and truth are on full display, people will still deny Him. The final Magog rebellion of Revelation 20:7-10 proves how sin over time can turn a Utopian society into hell on earth. God in His foreknowledge understood this from the beginning, but He had to let mankind learn it over time the hard way.

Unfortunately, it took 7000 years, but in the end analysis only those who still believe in God's worship worthiness go forward into the Eternal Order. The last act of officiating happens next in the WHITE THRONE JUDGMENT.

19

The Great White Throne Judgment

"And as it is appointed for men to die once, but after this the judgment." (Hebrews 9:27)

The last thing to happen in the Aftermath Age is the final judgment of all the unbelievers throughout time and the abolishment of Death forever. With Satan, who caused death for man by tempting the first parents, confined forever in the Lake of Fire, now it's time for the Lord to deliver Death its final blow. Once Death is eradicated, the Eternal Order can commence.

> "The last enemy *that* will be destroyed *is* death." (1 Corinthians 15:26)

The Great White Throne Judgment verses are included below and then explained throughout the remainder of the chapter.

> "Then I saw a great white throne and Him who sat on it, from whose face the earth and the heaven fled away. And there was found no place for them. And I saw the dead, small and great, standing before God, and books were opened. And another book was opened, which is *the Book* of Life. And the dead were judged according to their works, by the things which were written in the books. The sea gave up the dead who were in it, and Death

and Hades delivered up the dead who were in them. And they were judged, each one according to his works. Then Death and Hades were cast into the lake of fire. This is the second death. And anyone not found written in the Book of Life was cast into the lake of fire." (Revelation 20:11-15)

The Great White Throne

(*Revelation 20:11*) "Then I saw a great white throne and Him who sat on it, from whose face the earth and the heaven fled away. And there was found no place for them."

The Apostle John sees "*a great white throne and Him who sat on it.*" We are not told who sits on this throne, but since it is dealing with judgment it's thought by many to be Jesus Christ. This conclusion is supported by the following Scriptures.

"For the (*Heavenly*) Father judges no one, but has committed all judgment to the Son, (*Jesus Christ*)." (John 5:22, NKJV; emphasis added)

" For as the Father has life in Himself, so He has granted the Son to have life in Himself, and has given Him authority to execute judgment, (*upon mankind*) also, because He is (*not only*) the Son (*of God, but also*) of Man." (John 5:26-27, NKJV; emphasis added)

"And He commanded us to preach to the people, and to testify that it is He, (*Jesus Christ*), who was ordained by God *to be* Judge of the living and the dead." (Acts 10:42, NKJV; emphasis added)

Matthew 19:28, 25:31 and Revelation 3:21 all speak of Jesus Christ's throne. These verses may not be identifying the specific

White Throne, but they do support the fact that Jesus Christ sits upon His throne.

This throne is "*White*," which likely symbolizes the purity of the one qualified to sit upon it. Lastly, the fact that this throne is "*Great*" seems to set it apart from the general thrones identified in Rev. 20:4.

> "And I saw thrones, and they sat on them,
> and judgment was committed to them."
> (Rev. 20:4a)

The Fleeing Away of the Earth and Heaven

Whoever is seated upon the Great White Throne, He is "*whose face the earth and the heaven fled away and there was found no place for them.*" This alludes to the departure of the present heaven and earth that were created way back in Genesis one. These domains were renovated for the Millennium, but became polluted all over again as evidenced by the final Magog revolt of Rev. 20:7-10. Thus, they need to be eliminated to make way for the new heaven and new earth of the Eternal Order.

> "Now I saw a new heaven and a new earth, (*created for the Eternal Order*), for the first heaven and the first earth had passed away. Also there was no more sea." (Rev. 21:1, NKJV; emphasis added)

The timing of the passing away of the present earth and heaven comes into question in Rev. 20:11. The inference is that the qualified judge first sits upon the White Throne and then the existing earth and heaven flee away from his presence. This verse, translated below in the New Century Version of the Bible especially gives this impression.

> "Then I saw a great white throne and the One who was sitting on it. Earth and sky ran away from him and disappeared." (Rev. 20:11, NCV)

This has caused some scholars to suggest that the actual White Throne Judgment happens somewhere in space. The Bible Knowledge Commentary: New Testament by John Walvoord and Roy Zuck comments on this verse that, *"It apparently is located neither in heaven nor earth but in space, as suggested by the statement, Earth and sky fled from His presence, and there was no place for them."*

Dr. David Jeremiah suggests the location could even possibly be on a distant planet.

> "It cannot take place on earth because at the appearance of the Lord, the earth and heaven will have fled away. And it cannot take place in heaven because no sinner can enter the presence of God there. So, the Great White Throne Judgment takes place somewhere between heaven and earth. Perhaps on some distant planet that we don't even know about, but it will take place."[78]

Somewhere in space is not likely because in Rev. 20:12 John sees the unbelievers *"standing before God."* This would imply that they are positioned upright on firm ground rather than suspended in limbo somewhere in outer space.

Dr. Jeremiah correctly states that the judgment *"cannot take place in heaven because no sinner can enter the presence of God there.* However, his distant planet scenario seems far-fetched because it lacks biblical precedent and depending on the expanse of the fleeing heavens alluded to by John, a distant planet may no longer exist at the time. If *there was found no place for them,* the first heaven and earth, then there's likely no place found for a distant planet either.

It could be space or a distant planet, but the other possible locations are, that the judgment happens on the existing earth before it flees away, or the new heaven and new earth if it has already been created by this point. The actual location is a secondary matter for the unbelievers because their primary concerns are that they will be *standing before God* in front of the White Throne and forced to give an account of their former lives.

The Resurrection of the Unbelievers

> "And I saw the dead, small and great, standing before God, and books were opened. And another book was opened, which is *the Book* of Life. And the dead were judged according to their works, by the things which were written in the books." (Rev. 20:11)

After seeing the White Throne, John sees "*the dead, small and great, standing before God.*" The terms *small and great* are used often in the Bible and five times in the book of Revelation. It's there to remind us that all classes and ranks of unbelievers will be present, no matter what their economic stature, social status or gender was in their former lives.

We can rule out all believers from this grouping because they are no longer classified as dead at the time. Whether they were Church Age, Old Testament, Tribulation or Millennial Saints, they will have already all been resurrected into immortal bodies in one of the four phases of the First Resurrection identified below.

Phase 1: The resurrection of Jesus Christ at the time of His First Coming – (Matt. 28:6-7, Mark 16:6, Luke 24:6) This phase also included, at about the same time, many saints who had previously died.

> "And the graves were opened; and many bodies of the saints who had fallen asleep were raised; and coming out of the graves after His resurrection, they went into the holy city and appeared to many." (Matthew 27:51-53).

Phase 2: The resurrection of Church Age believers at the Pre-Tribulation Rapture – (John 14:3, 1 Thess. 4:13-18, 1 Cor. 15:50-53).

Phase 3: The resurrection of the Two Witnesses at the Midpoint of the Trib-period – (Rev. 11:11-12). This phase will likely also include, but not necessarily at the same time, the 144,000 Jewish Evangelists – (Rev. 14:1-5).

Phase 4: The resurrection of the Old Testament Saints – (Daniel 12:1-2, Isaiah 26:19, and about the same time the Tribulation Saints – (Rev. 7:14; 20:4-6). Both of these groups resurrect in the 75-Day Interval Period.

Thus, all of these dead in Rev. 20:12 *standing before God* represent resurrected unbelievers. This would be the Second Resurrection. The fact that they are seen *standing* implies that they are fitted into physical bodies equipped with legs and feet, and no longer just a soul that had been confined to Hades. Other scriptural references to a Second Resurrection for the unbelievers are provided below.

"And many of those who sleep in the dust of the earth shall awake, Some to everlasting life, Some to shame *and* everlasting contempt." (Daniel 12:2)

"Do not marvel at this; for the hour is coming in which all who are in the graves will hear His voice and come forth—those who have done good, to the resurrection of life, and those who have done evil, to the resurrection of condemnation." (John 5:28-29)

'I have hope in God, which they themselves also accept, that there will be a resurrection of *the* dead, both of *the* just, (*at the First Resurrection*),

and *the* unjust, (*at the White Throne Judgment*)."
(Acts 24:15, NKJV; emphasis added)

The Second Resurrection will include billions, if not tens or hundreds of billions because it will include every unbeliever that existed on the earth for approximately 7000 years. This grouping will include the secular and religious, civil and uncivil, rich and poor, weak and strong, in other words any of the smallest of the small and greatest of the great.

The Books are Opened

John also sees "*books were opened and another book was opened, which is the Book of Life.*" These books were opened so that the unbelievers could be "*judged according to their works, by the things which were written in the books.*" This implies that the unbelievers will each experience a personal recounting of their former lives and that they will be judged according to their works.

If this is the case, it beckons the questions; How long will it take to rewind through the highlight reels of the autobiographies of billions of unbelievers? Since this could take some time, the next logical question becomes; How long is the Aftermath Age going to last? Will it take a day, week, month or more? We are not told, but this judgment process could take a considerable amount of time, that is if the dimension of time still exists at this juncture.

Some teach that the purpose of the open books at this judgment is to determine the degree of punishment that each unbeliever will receive. There are some Scriptures, such as Matthew 11:20-24, Luke 12:47-48 and John 19:11 that point out there are different measures of sinfulness and greater accountabilities depending on what light has been shown to an individual.

Undoubtedly, there will be different report cards for the billions of unbelievers throughout time. Some were guilty of mass murder, such as Adolph Hitler, while others lived more civilized lives. This latter grouping tried to live by the so-called "Golden Rule" that they believed was the common thread that united all the religions. Below is a quote from Wikipedia about the "Golden Rule."

> "*The Golden Rule is the principle of treating others as one wants to be treated. It is a maxim that is found in most religions and cultures. It can be considered an ethic of reciprocity in some religions, although different religions treat it differently.*
>
> *The maxim may appear as a positive or negative injunction governing conduct:*
>
> - *Treat others as you would like others to treat you (positive or directive form)*
>
> - *Do not treat others in ways that you would not like to be treated (negative or prohibitive form)*
>
> - *What you wish upon others, you wish upon yourself (empathetic or responsive form)*
>
> *The idea dates at least to the early Confucian times (551–479 BCE), according to Rushworth Kidder, who identifies the concept appearing prominently in Buddhism, Christianity, Hinduism, Islam, Judaism, Taoism, Zoroastrianism, and "the rest of the world's major religions.""*[79]

Whatever works any unbeliever did in their lives, it will be revealed to them at the White Throne Judgment that they were all sinners in need of THE SAVIOR. Remember that the One seated upon the White Throne, THE SAVIOR, made it clear in the passage below that the purposeful intent, even if it didn't manifest into a sinful action, qualified as a sin.

> "You have heard that it was said to those of old, 'You shall not commit adultery.' But I say to you that whoever looks at a woman to lust for her has already committed adultery with her in his heart. If your right eye causes you to sin, pluck it out and cast *it* from you; for it is more profitable for you that one of your members perish, than for your whole body to be cast into hell. And if your right hand causes you to sin, cut it off and cast *it* from you; for it is more profitable for you that one of your members perish, than for your whole body to be cast into hell." (Matthew 5:27-30)

We read a summary of the findings from the White Throne Judgment in the verse below.

> "But the cowardly, unbelieving, abominable, murderers, sexually immoral, sorcerers, idolaters, and all liars shall have their part in the lake which burns with fire and brimstone, which is the second death." (Rev. 21:8)

It is revealed to all of the unbelievers on trial that they fell into one or more of these categories above. As a result, they will be cast into the Lake of Fire, which is also stated in Rev. 20:15.

Perhaps visiting the known library of the holy books will provide some other insights into why they are present and opened at the time. In addition to the primary *Book of Life* and the 66 books in the Bible, one or all of the following books might also be among the open books,

The open books at the White Throne Judgment could include the Book of:

1.   *Records* – Ezra 4:15,
2.   *the Living* – Psalm 69:28,

3. *Remembrance* – Malachi 3:16,
4. *Life of the Lamb* or, *The Lamb's Book of Life* – Rev. 13:8, 17:8, 21:27,
5. *the Genealogy of Adam* – Gen. 5:21,
6. *the Covenant* – Exodus 24:7; 2 Kings 23:2, 21; 2 Chron. 34:30,
7. *the Wars of the LORD* – Numbers 21:4,
8. *the Law* – Deuteronomy 28:61, 29:11, 30:10, 31:26; Joshua 8:31-34; 2 Kings 22:8, 11; 2 Chron. 34:15; Nehemiah 8:3; Galatians 3:10,
9. *Jasher* – Joshua 10:13; 2 Samuel 1:18,
10. *the Law of Moses* – Joshua 23:6; 2 Kings 14:6; 2 Chron. 25:4, 35:12; Ezra 6:18; Nehemiah 8:1, 13:1; Mark 12:26,
11. *the Law of God (or the LORD)* – Joshua 24:26; 2 Chron. 17:9, 34:14; Nehemiah 8:18, 9:3,
12. *the Acts of Solomon* – 1 Kings 11:41,
13. *the Kings of Israel* – 1 Kings 14:19, 15:31, 16:5, 14, 20, 27, 22:39; 2 Kings 1:18,10:34, 13:8, 12, 14:15, 28, 15:11, 15, 21, 26, 31; 1 Chron. 9:1; 2 Chron. 20:34, 25:26, 27:7, 28:6, 32:32, 33:18, 35:27, 36:8,
14. *the Kings of Judah* – 1 Kings 24:29, 15:7, 23, 22:45; 2 Kings 8:23, 12:19, 14:18, 15:6, 36, 16:19, 20:20, 21:17, 25, 23:28, 24:5; 2 Chron. 16:11, 25:26, 27:7, 28:6, 32:32, 35:27, 36:8,
15. *Samuel the Seer* – 1 Chron. 29:29,
16. *Nathan the Prophet* – 1 Chron. 29:29; 2 Chron. 9:29,
17. *Gad the Seer* – 1 Chron. 29:29,
18. *Shemaiah the Prophet* – 2 Chron. 12:15,
19. *Iddo the Seer* – 2 Chron. 12:15,
20. *Jehu* – 2 Chron. 20:34,
21. *the Lord* – Isaiah 34:16,
22. *the Genealogy of Jesus Christ* – Matthew 1:1,
23. *of this* (Revelation) *Prophecy* – Rev. 21:27.

Supposedly, somewhere in one of these or other various holy books, a record of each person's life has been written. As an example, the evil Assyrian King Sennacherib is recorded in 2 Kings

19:23–28 and Isaiah 37:24–29. His report card isn't going to look good at the White Throne Judgment.

Then, there's Queen Jezebel, one of the most wicked women to have ever existed. Her life story shows up at least 18 times in 1 Kings 16:31, 18:4, 13, 19:1-2, 21:5, 7, 11, 14-15, 23, 25; and 2 Kings 9:7, 10, 22, 30, 36-37. You can read these Jezebel verses to get a sneak preview of what her visitation at the White Throne will be like.

These two examples are of the "*great*" unbelievers in prominence of the past, but what about the "*small*" unbelievers that didn't even make it on the pages of the Bible? Take as an example, someone near and dear to you who is just an average unbeliever with no greatness of stature or fame. Unless they get saved before they die, then they will also be judged according to their works at the White Throne.

The Book of Life vs The Lamb's Book of Life

There are important distinctions to be made between the *Book of Life*, the *Lamb's book of Life* and all of the other books above in the Holy Library. The *Book of Life* includes the names of everyone according to the Psalm passage below.

> "Your eyes saw my substance, being yet unformed. And in Your book (*of Life*) they all were written, The days fashioned for me, When *as yet there were* none of them." (Psalm 139:16, NKJV; emphasis added)

Believers are blessed to have their names retained in the *Book of Life* as per the Revelation verse below.

> "He who overcomes shall be clothed in white garments, and I, (*Jesus Christ*), will not blot out his name from the Book of Life; but I will confess

his name before My Father and before His angels."
(Rev. 3:5, NKJV; emphasis added)

As this above verse points out, the names inscribed in the *Book of Life* can be blotted out by Jesus Christ. The next verse points out that unbelievers are those that get blotted out.

"Let them be blotted out of the book of the living,
And not be written with the righteous." (Psalm 69:28)

The *Lamb's Book of Life*, or the Book of the Life of the Lamb, is a different book. The *Lamb's Book of Life* seemingly contains the names of, and exclusively of, born-again believers. Thus, these are people who became believers by receiving Christ as their Savior. These born-again believers are also in the *Book of Life*, as are the names of the Old Testament Saints. However, the names of the Old Testament Saints are not written in the *Lamb's Book of Life*.

The verse below points out that the names of born-again believers are also in the *Book of Life*.

"And I, (*the Apostle Paul*), urge you also, true companion, help these (*Christian*) women who labored with me in the gospel, with Clement also, and the rest of my fellow workers, whose names are in the Book of Life." (Philippians 4:3, NKJV; emphasis added)

The verses below point out that the names in *The Lamb's Book of Life* were inscribed in this holy book before the earth was created.

"All who dwell on the earth will worship him, (*the Antichrist*) whose names have not been written in the Book of Life of the Lamb slain from the foundation of the world." (Rev. 13:8, NKJV; emphasis added)

"The beast, (*Antichrist*), that you saw was, and is not, and will ascend out of the bottomless pit and go to perdition. And those who dwell on the earth will marvel, whose names are not written in the (*Lamb's*) Book of Life from the foundation of the world, when they see the beast that was, (*alive in Rev. 13:1*) and is not, (*died by a mortal head wound as per Rev. 13:3*), and yet is (*resurrected by Satan in Rev. 13:3, 14*)." (Rev. 17:8, NKJV; emphasis added)

The fact that all born-again believers names' are written in the *Lamb's Book of Life* and *from the foundation of the world*, means that before each believer was even born, Jesus Christ, in His foreknowledge, knew who WOULD become a born-again believer. It also means that Jesus knew in advance who WOULD NOT become born-again.

This predestination understanding isn't about favoritism because Jesus Christ died for everyone's sins. John 3:16 explains that God loves everyone and wishes that none would perish, but all would have eternal life by receiving Jesus Christ. In Rev. 3:20 Jesus Christ extends a personal invitation to everyone to become born-again.

"Behold, I stand at the door and knock. If anyone hears My voice and opens the door, I will come in to him and dine with him, and he with Me."

The key word in this passage is "anyone." However, Jesus Christ foreknew that not everyone would receive Him. He compared being born-again to entering through a *narrow gate*, but He acknowledged that most would take the broader way that leads to the White Throne Judgment.

"Enter by the narrow gate; for wide *is* the gate and broad *is* the way that leads to destruction,

and there are many who go in by it. Because
narrow *is* the gate and difficult *is* the way which
leads to (*eternal*) life, and there are few who find
it." (Matthew 7:13-14, NKJV; emphasis added)

What is the Basis of Salvation in the Old Testament?

Since the *Lamb's Book of Life* only includes born-again believers
of Jesus Christ, then how do the people prior to the First Coming
of Christ prevent their names from being blotted out of the *Book
of Life* by Jesus Christ? Remember, the *Book of Life* is apparently
a registry of all names. It's like a spiritual birth certificate and it
includes the small, great, good, evil, righteous and unrighteous
throughout all time.

The paramount goal of an individual born before the First
Advent of Jesus Christ, was to do whatever was required to ensure
that their name would never be blotted out of the *Book of Life*. How
was this feat possible? The simple answer is they had to exercise faith
and become a believer in Yahweh, the God of the Old Testament.

How was this belief in Yahweh accomplished? Was it by strictly
following the Ten Commandments, which were a portion of the 613
commandments of the (Levitical) Law? The answer is NO because
the New Testament points out that men in the flesh with their sin
nature were unable to fulfill the Law in its entirety. If fulfilling the
Law was the guarantee of keeping one's name in the Book of Life,
then every man's name would be blotted out. The Law merely served
as a tutor to mankind to inform it that it needed a Savior.

> "Therefore the law was our tutor *to bring us* to
> Christ, that we might be justified by faith."
> (Galatians 3:24)

Additionally, King David violated two of the Ten
Commandments by committing adultery in 2 Samuel 11:4-5 and
murder in 2 Samuel 11:14-17, but according to Ezekiel 37:24-

25 and elsewhere, King David will be among the resurrected Old Testament Saints, which means his name did not get blotted out of the *Book of Life* for his offenses.

Moreover, it's estimated that the Law was issued about 3500 years ago, which meant that Abraham, who lived about 4000 years ago, would not even have knowledge of the Ten Commandments and the 613 Levitical Laws. So then, is the means of keeping an Old Testament person's name in the *Book of Life*, integrated in the Abrahamic Covenant, which was issued about 500 years prior to the time of Moses?

After all, Genesis 12 says that God will bless those who bless Abraham and that through him all of the families of the earth would be blessed.

> "I will bless those who bless you, (*Abraham*), And I will curse him who curses you; And in you all the families of the earth shall be blessed." (Genesis 12:3, NKJV; emphasis added)

The answer is again NO, because Enoch lived about 1400 years before the Abrahamic Covenant was issued and he was Raptured by God, which means his name is still in the *Book of Life*. Enoch had no physical way of blessing Abraham.

> "And Enoch walked with God; and he *was* not, for God took him." (Genesis 5:24)

Therefore, for anyone dating back to the time of Adam and Eve until the First Coming of Christ to retain their name in the Book of Life, they had to manifest one common thing. FAITH! They had to have faith in God. Without faith in God it's impossible to please God.

> "But without faith *it is* impossible to please *Him,* for he who comes to God must

believe that He is, and *that* He is a rewarder of those who diligently seek Him." (Hebrews 11:6)

God's grace in conjunction with man's faith are the two essential ingredients in everyone's salvation. This is also the case for born-again believers.

"For by grace you have been saved through faith, and that not of yourselves; *it is* the gift of God, not of works, lest anyone should boast." (Ephesians 2:8-9)

Hebrews chapter 11, which is also sometimes called the "Hall of Faith," provides examples of how certain men and women of faith pleased God. This chapter points out how various patriarchs' and matriarchs' faith in God served as a testimony of courage, divine reward and in many instances a cause of severe suffering for the greater good.

"These all, (*Abel, Enoch, Noah, Abraham, Isaac, Jacob, and Sarah*), died in faith, not having received the promises, but having seen them afar off were assured of them, embraced *them* and confessed that they were strangers and pilgrims on the earth." (Hebrews 11:13, NKJV; emphasis added)

"But now they desire a better, that is, a heavenly *country.* Therefore God is not ashamed to be called their God, for He has prepared a city for them." (Hebrew 11:16)

"Women (*of faith*) received their dead raised to life again. Others were tortured, not accepting deliverance, that they might obtain a better resurrection." (Hebrews 11:35, NKJV; emphasis added)

"And all these, (*including Moses, Rahab, Gideon, Barak, Samson, Jephthah, David, Samuel, the prophets and many more*), having obtained a good testimony through faith, did not receive the promise, God having provided something better for us, (*born-again believers*), that they should not be made perfect apart from us." (Hebrews 11:39-40, NKJV; emphasis added)

Faith in God is the essential requirement of retaining one's name in the *Book of Life*. Faith in Jesus Christ is the prerequisite condition for having a person's name written in the *Lamb's Book of Life*.

What are the resurrected unbelievers judged upon at the White Throne? It's not faith, which they lacked, but it's their works as outlined in the open books at the White Throne Judgment.

"And the dead were judged according to their works, by the things which were written in the books." (Rev. 20:12d)

When are the Names of Unbelievers Blotted Out of the Book of Life?

Before addressing when the names of unbelievers are blotted out of the Book of Life, it's important to point out that the resurrected unbelievers at the White Throne Judgment included those who came out of both the sea and Death and Hades.

"The sea gave up the dead who were in it, and Death and Hades delivered up the dead who were in them. And they were judged, each one according to his works. Then Death and Hades were cast into the lake of fire. This is the second death. And anyone not found written in the Book of Life was cast into the lake of fire." (Rev. 20:13-15)

The reference to the sea, could simply apply to unbelievers who died at sea, or according to the typological precedent presented in Daniel 7:2-3, the sea could represent the Gentile world at large. Daniel had a vision of four beasts arising out of the Great Sea and these beasts represented the historical Gentile Empires of Babylon, Medo-Persia, Greece and Rome.

The mention of Death and Hades could apply to the unbelievers killed by the fourth horseman of the apocalypse in Rev. 6:7-8, but more than likely it alludes to the unbelievers who were confined to Hades after their earthly deaths. In the New Testament, when Hades is used in the context of a habitation it identifies the temporary abode of the souls of the unsaved dead.

In both cases, the sea and Death and Hades, the dead they give up are all unbelievers who are going to be judged for their works at the White Throne Judgment. After delivering up its host of unbelievers, *"Death and Hades were cast into the lake of fire."*

This becomes a necessary act because from that point forward there will no longer be any unmanned souls in need of an abode. All souls, whether they belong to believers or unbelievers, will be resurrected into immortal bodies. Thus, Death and Hades are evicted from their old address and cast into the Lake of Fire.

> *"And anyone not found written in the Book of Life was cast into the lake of fire."* (Rev. 20:15)

At some point an unbeliever's name will be blotted out of the *Book of Life* and as a result their final destination will become the Lake of Fire. One possibility is that the blotting out of an unbeliever's name from the *Book of Life* occurs at the point of their death. Thus, when the *Book of Life* gets opened at the White Throne Judgment, their name does not appear in it because it was already erased.

This is a possibility, but I believe that the unbeliever's name is blotted out at the White Throne Judgment. The process would be that the person has had his or her works judged via the review of the other open books, that they are found wanting. Their works will evidence their lack of faith in either God, if they dwelt in Old Testament times, or Jesus Christ, if they lived during New Testament times.

I think it's possible that it is then, after their works are judged, the last sound they hear and last sight they see before being cast alive into the Lake of Fire, will be something like the deliberate swipe of an eraser on a chalkboard causing a puff of chalk to drift away. All that will remain is an illegible smudge after their names are erased off the pages of the *Book of Life*. I believe the blotting out of the names happens at the White Throne Judgment for the three primary reasons below.

First, Revelation 20:15, which says *"and anyone not found written in the Book of Life was cast into the lake of fire,* is the last verse dealing with the Aftermath Age. It concludes Revelation chapter 20. Then, the next chapter, Revelation 21 begins by introducing the new heaven and new earth of the Eternal Order. It seems fitting that the grand finale of the Aftermath Age would be the blotting out of the names of all unbelievers at the White Throne Judgment.

It also appears appropriate, that when the *Book of Life* is opened at the White Throne, the unbelievers see their names inscribed upon its pages. This recognition, along with the fact that God kept records of their individual lives in the other open books, should invoke a fearful reverence for the ones on trial. The realization would be that God cared for them, but they placed no faith in Him. Therefore, by their own free will, they leave God no choice but to blot their names out of His special *Book of Life*.

Second, As per Rev. 3:5, which was quoted earlier in this chapter, it is Jesus Christ Who does the blotting out of the names in the *Book of Life*. If an unbeliever died after the First Advent of Jesus Christ, Jesus could blot his or her name out. However, if an unbeliever died before His First Coming, it seems unlikely that He would greet them at the gates of Hades and blot their name out at that time.

Third, the fulfillment of the two prophetic passages below, as far as they apply to all unbelievers, takes place at the White Throne Judgment. These individuals are resurrected and placed in front of Jesus Christ on His White Throne. Their lives and works are reviewed, they are found guilty of having no faith in God or Jesus Christ, and then they drop to a knee and confess that Jesus Christ is Lord. It seems likely that after that confession is made, that they witness the authority of Jesus Christ, over all things, as He blots their names out of the Book of Life.

> "That at the name of Jesus every knee should bow, of those in heaven, and of those on earth, and of those under the earth, and *that* every tongue should confess that Jesus Christ *is* Lord, to the glory of God the Father." (Philippians 2:10-11)

> "For it is written: "*As* I live, says the Lord, Every knee shall bow to Me, And every tongue shall confess to God."" (Romans 14:11)

20

The
Lake of Fire
and the
Second Death

"Those who are born twice will die only once. Those born only once will die twice." (Warren Wiersbe)[80]

What does this Wiersbe quote imply? It means that a believer only experiences a physical death one time, unless they are Raptured, but an unbeliever dies a physical death and a spiritual Second Death. This chapter will explain the Second Death and attempt to show the connections between the Second Death and the Lake of Fire.

> "Then Death and Hades were cast into the lake of fire. This is the second death." (Rev. 20:14)

Jesus stated that a person must be born again, alluding to a second birth, in order to become saved into the kingdom of God.

> "'Jesus answered and said to him, "Most assuredly, I say to you, unless one is born again, he cannot see the kingdom of God."'" (John 3:3)

This is impossible to do physically, so it must be accomplished spiritually. Jesus Christ explained that two births exist for mankind. The first is in the fleshly birth out from a mother's womb and the second is a spiritual birth into the Spirit.

> "That which is born of the flesh is flesh, and that
> which is born (*again*) of the Spirit is spirit." (John
> 3:7, NKJV; emphasis added)

Unbelievers cannot see the kingdom of God because they operate in their flesh and kingdom awareness requires spiritual discernment, meaning that a person must be born again into the Spirit.

> "But the natural man does not receive the things
> of the Spirit of God, for they are foolishness to
> him; nor can he know *them,* because they are
> spiritually discerned." (1 Corinthians 2:14)

The Apostle Paul explains below why this birth into the Spirit must take place in order to inherit the kingdom of God. He points out the limitations of the flesh.

> "Now this I say, brethren, that flesh and blood
> cannot inherit the kingdom of God; nor does
> corruption inherit incorruption." (1 Cor. 15:50)

When a person receives Christ, at that same time, they are born a second time and become indwelt by the Spirit, Who according to 2 Corinthians 1:22 seals up our hearts as a guarantee from God of our spiritual birth.

> "And I will pray the Father, and He will give
> you another Helper (*the Holy Spirit*), that He
> may abide with you forever— the Spirit of
> truth, whom the world cannot receive, because it
> neither sees Him nor knows Him; but you know
> Him, for He dwells with you and will be in you."
> (John 14:16-17, NKJV; emphasis added)

It is from that point forward that a person can begin to understand those things that can only be spiritually discerned.

> "These things I have spoken to you while being
> present with you. But the Helper (*the Holy Spirit*),
> the Holy Spirit, whom the Father will send in My
> name, He will teach you all things, and bring to
> your remembrance all things that I said to you."
> (John 14:25-26, NKJV; emphasis added)

Eventually at the time of a believer's physical death, like the umbilical cord detaches from the baby, the flesh will separate itself from their spirit. Subsequently, the believer will receive an immortal body at the First Resurrection for their spirit to inhabit throughout eternity. Thus, as Wiersbe stated, "*Those* (believers) *who are born twice will die only once.*"

In the next verse Jesus Christ promises that believers will not experience the Second Death.

> "He who has an ear, let him hear what the Spirit
> says to the churches. He who overcomes shall not
> be hurt by the second death." (Rev. 2:11)

This promise was made "*to the churches,*" meaning all true believers. Specifically, Jesus Christ stated this to comfort the Christian martyrs at the beginning of the Church Age. This period of persecution would lead to the deaths of many believers, so Jesus wanted them to be encouraged by the understanding that because they were born of the *Spirit,* they would *not be hurt by the second death.*

According to Rev. 2:8, the source of these comforting words was Jesus Christ, "*These things says the First and the Last, who was dead, and came to life.*" Jesus was reinforcing this important promise by quoting what the Spirit said in Rev. 2:11, "*hear what the Spirit says to the churches.*"

Thus, if you receive Jesus Christ as your personal Lord and Savior, then you are:

1. A believer,
2. Born again from the flesh into the Spirit,
3. Indwelt by the Helper, (*the Holy Spirit*),
4. A citizen in the kingdom of God,
5. Capable of understanding the things that require spiritual discernment,
6. Going to die, unless you're Raptured, and then be resurrected into an immortal body,
7. You will *NOT BE HURT BY THE SECOND DEATH*!

Since the Old Testament Saints and Tribulation Saints are also going to be part of the First Resurrection, they will be considered born again into immortality and thus they will also not be hurt by the Second Death.

Having just identified, *"those who are born twice* (and) *will die only once,"* now it's time to strongly warn, *"those born only once,* (but) *will die twice,"* what's in store for them!

What is the Lake of Fire?

The two quotes below from the book of Revelation inform us that the Lake of Fire is the Second Death.

> "Then Death and Hades were cast into the lake of fire. This is the second death." (Rev. 20:14)

> "But the cowardly, unbelieving, abominable, murderers, sexually immoral, sorcerers, idolaters, and all liars shall have their part in the lake which burns with fire and brimstone, which is the second death." (Rev. 21:8)

Therefore, in order to gain a greater understanding of the Second Death we need to comprehend what the Lake of Fire is. A mountain on fire is a volcano, a forest on fire is a wildfire, but a lake on fire is an oxymoron.

A body of water on fire on this present earth can result from an underwater oil or gas pipeline rupture, as was the case in July 2021 in the Gulf of Mexico, a toxic combustible waste hazard that happened in February 2018 in Bellandur, India or an overflowing volcanic lava flow, such as the eruption at Holuran in September 2014 that overtook the Jökulsá á Fjöllum river.

However, in all of these instances the fires were only temporary and ultimately extinguished, but the Lake of Fire appears to represent a body of water that burns continuously throughout eternity. Unlike many earthly lakes, this burning lake is not open for recreational use. There will be no boating, fishing or shoreline camping!

I point all of the above out in an attempt to get the reader to imagine what a massive lake, which is burning 24/7 with brimstone, or sulfur in some translations, looks like. There will be billions of resurrected unbelievers cast into this fiery lake, so it's safe to assume that this is no small pond. The area of all the Great Lakes is 95,160 square miles. If they all caught on a sulfur fire at the same time, what would that look like?

Moulton sulfur is highly flammable, explosive and emits poisonous gases into the atmosphere. Sulfur produces inextinguishable flames, smells like rotten eggs and the smoke it produces in a fire is extremely hazardous to breathe.

I live in a town near Palm Springs, CA, which is about forty miles to the west of the Salton Sea. Every once in a while this sea emanates a terrible odor that smells like rotten eggs. The closer one travels toward this salty lake, the more prevalent the odor becomes. The advisory quote below from the local newspaper called the Desert Sun explains the scenario.

> *"The South Coast Air Quality Management District has issued an odor advisory for the eastern region due to elevated levels of hydrogen sulfide coming from*

> *the Salton Sea. It happens on a relatively regular basis throughout the year and typically produces a stench similar to rotten eggs.*"[81]

Hydrogen sulfide is a sulfur oxoanion. It is formed as part of sulfuric acid. This smell can sometimes be unbearable to those traveling close by, and the Salton Sea is not a body of water burning with fire.

Geographically, the Lake of Fire is an unimaginably horrifying place to live, but geopolitically it's even worse, as it is filled with *"the cowardly, unbelieving, abominable, murderers, sexually immoral, sorcerers, idolaters, and all liars."*

The thought of an unbeliever spending an eternity in such a location should cause someone to want to become a born-again believer in Jesus Christ, just to escape this place of torment. The point dear reader is don't go to the Lake of Fire. You won't need to ever come near to it if you receive Jesus Christ as your Savior.

The Lake of Fire, which is also called the lake that burns with fire, appears five times in the book of Revelation. These verses are provided and explained below.

> "Then the beast, (*the Antichrist*), was captured (*by Jesus Christ*), and with him the false prophet who worked signs in his presence, by which he deceived those who received the mark of the beast and those who worshiped his image. These two were cast alive into the lake of fire burning with brimstone." (Rev. 19:20, NKJV; emphasis added)

The first two inhabitants to enter the Lake of Fire are the Antichrist and False Prophet. They get cast ALIVE into this place prior to the start of the Millennium. They spend over 1000 years in this unbearable location before the next resident arrives, which is Satan.

> "The devil, who deceived them, was cast into the
> lake of fire and brimstone where the beast and the
> false prophet *are*. And they will be tormented day
> and night forever and ever." (Rev. 20:10)

While the Antichrist and False Prophet were tormented day
and night in the burning lake, Satan spent the same 1000-year
period in the abyss as per Rev. 20:1-3. Notice that Rev. 20:10
points out that *"the beast and the false prophet are"* still ALIVE in
the Lake of Fire. In other words they weren't cast into the burning
lake, burned up and cremated. So, the Second Death, at least for
them, did not result in a physical death.

In Rev. 20:7-10 the Devil comes out of the Abyss and leads a
rebellion against God, but he gets soundly defeated. Then, Satan
is cast into the Lake of Fire where he gets reacquainted with the
Antichrist and False Prophet. Thus, the unholy trinity is once again
reunited and just in time for the arrival of the next occupants, who
are Death and Hades.

> "The sea gave up the dead who were in it, and
> Death and Hades delivered up the dead
> (*unbelievers*) who were in them. And they were
> judged, each one according to his works. Then,
> (*after the unbelievers are judged*), Death and
> Hades were cast into the lake of fire. This is the
> second death." (Rev. 20:13-14, NKJV; emphasis
> added)

The dead that Death and Hades delivered up were the souls of
those who were *born only once* in the flesh and not born-again in
the Spirit. They are unbelievers whose souls went into temporary
confinement in Hades after the death of their physical bodies.
Hence, these individuals experienced Death and then Hades.
They are delivered up and get resurrected at the time of the White
Throne Judgment.

Once Death and Hades have delivered up their dead, they will serve no further purpose and the Lord will get rid of them. Their functionality ceases from that point forward because nobody will ever die the first death again; SAY GOODBYE DEATH, and the unsaved souls will be re-embodied at the Second Resurrection making it impossible to ever enter into Hades again; SAY GOODBYE HADES.

A point made earlier in this book was that nobody gets into Hades alive, and on the flip side, no one dead gets cast into the Lake of Fire. The Antichrist, False Prophet and Satan are all alive when they are cast into the Lake of Fire.

With the unholy trinity reunited, and Death and Hades relocated, it's time to usher in the rest of the occupants into the Lake of Fire, *"the cowardly, unbelieving, abominable, murderers, sexually immoral, sorcerers, idolaters, and all liars."*

> "And anyone not found written in the Book of
> Life was cast into the lake of fire." (Rev. 20:15)

The close of the prior chapter explained that those *not found written in the Book of Life* were all the resurrected unbelievers throughout time. It's their turn to be cast ALIVE into the Lake of Fire. By the time these unbelievers arrive to their eternal hellfire destination they will undoubtedly have some extremely harsh and unkind words for their welcoming committee, the unholy trinity. They will likely angrily shout out the sentiments recorded below by Isaiah the prophet. The personage Isaiah speaks negatively about is Satan, but we can also include the Antichrist and / or the entire unholy trinity into much of this demeaning quote.

> "In the place of the dead there is excitement over
> your arrival. The spirits of world leaders and
> mighty (*unsaved*) kings long dead stand up (*in
> the Second Resurrection*) to see you (*in the Lake
> of Fire*). With one voice they all cry out, 'Now

you are as weak as we are! Your might and power were buried with you. The sound of the harp in your palace has ceased. Now maggots are your sheet, and worms your blanket.' "How you are fallen from heaven, (*Satan*), O (*you once upon a time*) shining star, son of the morning! You have been thrown down to the earth, (*at the Midpoint of the Trib-period as per Rev. 12:9*), you who destroyed the nations of the world. For you said to yourself, 'I will ascend to heaven and set my throne above God's stars. I will preside on the mountain of the gods far away in the north. I will climb to the highest heavens and be like the Most High.' Instead, you will be brought down to the place of the dead, down to its lowest depths. Everyone there will stare at you and ask, Can this be the one who shook the earth and made the kingdoms of the world tremble? Is this the one who destroyed the world and made it into a wasteland? Is this the king who demolished the world's greatest cities and had no mercy on his prisoners?' "The kings of the nations lie in stately glory, each in his own tomb, but you will be thrown out of your grave like a worthless branch." (Isaiah 14:9-19a, HCSB; emphasis added)

The Gehenna and Lake of Fire Connections

> "*The Lake of Fire is the same as Gehenna. Gehenna is the proper name and the Lake of Fire is a descriptive name.*" (Dr. Arnold Fruchtenbaum).[82]

The Greek word *Gehenna* comes from the Hebrew words *Gei Hinnom*, which means "*the Valley of Hinnom.*" In the Old Testament this valley was notorious for being the place where the wicked kings of Israel practiced human sacrifices as burnt offerings to pagan gods.

"He offered sacrifices in the valley of Ben-Hinnom, even sacrificing his own sons in the fire. In this way, he followed the detestable practices of the pagan nations the Lord had driven from the land ahead of the Israelites." (2 Chronicles 28:3)

"They have built pagan shrines at Topheth, the garbage dump in the valley of Ben-Hinnom, and there they burn their sons and daughters in the fire. I have never commanded such a horrible deed; it never even crossed my mind to command such a thing!" (Jeremiah 7:31)

So in the New Testament *Gehenna* symbolizes the eternal location of the burning of human souls.

There are twelve references to Gehenna in the New Testament. They are summarized below. These scriptures seem to provide additional details about the Lake of Fire. Thus, Gehenna finds connections with the Lake of Fire, and seems to be alluding to the same place.

- Matthew 5:22 and Mark 9:47 – speaks about the danger of Gehenna hellfire.

- Matthew 5:29-30, 18:9 – explains that sin can result in the body being cast into Gehenna.

- Matthew 10:28 – points out that a sinner's soul and body both go into Gehenna.

- Matthew 23:15 – warns that the apostate scribes and Pharisees will be in Gehenna.

- Matthew 23:33 – clarifies that Gehenna is a place of condemnation.

- Mark 9:43, 45 – declares that Gehenna hosts a fire that can never be quenched.

- Luke 12:5 – states that God can cast someone into Gehenna.

- James 3:6 – compares a spiteful tongue to the hellfire in Gehenna. The first part of this verse reads, *"And the tongue is a fire, a world of iniquity."*

Concerning these above Gehenna uses, Dr. Arnold Fruchtenbaum states the following:

> *"From these twelve references in the Greek New Testament, four deductions can be drawn. First: Gehenna is the eternal abode of the lost, both angels and men. Second: the punishment in Gehenna includes both soul and body. That is why Gehenna must not be translated as "Hell.".... Hell is a temporary place and it is for the soul only, but Gehenna is an eternal place and it includes both the soul and the body. Third: it is an eternal torment. Fourth: Gehenna is associated with fire and fire is the source of torment."*[83]

To clarify the meaning of Hell, it is an old English expression for the Greek term Hades and the Hebrew word Sheol. Thus, Hell is often used interchangeably with the word Hades. Fruchtenbaum is distinguishing between Gehenna and Hades when he says, *"Hell is a temporary place and it is for the soul only, but Gehanna is an eternal place and it includes both the soul and the body."*

In summary, the Lake of Fire, also known as Gehenna, is where resurrected unbelievers go after they are judged and have their names blotted out from the Book of Life. This all happens at the time of the White Throne Judgment. Being resurrected individuals, they each possess a body and soul. This is different than Hades, also known as Hell, which could only accommodate unsaved souls and not physical bodies.

The Lake of Fire is also the place where Satan and the fallen angels are confined. Together, resurrected unbelievers and fallen angels spend eternity in this burning place of torment.

What is the Second Death?

Taking into consideration all of what's been written in this and the prior chapter about the White Throne Judgment, it's time to define what is meant by the Second Death. Rev. 20:14 and 21:8 inform that the lake that burns with fire is the Second Death, which means that only unbelievers will experience this specific death. No believers in God are cast into the Lake of Fire, but all of them will have experienced a rebirth in the Spirit prior to the White Throne Judgment.

The fate of every human unbeliever is to die once and then have their soul sent into Hades. Since only God can kill the soul, and He doesn't plan on killing any souls in Hades prior to the White Throne Judgment, this means that every unsaved soul gets re-embodied, judged and then cast into the Lake of Fire.

> "Don't be afraid of those who want to kill your
> body; they cannot touch your soul. Fear only God,
> who can destroy both soul and body in (*Gehenna*)
> Hell." (Matthew 10:28, NLT)

Once a resurrected unbeliever's name is blotted out of the Book of Life and their unsaved embodied soul is cast into the Lake of Fire, they have become dead to God. In essence, they have died a spiritual death. The Warren Wiersbe quote at the top of this article addressed this as, "*Those born only once will die twice.*"

Now we can understand that every unbeliever was born one time, then they died once in the flesh and then at the White Throne Judgment they were cast into the Lake of Fire, which is when they died a subsequent Second Death spiritually.

Is the Lake of Fire an Eternal Abode?

So, the Second Death is a spiritual phenomenon. Once unbelievers are cast into the Lake of Fire they are incapable of being born again in the Spirit. John 14:16-17 says that the Holy Spirit, referred to as the Helper, abides WITH the believer FOREVER, but on the flip side at the Second Death every unbeliever will abide WITHOUT the Holy Spirit FOREVER.

FOREVER is a long time, but is it an eternity for the spiritually dead unbelievers in the Lake of Fire? Verses like Galatians 6:8 and Romans 6:23 point out that believers will exist eternally, but will God, Who has the ability to kill the body and soul, cut some slack on the suffering of the unbelievers in the Lake of Fire? There are some people who think this might be the case. They hold the "Conditionalist View."

There are two views about this. The Traditionalist View believes that the Lake of Fire is a place of eternal, conscious torment for unbelievers. Whereas the Conditionalist View teaches that it is only a temporary suffering scenario.

The Traditionalist View of the Lake of Fire

In addition to Mark 9:43-45 that says the fire of Gehenna can never be extinguished, the Traditionalist will quote verses like the ones below to defend their position.

> "He who believes in the Son has everlasting life; and he who does not believe the Son shall not see life, but the wrath of God abides on him." (John 3:36)

> "And these (unbelievers) will go away into everlasting punishment, but the righteous (believers) into eternal life." (Matthew 25:46, NKJV; emphasis added)

> "The devil, who deceived them, was cast into the lake of fire and brimstone where the beast and

the false prophet *are*. And they will be tormented day and night forever and ever." (Rev. 20:10)

"And the smoke of their torment ascends forever and ever; and they have no rest day or night, who worship the beast and his image, and whoever receives the mark of his name." (Rev. 14:11)

These are just a few of the verses that imply a person who ends up in the Lake of Fire is doomed to a never-ending existence of excruciating pain and suffering. These passages portray a place of no escape and no hope.

The Conditionalist View of the Lake of Fire

The Conditionalist View, held by Dr. David Reagan and some others teaches that the unrighteous will be resurrected and judged according to their works at the White Throne Judgment. Then they will be punished in the Lake of Fire, but only for a period of time that is proportional to their sins, after which, they suffer destruction of their body and soul.

The Conditionalist will point to verses like:

- 2 Thess. 1:9 – that says sinners will be punished with everlasting destruction, which implies that they will ultimately be destroyed.

- John 3:16 – which seemingly suggests that people who don't receive eternal life through Jesus Christ might eventually perish.

- Matthew 7:13 – Whereby Jesus Christ warned people to not go through the wide gate, which represents unbelief in God, because it leads to destruction.

- Matthew 10:28 – that says God can destroy the body and soul.

If you are interested in this topic, I encourage you to study Dr. Reagan's entire article, which is available to read online at this link: *https://christinprophecy.org/articles/the-nature-of-hell/*.

Traditionalist *vs* Conditionalist, which view is correct? I'm a Traditionalist, who believes in a literal interpretation of verses that talk about "everlasting punishment," "they will be tormented day and night forever and ever," "and the smoke of their torment ascends forever and ever." These are references that have eternal consequences.

It's important to note that when the Bible uses words like eternal, eternity, everlasting and forever and ever, they are the same terms and meanings whether they apply to the saved or the unsaved. If the Lake of Fire is temporary and conditional, then does that likewise mean that everlasting life in Christ also comes with terms and conditions? If so, should we paraphrase Matthew 25:46 below to read:

> "And these UNBELIEVERS will go away into everlasting punishment and after their probationary period, which was predetermined by their past works, their suffering will end and they will perish, but the righteous believers will receive eternal life and at the end of their probationary period, their rejoicing will come to an end."

Understanding the terrifying nature of the eternal Lake of Fire should Light a Fire under all of us to preach the Gospel while we still can. Certainly, Satan, the Antichrist and False Prophet deserve to be there, but what about your lost loved ones who are clueless about this eternal Lake of Fire? Do they belong there? Are they headed there?

Tell them the GOOD NEWS GOSPEL of JESUS CHRIST, so that they can be spared from the BAD NEWS of THE SECOND DEATH and the LAKE of FIRE!

21

The Eternal Order and the New Jerusalem

"While the Messianic Kingdom is the high point of Old Testament Prophecy, the Eternal Order is the high point of New Testament Prophecy." (Dr. Arnold Fruchtenbaum)[84]

Thus far, this book has attempted to chronicle the events that happen in the Seventy-Five Day Interval, the Millennium and the Aftermath Age. Now it's time to explore the last two chapters in the Bible and take a sneak peek into eternity.

Dr. Fruchtenbaum states that, *'the Eternal Order is the high point of New Testament Prophecy."* Below are the top ten high points. These are listed in the order that they appear in Revelation 21-22 and some of these high points will be explained subsequently.

1. There will be a new heaven and a new earth (Revelation 21:1),
2. There will be a new holy city called NEW JERUSALEM (Rev. 21:2),
3. God the Father will dwell amongst His people (Rev. 21:3),
4. There will be no more death, sorrow, crying or pain (Rev. 21:4),
5. All things will be made new (Rev. 21:5),
6. God's people will be treated as sons and become heirs to all things (Rev. 21:7),

7.   There won't be a Fifth Jewish Temple in it, for the Lord God Almighty and the Lamb are its Temple (Rev. 21:22),
8.   There will be a crystal-clear pure River of Life (Rev. 22:1),
9.   There will be a healing Tree of Life (Rev. 22:2),
10. There will be no more sin and thus no more curse (Rev. 22:3).

There will be a new heaven and a new earth

> "Now I saw a new heaven and a new earth, for the first heaven and the first earth had passed away. Also there was no more sea." (Rev. 21:1)

The first thing that needs to happen to inaugurate the Eternal Order is for the Lord to create a sin-free environment. Since God the Father will Personally dwell amongst His people and call them His sons, the earth has to be void of all unrighteousness. This requires the creation of a new earth.

In Rev. 21:1, John acknowledges the existence of the first heaven and earth, but confirms that they will be replaced by a completely new second heaven and earth. The initial heaven and earth phases out in two stages and ultimately flees away at the time of the White Throne Judgment.

> "Then I saw a great white throne and Him who sat on it, from whose face the earth and the heaven fled away. And there was found no place for them." (Rev. 20:11)

The present earth gets destroyed according to:

- Isaiah 51:6 - says that "*the heavens will vanish away like smoke*" and "*the earth will grow old like a garment.*"

- 2 Peter 3:10 - informs "*the heavens will pass away with a great noise, and the elements will melt with fervent heat; both the earth and the works that are in it will be burned up.*"

Then this earth undergoes a renovation for the Millennium as per these following verses:

- 2 Peter 3:13 - clarifies that after the earth is "burned up," that "Nevertheless we, according to His promise, look for new heavens and a new earth in which righteousness dwells."

- Isaiah 65:17 and 66: 22 - states that God will "create new heavens and a new earth."

Since the sin nature will be present on the earth during the Millennium, a restored inhabitable earth is apparently all that's required. Over the course of the 1000-years the renovated stage two earth also becomes corrupted by sin. This is why it will necessarily flee away from the righteous face of the One seated on the White Throne as per Rev. 20:11.

When the restored earth flees away, sin will no longer have a planet to be performed upon. At that time all sinners will be confined to the Lake of Fire. With sin and sinners removed, God the Father can Personally dwell in righteousness amongst His people.

The NEW JERUSALEM

"Then I, John, saw the holy city, New Jerusalem, coming down out of heaven from God, prepared as a bride adorned for her husband." (Rev. 21:2)

Can you imagine watching an entire city descend downward from the sky, rather than being built from the ground up? Not just a city, but according to Rev. 21:16 the largest city that will ever be known to man?

This city comes down at the beginning of the Eternal Order,

but it could possibly already exist. John sees the actual city, not a blueprint of the city. Some believe that it is the city that Abraham waited for as part of the covenant that God made with him.

> "By faith he, (*Abraham*), dwelt in the land of promise as *in* a foreign country, dwelling in tents with Isaac and Jacob, the heirs with him of the same promise; for he waited for the city which has foundations, whose builder and maker *is* God." (Hebrews 11:9-10, NKJV; emphasis added)

This above verse says that Abraham awaited for a city, *which has foundations*, as if to suggest the city, or at least its foundations, may have existed as far back as about four thousand years ago when Abraham lived. Below is a relevant quote from The Bible Knowledge Commentary: New Testament about the possibility that the NEW JERUSALEM may already exist.

> "*Many expositors regard the promise of Christ in John 14:2, "I am going there to prepare a place for you," as referring to this city. The suggestion has been made that if the New Jerusalem is in existence during the millennial reign of Christ, it may have been suspended in the heavens as a dwelling place for resurrected and translated saints, who nevertheless would have immediate access to the earth to carry on their functions of ruling with Christ. J. Dwight Pentecost, for instance, quotes F.C. Jennings, William Kelly, and Walter Scott as supporting this concept of the New Jerusalem as a satellite city during the Millennium.[85] In the Millennium the New Jerusalem clearly does not rest on the earth, for there is an earthly Jerusalem and an earthly temple (Ezek. 40-48).*
>
> *The New Jerusalem then will apparently be withdrawn from its proximity to the earth when the*

> *earth will be destroyed at the end of the Millennium, and then will come back after the new earth is created. Though this possibility of a satellite city has been disregarded by most commentators and must be considered as an inference rather than a direct revelation of the Bible, it does solve some problems of the relationship between the resurrected and translated saints to those still in their natural bodies in the Millennium, problems which otherwise are left without explanation."*[86]

This above quote starts with this intriguing comment, "*Many expositors regard the promise of Christ in John 14:2.*" This passage of scripture is worth quoting and explaining in its full context to see how it might apply to the Church Saints, the Rapture and the NEW JERUSALEM.

> "Let not *your* heart be troubled; *you* believe in God, believe also in Me. In My Father's house are many mansions; if it were not so, I would have told *you*. I go to prepare a place for *you*. And if I go and prepare a place for *you*, I will come again and receive *you* to Myself; that where I am, there *you* may be also. And where I go *you* know, and the way *you* know." (John 14:1-4, NKJV; emphasis added)

Firstly, please note that these four verses convey a very personal message from Jesus Christ to His believers. He uses the words *you* and *your* nine times to qualify who He's addressing and comforting. If *you* are a believer, then let not *your* heart be troubled because these promises are for *you!*

Secondly, the mansions being prepared for *you* as a believer are in *My Father's house*, which places their location where Jehovah dwells. According to Rev. 21:2-3, 22-23, God the Father will dwell in the Eternal Order among His people in the golden holy city of

NEW JERUSALEM. Perhaps, this is the zip code that Jesus Christ is presently preparing a place for *you*.

If the NEW JERUSALEM already exists, and if this is the place Jesus Christ is preparing for *you*, then when *you* are Raptured, whether you are asleep in Christ or alive and remain on the earth at that time,[87] then the instant you are caught up to be with Christ, this is likely where you are going. According to 1 Corinthians 15:52 this happens as fast as the "*twinkling of an eye.*"

In other words, "*Here today, in NEW JERUSALEM tomorrow,*" alluding to the unknown tomorrow when the Rapture occurs.

Lastly, it's important to note that the way to be carried over the threshold of *your* mansion, which may be located in the NEW JERUSALEM, is through the Preparer of *your* mansion, Jesus Christ.

> "Jesus said to him, "I am the way, the truth, and the life. No one comes to the Father except through Me." (John 14:6)

Rev. 21:2 uses the illustration of the NEW JERUSALEM "*as a bride adorned for her husband.*" This may be a hint that this is where the Church Saints go after being Raptured because in 2 Cor. 11:2 the Church is pictured as the Bride of Christ.

Because the Church is portrayed in scripture as Christ's Bride, some teach that the inhabitants in the NEW JERUSALEM are exclusively Church saints. However, the use of marriage in the Bible as an illustration does not only relate to Jesus Christ and His Church but also Jehovah and His people Israel. Some suggest that details provided by John about the city identifies that the inhabitants include Jews, Angels and Church Saints, which are comprised of Jews and Gentiles. This point is explained later in this chapter.

John describes this holy city throughout most of Revelation chapter 21. Below are some details about the NEW JERUSALEM.

It will:

- descend down from heaven (Rev. 21:2,10),

- be situated on a great and high mountain (Rev. 21:10),

- be constructed of pure gold, which includes a main street of gold (Rev. 21:18, 21),

- be filled with the Shekinah Glory of God (Rev. 21:11),

- be illuminated by God and Jesus Christ and not the sun or moon (Rev. 21:11, 23),

- be laid out as a square with a length, breadth, and height that are equal (Rev. 21:16),

- measure about 12,000 furlongs, which is about 1500 miles (Rev. 21:16),

- have a massively high wall (Rev. 21:12). This wall will be comprised of:

  A. the jasper stone (Rev. 21:18),

  B. twelve pearl gates, which bear the names of the twelve tribes of Israel that are monitored by angels and always kept open to visitors (Rev. 21:12, 21),

  C. twelve foundations and on them are the names of the twelve apostles. These foundations are made of the following twelve precious stones (Rev. 21:14, 19-20),

1. *Jasper* – is usually opaque reddish-brown in color,

   (*high value estimate is about $5.00 per carat, which is $705 per ounce*),

2. *Sapphire* – generally known as a blue gemstone,

   (*high value est. is about $1600.00 per carat, which is $225,600 per ounce*),

3. *Chalcedony* – most commonly seen as white to gray or grayish-blue,

   (*high value est. is about $100.00 per carat, which is $14,100 per ounce*),

4. *Emerald* – mostly green with hues ranging from yellow-green to blue-green,

   (*high value est. is about $9,800 per carat, which is $1,381,800 per ounce*),

5. *Sardonyx* – characteristically a light yellow-red to reddish-brown color,

   (*value estimate is undetermined by this author*),

6. *Sardius* – was the first stone on the breastplate of the Jewish high priest, and is probably equivalent to a red ruby,

   (*Ruby mid-value est. is about $650 per carat, which is $91,650 per ounce*),

7. *Chrysolite* – comes from volcanic rocks and are light green to yellow-green,

   (*value estimate is about $80 per carat, which is $11,280 per ounce*),

8. *Beryl* – can be colorless, but could also be a tinted aqua-green,

   (*value estimate is about $150 per carat, which is $21,150 per ounce*),

9. *Topaz* – has a wide color range that, besides brown, includes various tones and saturations of blue, green, yellow, orange, red, pink, and purple,

   (*value estimate is about $25.00, which is $3,525 per ounce*),

10. *Chrysoprase* – its color is normally apple-green, but varies to deep green,

    (*value estimate is undetermined by this author*),

11. *Jacinth* – is somewhere between violet and orangish-red and in Exodus 28:19 is listed as the first stone of the third row in the breastplate of the Jewish high priest, (*value estimate is undetermined by this author*),

12. *Amethyst* – is a strong reddish-purple or purple color,

    (*high value estimate is about $70.00 per carat, which is $9,870 per ounce*).

(CAVEAT: The precious stones value estimates above, which came from various Internet sites, change frequently and could be wrong).

It's worth noting that some of these twelve stones adorning the foundations of the NEW JERUSALEM were also incorporated into the breastplate of the Jewish High Priest, which also included twelve gemstones. The breastplate hosted four rows with three stones in each row.

> "And you shall put settings of stones in it, four
> rows of stones: *The first* row *shall be* a sardius, a
> topaz, and an emerald; *this shall be* the first row;
> the second row *shall be* a turquoise, a sapphire,
> and a diamond; the third row, a jacinth, an agate,
> and an amethyst; and the fourth row, a beryl,
> an onyx, and a jasper. They shall be set in gold
> settings." (Exodus 28:17-20)

The purpose of including the assorted gemstone colors and value guesstimates of these precious stones above is to illustrate that the twelve foundations with the names of the twelve apostles will be:

1.   Structurally sound,

2.   Extremely ornate and colorful,

3.   Worth an incalculable amount of money in today's marketplace.

The NEW JERUSALEM is made of gold, which is presently worth about $1800 per ounce, pearly gates and all of these twelve precious stones listed above. None of these items are currently considered common-place construction materials. Presently, there are about twenty structures, not entire cities, in the world that are made of gold, but in some cases these are of a more synthetic gold, like copper-aluminum alloy.

The high point of this topic is that God spares no expense to ensure that His holy city is the greatest city ever constructed. Obviously, money is no object to God when it comes to the NEW JERUSALEM. Not only will it be the sturdiest, costliest and most aesthetic city ever built, but it will be the largest city ever to be inhabited.

> "The city is laid out as a square; its length is as
> great as its breadth. And he measured the city
> with the reed: twelve thousand furlongs. Its

length, breadth, and height are equal. Then he measured its wall: one hundred *and* forty-four cubits, *according* to the measure of a man, that is, of an angel." (Rev. 21:16-17)

Some scholars believe this holy city will be designed as either a perfect cube or a pyramid.

> "*An angel measured the city with a measuring rod of gold, about 10 feet in length. The city is 12,000 stadia in length and width, approximately 1,400 miles on each side. Tremendous as is the dimension of the city, the amazing fact is that it is also 1,400 miles high. Commentators differ as to whether the city is a cube or a pyramid. The descriptions seem to favor the pyramid form.*" (John Walvoord and Roy B. Zuck)[88]

Some interpreters have comparatively scaled the size of the NEW JERUSALEM to be about two-thirds the size of the United States.

> "*The dimensions and descriptions of the city stagger our imagination. "Foursquare" means "equal on all sides"; which may mean the city is a perfect cube, a "holy of holies" radiant with the presence of God. Or, it could be a pyramid. In either case, the city measures about 1,500 miles each way, or two-thirds the size of the United States!*" (Warren Wiersbe)[89]

The fact that the gates identify the twelve tribes of Israel and the foundations are named after the apostles, implies that the holy city unites Israel and the Church.

> "*Note that the city unites God's people of the Old Testament and the New Testament, Israel and the*

> *church. The tribes of Israel are named on the gates, and the twelve apostles are named on the foundation stones."* (Warren Wiersbe)[90]

Concerning the gates named after the twelve tribes of Israel, the passage below designates three gates per each side of the city.

> "Also she had a great and high wall with twelve gates, and twelve angels at the gates, and names written on them, which are *the names* of the twelve tribes of the children of Israel: three gates on the east, three gates on the north, three gates on the south, and three gates on the west." (Rev. 21:12-13)

Ezekiel 48:30-35 may provide more details about the size of the gates and which tribe gets assigned to each one. This topic was addressed in a prior chapter entitled, "*The Millennial Jerusalem, Temple and Tribal Territories.*"

Interestingly, the twelve gates are each monitored by angels, which suggests that some, if not all, of the good angels, including Michael and Gabriel, will also dwell inside the NEW JERUSALEM. Another important aspect about the NEW JERUSALEM is that the gates are opened all day and there will be no night there.

> "Its gates shall not be shut at all by day (there shall be no night there)." (Rev. 21:25)

God the Father will dwell amongst His people

In the Millennium, Jesus Christ will personally dwell among His people, but only the glory of God the Father will be present on earth during those one-thousand years. However, the curse of sin will be gone in the Eternal Order, meaning that God the Father and Jesus Christ the Son can both dwell amongst their people.

"And there shall be no more curse, but the throne of God and of the Lamb shall be in it, and His servants shall serve Him." (Rev. 22:3)

"And I heard a loud voice from heaven saying, "Behold, the tabernacle of God *is* with men, and He will dwell with them, and they shall be His people. God Himself will be with them *and be* their God." (Rev. 21:3)

Not only will God the Father dwell amongst His people, but He will also treat them like sons and they will inherit all things.

"He who overcomes shall inherit all things, and I will be his God and he shall be My son." (Rev. 21:7)

There will be no more death, sorrow, crying or pain

With no more curse, the things that resulted from the curse will be eliminated and all things will be made new.

"And God will wipe away every tear from their eyes; there shall be no more death, nor sorrow, nor crying. There shall be no more pain, for the former things have passed away." Then He who sat on the throne said, "Behold, I make all things new." And He said to me, "Write, for these words are true and faithful."" (Rev. 21:4-5).

The Lord God Almighty and the Lamb are its Temple

When the earth flees away at the time of White Throne Judgment in Rev. 20:11, the Millennial Temple will cease to further exist. This will be the fourth and final Jewish temple to be destroyed.

1.　*Temple #1*, the Solomonic Temple, was destroyed by the Babylonians in 587/586 BC.

2.　*Temple #2*, the Herodian Temple, was destroyed by the Romans in 70 AD.

3.　*Temple #3*, the Tribulation Temple, seems to get destroyed by Jesus Christ shortly after His Second Coming. This will apparently happen on the 30th day of the 75-Day Interval as per Daniel 12:11.

4.　*Temple #4*, the Millennial Temple, will get destroyed when the earth flees away at the White Throne Judgment during the Aftermath Age.

5.　*Temple #5,* will not exist as per Rev. 21:22, which says, *"But I saw no temple in it, for the Lord God Almighty and the Lamb are its temple."*

There will be a crystal-clear pure River of Life

"And he showed me a pure river of water of life, clear as crystal, proceeding from the throne of God and of the Lamb." (Rev. 22:1)

This river is not the Millennial River described in Ezekiel 47:1-12 that flowed from under the threshold of the temple and brought life to the Dead Sea. When the earth flees away in the Aftermath Age, the Millennial River has no place to continue its flow. This is apparently a newly created river that proceeds from the throne of God the Father and Jesus Christ the Lamb of God.

There will be a healing Tree of Life

"In the midst of the street (*of gold*) thereof. And on this side of the river (*of Life*) and on that was the tree of life, bearing twelve *manner of* fruits,

yielding its fruit every month: and the leaves of
the tree were for the healing of the nations." (Rev.
22:2, ASV; emphasis added)

The Tree of Life dates back to the Garden of Eden in Genesis
2:9; 3:11, 24. It will return in the Eternal Order. It will bear twelve
fruits every month. The reference to a month suggests that some
type of a dating system will still exist during the Eternal Order.
This is also implied in Rev. 21:25 that says the gates of NEW
JERUSALEM are not shut during the day.

Presently, there are estimated to be over 2000 fruit varieties
throughout the world. Man has even invented a "Fruit Salad" tree
that bears up to 8 fruits through grafting fruits within the same
family. However, in the Eternal Order, the Tree of Life is all natural
and made from God and not man's grafting techniques.

There may still be that many fruit types in the Eternal Order,
but the Tree of Life apparently bears the top twelve and presumably
these are all edible. The other important information is that the
leaves from the Tree of Life are used for *the healing of the nations.*

This beckons the question, since Rev. 21:4 states there will be
no death, sorrow, crying or pain, which also implies no sicknesses,
then why do the nations need the leaves from the Tree of Life
for healing purposes? Below are quotes that may provide possible
answers.

> *"The Greek word translated healing is the source of*
> *the modern English word "therapeutic." The purpose*
> *of the leaves is not to heal existing sicknesses, for they*
> *will not exist in the Eternal Order; rather, they will*
> *be for health-giving to the nations."* Dr. Arnold
> Fruchtenbaum.[91]

> *"It is, of course, not implied that there is, in the new*
> *Jerusalem, any disease which needs healing, but the*

tree of life is put forward as the means by which the perpetual health and life and general well being of the inhabitants are sustained." The Pulpit Commentary[92]

The mention of *the healing of the nations* implies that there will be peoples and / or angels residing outside of the NEW JERUSALEM that live within the nations. This point is also made self-evident in the following verse.

"And the nations of those who are saved shall walk in its light, and the kings of the earth bring their glory and honor into it, (*the NEW JERUSALEM*)."
(Rev. 21:24, NKJV; emphasis added)

If some of the Angels, at least the twelve monitoring the twelve gates, the Jews and the Church Saints live inside the golden holy city, then who is dwelling among the nations? These non-NEW JERUSALEM citizens are saved as per Rev. 21:4. Thus, they likely include the saved Gentiles that come out of the Millennium. Since the Millennial earth and the nations therein will have fled away, then these Millennial citizens will be in need of new national homelands in the Eternal Order, and they will be the recipients of the therapeutic leaves from the Tree of Life.

A Few Final Observations

As this book concludes, there are a few more points to acknowledge.

- All saved souls will see God's face, bear His name on their foreheads and reign with Him forever (Rev. 22:4-5). This may not imply that a visible marking is displayed on the outer forehead, but likely alludes to the inscription of God's law on the inner mind as described in the New Covenant passages below.

"But this *is* the covenant that I will make with the house of Israel after those days, says the Lord: I will put My law in their minds, and write it on their hearts; and I will be their God, and they shall be My people." (Jeremiah 31:33)

"This *is* the covenant that I will make with them after those days, says the Lord: I will put My laws into their hearts, and in their minds I will write them." (Hebrews 10:16)

• All of the biblical verses in the book of Revelation are faithful and true (Rev. 22:6).

• Jesus Christ is coming quickly and blessed *is* he who keeps the words of the prophecy of the book of Revelation (Rev. 22:7).

• Jesus Christ comes quickly and with His reward to give to every one according to his work (Rev. 22:12).

• Blessed are those who do the commandments of Jesus Christ (Rev. 22:14).

"Jesus said to him, "'You shall love the Lord your God with all your heart, with all your soul, and with all your mind.' This is *the* first and great commandment. And *the* second *is* like it: 'You shall love your neighbor as yourself.' On these two commandments hang all the Law and the Prophets.'"" (Matthew 24:37-40).

Lastly and of utmost importance:

"And the Spirit and the bride say, "Come!" And let him who hears say, "Come!" And let him who thirsts come. Whoever desires, let him take the water of life freely." (Rev. 22:17)

"He who testifies to these things says, "Surely I am coming quickly.""

Amen. Even so, come, Lord Jesus! The grace of our Lord Jesus Christ *be* with you all. Amen." (Rev. 22:20-21)

Appendix

The Fate of the Fallen Angels and Demons

This appendix includes some thoughts from a handful of today's top Bible prophecy teachers on the topic of the final fates of the fallen angels and demons. The panel of experts includes Dr. David Reagan, Dr. Ron Rhodes, Dr. Mark Hitchcock, Dr. Andy Woods and TV Hosts Gary Stearman, LA Marzulli and Nathan Jones.

On January 15, 2021, I sent the following email inquiry to these qualified individuals.

> *"I'm doing some research for my new book and have a question for you. In all of your years of research, did you discover the fates of the fallen angels and demons during the Millennium?*
>
> *Satan gets chained in the Abyss and the Antichrist and False Prophet get cast into the Lake of Fire, but where do these bad angels and demons go?*
>
> *Some, like Arnold Fruchtenbaum teach that they could be the wild beasts of the desert, the foul birds and the doleful creatures in Babylon and Edom, which are desolate spots during the Millennium. (Isaiah 13:20-22, 34:8-15, Jeremiah 50:39-40, 51:41-43, Revelation 18:1-2).*
>
> *If you agree, do you think these verses are inclusive of the entire fallen angelic and demonic populations? Do you think some of them will be delivered into the abyss alongside Satan, or elsewhere at that time?*
>
> *What say you?...*
>
> *Bill Salus"*

Read the assorted comments below. The shorter responses are listed on top. The most lengthy and detailed response came from Dr. Ron Rhodes and is included at the bottom of this appendix.

Dr. David Reagan – The host of Christ in Prophecy TV

> "Matthew 25:41: *Then he will say to those on his left, 'Depart from me, you cursed, into the eternal fire prepared for the devil and his angels...Hell was designed by God for Satan and his angels. So, I believe that all of them will be consigned to hell, most likely at the beginning of the Millennium at the same time that Satan is locked up to await his final demise. If Satan is going to be restrained during the Millennium, then certainly his demons will also be.*"

Nathan Jones – The co-host of Christ in Prophecy TV

> "Satan is confined to the Pit and then released to be defeated once more. And since the demons are not active during the Millennial Kingdom, the only conclusion I can draw is that they're cast into the Lake of Fire along with the Antichrist and False Prophet...Well, there's one possible clue in 1 Corinthians 6:3, "Do you not know that we shall judge angels? How much more, things that pertain to this life?" At what point would Christians be judging angels? It could either be at the Sheep-Goat Judgment or at the Great White Throne. I believe the former fits the timeline better. But it's just a hypothesis."

Dr. Mark Hitchcock – Senior pastor of Faith Bible Church in Edmond, Oklahoma

> *"I've always assumed that demons are bound in the abyss with Satan for 1,000 years, although I have to admit the text doesn't say that specifically. Rev 20:10 only mentions Satan being cast into the lake of fire, but we know that demons must be cast there at that time too since there is no mention of them after that point... One argument I would make is that the text is focusing on the false trinity (Satan, beast and false prophet) and while demons are not mentioned specifically they are part of whatever happens to Satan who is their leader."*

Dr. Andy Woods – Senior pastor of Sugar Land Bible Church

> *"I'm not sure we have enough biblical data to be dogmatic on the subject one way or the other. My working assumption has always been that the demons will be with Satan in the abyss (Rev. 20:2-3) since, according to passages like Matthew 25:41 and Revelation 12:7, the demons, or the fallen angels, seem to be under Satan's authority. So, wherever Satan is they will be also. However, this is just assumption on my part."*

LA Marzulli – Author, filmmaker and TV host of Politics, Prophecy and the Supernatural

> *"They have to go somewhere don't they! It would be speculative on my part. They could be bound in the Abyss for the millennium. They could be buried in the desert wastelands like Azazel with stones piled on top of them. I don't believe they are free to do what they did before the second coming."*

Gary Stearman – The host of Prophecy Watchers TV

"Looking at Revelation 12:7 and following, we see the famous "war in heaven." This is the ultimate retribution of God's holy angels against Satan and the fallen angels. It comes right after the "second woe" and the "seventh trumpet," and I believe that it's interesting that it comes before the Beast out of the Sea, It's curious that they're banished into the Earthly dimension ("cast out into the earth") before the Antichrist comes to power, or so it seems.

Anyway, the fascinating thing is that in Rev. 12:9, we have Satan cast out into the Earth and his angels with him. So it seems that he no longer has the ability to escape into the realms of heaven, but must fight in the earthly dimension. Then come the beasts out of the sea and out of the earth. The fight is brought to the surface of the Earth. The last time the fallen angels are directly referenced, is in Rev. 12:9. After that, they are forbidden to escape into the heavens, as they can do now.

It makes sense to me that they remain locked into the Earthly dimension until Satan is cast into the bottomless pit in Revelation 20. I think the fallen angels go with him. (Remember, the last time they're referred to is in Revelation 12:9.) The "doleful creatures of Babylon and Edom" could well be idioms for these angels. At the moment, and until just after the middle of the Tribulation, they are free to do their evil in both heavens and Earth. After Revelation 12:9, all that is changed, and they're banned from the heavens, along with the great dragon.

That's my take on it, just looking at Scripture. I think that ultimately the fallen angels will be banished to the "Lake of Fire" (Rev. 20:10). with Satan for ever and ever."

Dr. Ron Rhodes – Bestselling author

"Fruchtenbaum's idea is interesting. The reality of Babylon's desolation and the statement that Babylon has become "a dwelling place for demons" (Rev. 18:2) *might* lend some credence to that view…We know with certainty that the demons will ultimately be locked up.

Demons said to Jesus: "What have you to do with us, O Son of God? Have you come here to torment us before the time?" (Matthew 8:29)… "The time" may be their future incarceration in the lake of fire, where they will experience never ending torment.

We know the lake of fire is their ultimate destiny because following the second coming, Jesus will say to the "goats" (unbelievers): "Depart from me, you cursed, into the eternal fire prepared for the devil and his angels." (Matthew 25:41).

The locality of demons during the millennial kingdom is a difficult matter. My general policy is: "Where Scripture is silent, I am silent." As you know, most commentators are silent on this issue.

There is always the possibility that they might be incarcerated in the Abyss along with Satan. Since there is no direct statement in Scripture to this effect, this view would rest entirely on conjecture and a few theological inferences. But there can be no dogmatism here.

Here is what I am referring to:

* *We know that the fallen angels are in subjection to Satan, and they serve his ends. Revelation 12:7 thus makes reference to "the dragon and his angels" (see also Matthew 12:41). The "messenger of Satan" who afflicted Paul would be an example of a demon doing Satan's bidding (2 Corinthians 12:7). This is significant, because if the devil were locked up — and demons were still free — they could still do his bidding on the earth.)*

* *We also know that Satan is not a "lone ranger" when it comes to deception. Fallen angels deceive too. We read about "doctrines of demons" in 1 Timothy 4:1. This points to the need to "test the spirits" (1 John 4:1). So, people on earth are deceived not just by Satan but also by fallen angels, who do Satan's bidding.*

* *The purpose of Satan's incarceration during the millennial kingdom is so that he might not "deceive the nations any longer." If Satan's angels (fallen angels) were still on the loose, the nations would surely still be subject to deception. One might therefore infer that perhaps Satan's fallen angels might be locked up with him, in order to prevent such deception.*

* *We also know that the millennial kingdom will be characterized by great spiritual blessing (the Holy Spirit will be present and will indwell all believers; righteousness will prevail around the world; obedience to the Lord will prevail; holiness will prevail; faithfulness will prevail; God's presence will be made manifest; etc. — see my book, THE END TIMES IN CHRONOLOGICAL ORDER). It's a bit hard to see how all this could be true with fallen angels still roaming around all over the earth.*

Of course, I could be wrong. This, again, is conjecture… I suppose that if Fruchtenbaum were correct, one might also surmise that with the massive outpouring of the Holy Spirit during the millennium, demonic deception will be restrained and possibly confined to the desolate remains of Babylon. This, too, is conjecture."

My view of this is presented in the chapter entitled, "*The Final Destinations of Satan, the Fallen Angels and Demons.*" As the title implies, I attempt to track the final destinations of all three of these wicked satanic forces.

Endnotes

1   Tim Drake quote taken on 4/29/19 from this website: https://legatus.org/do-catholics-believe-in-the-rapture/.

2   "Armageddonites is the author's unique word construct that describes the Antichrist and his world armies assembled at Armageddon. It is not to be confused with "Armageddonist," which basically means someone who believes the New Testament end of times is imminent."

3   Meyers NT Commentary quote taken on 1/20/21 from this website: https://bible-hub.com/commentaries/revelation/20-1.htm.

4   Missler/Eastman quote taken from their book entitled, Alien Encounters: The Secret Behind The UFO Phenomenon, pg. 239.

5   Brenton Septuagint translation taken on 2/1/21 from this website: https://bible-hub.com/sep/isaiah/13.htm.

6   Strong's Lexicon translation was paraphrased and taken on 2/1/21 from this website: https://biblehub.com/strongs/isaiah/13-21.htm.

7   Fausett's quote taken on 2/1/21 from this website: https://www.bible-history.com/faussets/s/satyrs/.

8   Eugene McCarthy quote taken on 2/1/21 from this website: http://www.macroevolution.net/caprinid-human-hybrids.html#:~:text=The%20Greeks%20used%20the%20word,horse%2C%20more%20like%20a%20centaur.

9   The Footsteps of the Messiah by Arnold Fruchtenbaum pages 513-514.

10   Garland quote taken on 1/30/21 from this website: https://www.biblestudytools.com/commentaries/revelation/revelation-18/revelation-18-2.html.

11   Fruchtenbaum: The Footsteps of the Messiah, pg. 409.

12   Greek interpretation came from NAS Exhaustive Concordance: https://biblehub.com/hebrew/1419.htm.

13   Promised Land size estimate taken from this website: https://www.bible.com/reading-plans/17945-joshua-inheritance/day/1.

14   Israel's population ranking taken on 2/9/21 from this website: https://www.worldometers.info/world-population/population-by-country/.

15   Size ranking of Israel came from this Wikipedia website: https://en.wikipedia.org/wiki/List_of_countries_and_dependencies_by_area.

16   The Resurrection lists were taken in large part on 2/12/21 from this website: https://www.petergoeman.com/full-list-of-resurrections-in-the-bible/.

17   The link to the Jewish Wedding model is: http://www.prophecydepotministries.net/2012/the-bride-of-christ-and-the-jewish-wedding-models/.

18   Fruchtenbaum quote taken from pg. 376 of the Footsteps of the Messiah book.

19   Fruchtenbaum quote taken from pg. 377 of the Footsteps of the Messiah book.

20   Charlie Trimm article was taken on 2/16/21 from this website: https://www.biola.edu/blogs/good-book-blog/2014/non-israelite-followers-of-yhwh-in-the-old-testament.

21   Christian Post article was taken on 2/23/21 from this website: https://www.christianpost.com/news/record-low-number-of-americans-hold-biblical-worldview-survey-says.html.

22   Kumbh Mela 2013 pilgrimage was taken from this website: https://largest.org/people/gatherings-of-people/.

23   William McDonald - Believer's Bible Commentary Thomas Nelson publisher pages 1299-1300.

24   Pelosi quote taken on 2/25/21 from this website: https://www.theblaze.com/news/nancy-pelosi-exploits-bible-prisoner-release.

25   Fruchtenbaum quote is from the Footsteps of the Messiah book, A Study of the Sequence of Prophetic Events. Pgs. 371-372.

26   Walvoord quote is from The Bible Knowledge Commentary: New Testament.

27   Wiersbe's quote came from his commentary entitled, Wiersbe's expository outlines on the New Testament.

28   Jewish population numbers were taken on 2/25/21 from this website: https://en.wikipedia.org/wiki/Historical_Jewish_population_comparisons.

29   Missler quote was taken on 3/10/21 from this web link: https://www.khouse.org/articles/2003/449/#notes.

30   Jewish Encyclopedia quote was taken on 3/10/21 from this web link: https://www.jewishencyclopedia.com/articles/7941-huppah.

31   LaHaye quote taken from his book, Revelation Unveiled, pages 294-295.

32   Reagan quote taken on 3/10/21 from this web link: https://christinprophecy.org/articles/the-marriage-feast-of-the-lamb/.

33   Ibid.

34   Ice quote taken on 3/10/21 from this weblink: https://www.raptureready.com/2015/11/10/the-marriage-supper-of-the-lamb-by-thomas-ice/.

35   MacArthur quote taken on 3/10/21 from this weblink: https://www.gty.org/library/sermons-library/66-68/heavenly-hallelujahs-part-3.

36   Rhodes quote from his book entitled, The Popular Dictionary of Bible Prophecy, page 190.

37   Fruchtenbaum quote taken from pg. 376 of the Footsteps of the Messiah book.

38   Commentary on 2 Thess. 1:7-8.

39   Commentary on Matt. 13:36-43.

40   The Coming Kingdom, What Is the Kingdom and How Is Kingdom Now Theology Changing the Focus of the Church? Publisher Grace Gospel Press, Duluth, MN 2016.

41   The Coming Kingdom page 103.

42   Quote taken on 8/14 from this weblink: https://www.biblegateway.com/resources/encyclopedia-of-the-bible/Valley-Jehoshaphat.

43   MacArthur Part 1 taken from this weblink: https://www.gty.org/library/sermons-library/2378/the-judgment-of-the-nations-part-1.

44   MacArthur Part 2 taken from this weblink: https://www.gty.org/library/sermons-library/2379/the-judgment-of-the-nations-part-2.

45 Hebrew definitions for restored fortunes was taken from Strong's Lexicon at this website: https://biblehub.com/strongs/jeremiah/49-39.htm.

46 The Edomites have ethnic representation within the Palestinians. Not all Palestinians are of Edomite descent, but many of them can trace their genealogies back to Esau, who fathered the Edomites according to Genesis 36:1, 8-9.

47 POWs is a common acronym for prisoners of war.

48 Egypt's military ranking was taken on 4/5/21 from this website: https://www.globalfirepower.com/countries-listing.php.

49 Quotes from John Walvoord and Roy B. Zuck from their commentary on Isaiah 60:1-3 and 4-9.

50 Shekinah Glory quote taken from this website on 5/10/21: https://www.christianity.com/wiki/christian-terms/what-is-the-meaning-of-shekinah-glory.html.

51 A neuralyzer is a fictional gadget featured in the Men in Black movies that wipes away the memory of a target.

52 Footsteps of the Messiah book, page 388.

53 The European Space Agency website is: http://www.esa.int/.

54 Alexa Answers website is: https://alexaanswers.amazon.com/.

55 Worldometer: https://www.worldometers.info/world-population/.

56 Promised Land size estimate taken from this website: https://www.bible.com/reading-plans/17945-joshua-inheritance/day/1.

57 Size of Turkey taken on 5/18/21 from this website: https://www.nationmaster.com/country-info/stats/Geography/Land-area/Square-miles.

58 Turkey population taken on 5/20/21 from this website: https://www.worldometers.info/world-population/turkey-population/.

59 The Footsteps of the Messiah, A Study of the Sequence of Prophetic Events – pg. 393.

60 H7489 Hebrew word ra'a' defined in the Strong's Hebrew and Greek Dictionaries at this weblink: https://www.htmlbible.com/sacrednamebiblecom/kjvstrongs/STRHEB74.htm.

61 Greek word definitions from Strong's Hebrew and Greek Dictionaries.

62 H7626 shebet is defined in the Strong's Hebrew and Greek Dictionaries at this weblink: https://www.htmlbible.com/sacrednamebiblecom/kjvstrongs/STRHEB76.htm.

63 Kathath: 3807 in the NAS Exhaustive Concordance.

64 Quote from John Walvoord and Roy B. Zuck on Revelation 2:26-27.

65 Solomon article taken on 5/30/21 from this website: https://www.lovemoney.com/gallerylist/51988/the-20-richest-people-of-all-time.

66 Fruchtenbaum's quote about Zerubbabel is on page 405 of his Footsteps of the Messiah book.

67 The Footsteps of the Messiah, A Study of the Sequence of Prophetic Events – pg. 407.

68 The Footsteps of the Messiah, A Study of the Sequence of Prophetic Events – pg. 400.

69   Pulpit Commentary Quote found at this weblink: https://biblehub.com/commentaries/revelation/7-14.htm.

70   The Footsteps of the Messiah, A Study of the Sequence of Prophetic Events – pgs. 401-402.

71   JP headline came from this weblink: https://www.jpost.com/israel-news/israel-welcomes-record-breaking-455-million-tourists-in-2019-612456.

72   I24 headline was taken from this weblink: https://www.i24news.tv/en/news/israel/1609448004-israel-in-severe-hit-by-covid-19-crisis-tourism-decreased-by-81-3-in-2020.

73   Times of Israel headline taken from this website: https://www.timesofisrael.com/up-to-60000-israeli-businesses-may-close-in-2021-amid-covid-19-fallout-report/.

74   Dr. Fruchtenbaum quote taken from page 458 of his book entitled, The Footsteps of the Messiah.

75   The Footsteps of the Messiah page 465.

76   Feast quotes came from Dr. John Walvoord and Roy B. Zuck.

77   The Footsteps of the Messiah book on pages 520-521.

78   Dr. David Jeremiah quote taken on 7/9/21 from this weblink: https://davidjeremiah.blog/what-is-the-great-white-throne-judgment-in-revelation/.

79   Golden Rule quote taken on 7/14/21 from this weblink: https://en.wikipedia.org/wiki/Golden_Rule.

80   Wiersbe's quote on the Second Death: Wiersbe's Expository Outlines on the New Testament.

81   Dessert Sun quote taken on 7/20/21 from this weblink: https://www.desertsun.com/story/news/environment/2020/06/21/odor-advisory-issued-palm-springs-area-due-salton-sea/3232791001/.

82   Footsteps of the Messiah book page 753-754.

83   Footsteps of the Messiah book page 753.

84   Footsteps of the Messiah book page 531.

85   (Things to Come. Grand Rapids: Zondervan Publishing House, 1958, pp. 577-79).

86   Quote from Dr. John Walvoord and Roy B. Zuck.

87   Read the related Rapture verses in 1 Thessalonians 4:15-18 and 1 Corinthians 15:50-52.

88   Quote from the Bible Knowledge Commentary: New Testament.

89   Wiersbe's expository outline on the New Testament.

90   Wiersbe's expository outline on the New Testament.

91   Footsteps of the Messiah book page 539.

92   Pulpit Commentary quote came from this weblink: https://biblehub.com/commentaries/revelation/22-2.htm.

Order your copies of this entire end times book series at our online bookstore located at www.prophecydepot.com.

The NOW Prophecies

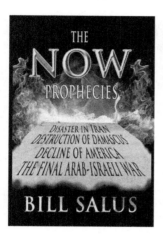

These are the biblical predictions that lack preconditions and could happen NOW! These prophecies include:

- Disaster in Iran

- Destruction of Damascus

- Final Arab-Israeli War – (Psalm 83)

- Toppling of Jordan

- Terrorization of Egypt

- Emergence of the exceedingly great Israeli army

- Expansion of Israel

- Vanishing of the Christians

- Emergence of a GREATER and SAFER Israel

- The Decline of America

The NEXT Prophecies

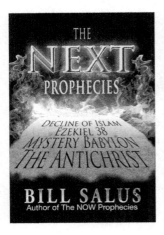

These are the biblical predictions that have minor preconditions and will follow the fulfillment of the NOW Prophecies. These prophecies include:

• 	Gog of Magog invasion (Ezekiel 38)

• 	Decline of Islam

• 	Unrestrained supernatural satanic deception

• 	Arrival of the Antichrist

• 	World Wars and global famines and pestilences

• 	"Mystery Babylon," the Harlot world religion

• 	Post-Rapture Christian martyrdom

• 	True content of the False Covenant

• 	Two phases of the "Overflowing Scourge"

• 	Start of the third Jewish Temple's construction

The LAST Prophecies

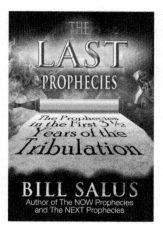

These are the biblical prophecies that happen in the first 3 ½ years of the Seven-Year Tribulation Period. These prophecies include:

- The Terminal Generation (What it is and How to Escape it)

- How Israel Gains World Renown after Ezekiel 38

- The Coming Third Jewish Temple

- Supernatural Signs and Lying Wonders

- The Harlot Religion of "Mystery Babylon"

- The 144,000 Hebrew Evangelists

- The Two Witnesses

- A Worldwide Christian Revival

- The 3 Phases of Christian Martyrdom in the Tribulation

- The Seven Seal Judgments

- The Seven Trumpet Judgments

- The Unholy Harlot and Antichrist Alliance

- The Ten Kings and Other Kings in the Tribulation

The FINAL Prophecies

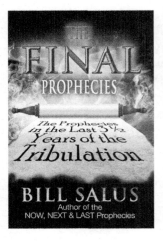

The FINAL Prophecies, The Prophecies in the Last 3 ½ Years of the Tribulation, is book four of an end time series and below are just a few of the prophecies it explores:

• Satan and the fallen angels are cast down to the earth

• Mystery Babylon and the Harlot world religion

• The rise of the Antichrist and False Prophet

• The Image of the Beast and Mark of the Beast

• The cashless global economy of the Antichrist

• The Antichrist attempts Jewish and Christian genocide

• The WRATH of GOD pours out of the Seven Bowl Judgments

• The Antichrist assembles his armies for Armageddon

• The Second Coming of JESUS CHRIST!

Printed in Great Britain
by Amazon

36047826R00195